CHURCH GROWTH:
The State of the Art

C·H·U·R·C·H
GROWTH
State of the art

C. PETER WAGNER, EDITOR
WITH WIN ARN AND ELMER TOWNS

Tyndale House Publishers, Inc.
Wheaton, Illinois

Second printing, January 1988

Library of Congress Catalog Card Number 86-50487
ISBN 0-8423-0287-5
Copyright 1986 by C. Peter Wagner, Win Arn, and Elmer L. Towns
Printed in the United States of America

Dedicated to
Donald A. McGavran,
Father of the Church Growth Movement

CONTENTS

Part 3   Church Growth and the Body of Christ

Part 4   Church Growth and Church Planting

Part 5   Church Growth and Technology

INTRODUCTION

Church growth has been a vital issue in churches and denominations throughout the world. Numerous methods for stimulating church growth have been devised and tried, some very successfully. But many heroic efforts have failed. Some pastors have successfully motivated members to try another plan or program. Often, though, the result has been discouragement and a return to the status quo.

What was needed was not merely another plan but a new approach—an effective strategy, based on biblical principles, to bring the unsaved to conversion and to integrate them into the church. That need was the impetus for the Church Growth Movement.

Now over thirty years old, the Church Growth Movement has played an increasingly positive role in American Christian life, and indeed throughout the world. This book, written by sixteen of America's top church growth theoreticians and practitioners, will help you become better informed about the issues involved in church growth.

This book has been designed for two purposes. The first is to provide a resource for pastors and other church leaders who want fresh, practical ideas on how to help their churches grow. Never before has such a wide spectrum of church growth expertise been placed between two covers. Many of the authors—such as Win and Charles Arn, Kent Hunter, Charles Singletary, Carl George, Delmar Anderson, and Melvin Schell—are continually consulting with churches which have all kinds of growth potential and problems. They are familiar with churches like yours. Others—such as John Wimber, Thomas Younger, John Vaughan, and again Kent Hunter—are active pastors who have mastered the field of church growth and are applying it to their own churches. They are also in demand as speakers for seminars and as consultants. They are complemented by theoreticians and researchers—such as Peter Wagner, George Hunter, Medford Jones, Elmer Towns, Eddie Gibbs, and F. J. May—whose interaction with students in the classroom and with church leaders at conferences keeps them in touch with the grass roots and lends an authenticity to their remarks.

The second purpose is for this book to serve as a reference work for any who are studying in the field of church growth. The Glossary clarifies the technical church growth vocabulary that has developed over the last thirty years. The Who's Who section introduces the personalities who have risen to prominence in the Church Growth Movement. Special attention is given to the revered founder of the movement, Donald A. McGavran. The Reading List is an annotated bibliography of the major church growth books, in print and out of print.

The editors of and contributors to this book are excited about church growth. They are not out to defend a particular movement or to perpetuate one of the latest fads. Their underlying motivation is obedience to our Lord's Great Commission to go and make disciples of all nations. They believe that church growth principles are twentieth century instruments that God has given to his servants for implementing that commission in a more rapid and effective way for his glory. Thousands of pastors have applied these principles and have seen their churches grow. The possibilities for accelerated church growth will excite you also as you read.

Part 1

AN OVERVIEW

The name Donald A. McGavran is inseparable from the concept of church growth. In these first two chapters, C. Peter Wagner, McGavran's understudy and academic successor at Fuller Theological Seminary, examines the life of the man himself and then describes the movement he started. Part I is for both the initiated and the uninitiated. Those who have considered themselves a part of the Church Growth Movement and who have known Donald McGavran personally will enjoy the nostalgia, but will also be challenged afresh by McGavran's untiring vision for reaching the lost and bringing them into Christ's fold. For readers who are new to the Church Growth Movement, this part will set the context in which the subsequent chapters need to be understood.

1
DONALD A. McGAVRAN: A TRIBUTE TO THE FOUNDER

C. Peter Wagner

"We stand in the sunrise of missions."

This is perhaps the most characteristic phrase proclaimed through the years by Donald A. McGavran, regarded by many as the twentieth century's premier missiologist. At eighty-seven years of age, he still makes that statement with the twinkle in his eye and the determination on his lips that have always been a part of his outgoing and forceful personality.

Donald McGavran was born of missionary parents in India before the turn of the century. His grandparents had also been missionaries to India, sailing around Africa's Cape of Good Hope to get there. He is a graduate of Yale and Columbia. He has climbed the Himalayas. He has produced motion pictures. He was the director of a missionary agency. He managed a leprosarium and supervised a school system. He went one-on-one with a wounded tiger and met a wild boar in combat. He is fluent in Hindi and Chattisqarhee. He stopped a cholera epidemic. He was the founding dean of a prestigious missiological institution. He has written twenty-three books on missions and church growth. His travels have taken him to virtually every nation of the world.

When, one or two generations from now, historians of religion look back to the twentieth century, McGavran will most likely be remembered chiefly as the father of the Church Growth Movement. Seed thoughts for the movement began to germinate in the 1930s when he was executive secretary and treasurer for the United Christian Missionary Society in India. He was in charge of eighty missionaries, five hospitals, many high schools and primary schools, evangelistic work, and a leprosy home. It was a formidable missionary effort. But through decades of hard work the net result of the mission's work had been only twenty or thirty small nongrowing churches.

This was the pattern of many missionary groups in India at that time, and still is for some. But Donald McGavran could not live with it. The conventional wisdom among missionaries was that India was a resistant country and that they should not expect many converts. But McGavran did not agree. It occurred to him that obviously there was a way of doing missionary work so as to produce few or no churches. But there must also be other ways of doing missionary work that God would bless with the establishment of many churches. At the time McGavran did not know exactly how the methodologies of the two approaches differed, but he determined to find out. As he declared in the preface to a book he coauthored in the 1930s, he had dedicated himself to "discarding theories of church growth which do not work, and learning and practicing productive patterns which actually disciple the peoples and increase the household of God."

In order to gather the experience necessary to undergird the theories of church growth that were developing, McGavran left his administrative position and spent seventeen years in planting churches. The work bore substantial fruit, and some 1,000 Indians now owe their conversion, humanly speaking, to McGavran's efforts. More significant than the immediate results, however, were the strong convictions about the growth and nongrowth of churches that were forming in McGavran's mind. These convictions led in 1955 to the publication of *The Bridges of God* (rev. ed., Friendship Press, 1981), the landmark volume which launched the Church Growth Movement.

The book was read and discussed by missionaries and mission executives on all six continents. Its ideas were new and controversial. Four principal points of discussion were raised: a theological issue, an ethical issue, a missiological issue, and a procedural issue.

The theological issue suggests that the central purpose of missions was to be seen as God's will that lost men and women be found, reconciled to himself, and brought into responsible membership in Christian churches. Evangelism was seen not just as proclaiming the gospel whether or not something happened, but as making disciples for the Master.

The ethical issue is one of pragmatism. McGavran became alarmed when he saw all too many of God's resources—personnel and finances—being used without asking whether the kingdom of God was being advanced by the programs they were supporting. McGavran demanded more accountability in Christian stewardship. He wanted efforts evaluated by their results. His attitude reflects these words of Bishop Waskom Pickett, McGavran's mentor in the early years in India: "It is disturbing to read book after book about modern missions without finding so much as a hint about either what helped or what hindered church growth. In many books the author seems eager to prove that the missionaries have done everything according to God's leading and that if no church has come into being it means only that God's time for saving souls has not come: 'The disciples' duty is to sow the seed and leave it to God to produce.' How different this is from the command of Jesus, 'Make disciples of the nations!' "[1]

The missiological issue is McGavran's people movement theory. Before the days of the conscious application of cultural anthropology to evangelistic strategy, McGavran intuitively recognized the fact that decision-making processes are frequently quite different from one culture to the next. Whereas most Western missionaries and their converts were preaching an individualistic gospel and expecting people to come to Christ one by one against the social tide, McGavran, with Waskom Pickett's encouragement, concluded that this was not the way multitudes could or would come to Christ. Important decisions, according to their worldview, were community decisions. Therefore, the way to approach many of the world's peoples with the gospel had to be through the encouragement of a multi-individual, interdependent conversion process whereby members of families, extended families, clans, villages, and tribes would become Christian at the same time. This process was labeled a people movement.

A corollary of the people movement theory is the homogeneous unit principle. "People like to become Christians without crossing racial, linguistic, or class barriers," said McGavran. Conversion, he argued, should occur with a minimum of social dislocation. This principle has become the most controversial of all church growth principles because critics have interpreted it as classist or racist. Nothing could be further from McGavran's mind, however. As the prototype of a world Christian, McGavran does not have a racist bone in his body. The homogeneous unit principle is an attempt to respect the dignity of individuals and allow their decisions for Christ to be religious rather than social decisions. It is developed in detail in McGavran's magnum opus, *Understanding Church Growth* (rev. ed., Eerdmans, 1980).

The procedural issue is the distinction between discipling and perfecting as two discreet stages of Christianization. Discipling brings an unbelieving individual or group to commitment to Christ and to the body of Christ. Perfecting is the lifelong process of spiritual and ethical development in the lives of believers. McGavran warned that too many mission activities had been diverted to perfecting when the original mission charter demanded discipling. He never tires of pointing out that a full 70 percent of the world's population is not yet discipled and he urges Christian churches worldwide to get on with sending more laborers into those harvest fields.

Having laid the conceptual groundwork for the Church Growth Movement in the 1950s, McGavran's crowning achievement was the establishment of the institution which was to become his base of operations. In 1961 he started an Institute of Church Growth at Northwest Christian College in Eugene, Oregon. In 1965 he moved the Institute to Fuller Seminary and became the founding dean of the Fuller School of World Mission and Institute of Church Growth. Although he stopped teaching at the age of eighty-three, McGavran continues an active schedule of research, writing, traveling, and speaking, and works in his seminary office daily when he is in town. His school is the foremost institution of missiological training with a resident faculty of twelve full-time and thirty part-time members and a student body of over 500.

With over three billion of the world's people yet to believe in Jesus Christ, Donald McGavran sees the golden years of mission yet ahead. Resources for completing the task have never been greater. Missiological research and knowledge have never been so advanced. Peoples around the world have never been more open to the gospel. God is on the throne. Jesus said, "I will build my church," and he continues to do it. No wonder that Donald McGavran, with a twinkle in his eye and determination on his lips, says today with more verve than ever, "We stand in the sunrise of missions."

1. J. Wascom Pickett, *Christian Mass Movements in India* (Lucknow: Lucknow Publishing House, 1933).

2
THE CHURCH GROWTH MOVEMENT AFTER THIRTY YEARS
C. Peter Wagner

This book is a broad brush sketch of the state of the art of the Church Growth Movement, which Donald A. McGavran founded in 1955. All sixteen contributors regard themselves as participants in the Church Growth Movement. They would claim to have "church growth eyes." They respectfully and enthusiastically acknowledge the profound influence of Donald A. McGavran's life and teachings on their own ministries.

What is this Church Growth Movement?

I was first introduced to it in 1967 when, as a missionary on furlough from Bolivia, I enrolled in the Fuller Seminary School of World Mission to study under Donald McGavran. At that time, the third year of the school's existence, the student body numbered thirty-five, compared to five hundred today. As the academic year progressed I found myself irresistibly drawn to McGavran as a man whose burning passion to see the lost won to Jesus Christ had stimulated him to develop what, at that time, were absolutely revolutionary ideas about missions and missiology. In 1968 he invited me to become his teaching colleague in the field of church growth, and I was able to accept in 1971. I enjoyed ten years as his understudy until he retired from teaching in 1981. In 1984 I was installed as the first occupant of the Donald A. McGavran Chair of Church Growth.

It is from this perspective, then, that I see the Church Growth Movement. While this book deals principally with churches and church growth in North America, it must be remembered that the Church Growth Movement was born in the Third World and that for over fifteen years its research was directed almost exclusively to the advance of the gospel in Africa, Asia, and Latin America. Two contributors to this volume, Elmer Towns and Medford Jones, began doing research on American church growth sometime before McGavran and his immediate followers did, and they both eventually converged with the Church Growth Movement, Jones in the early days and Towns later.

Today the Church Growth Movement is serving two broad constituencies. On the one hand it serves those engaged in missions and missiology, the cross-cultural communication of the Christian faith. On the other hand, it serves those whose primary interest is in monocultural ministry, such as the great majority of American pastors. The recently formed North American Society for Church Growth attempts to bring together individuals from both of these constituencies under the banner of church growth.

In this effort to describe the Church Growth Movement, I will look first at its past, then at the present, and, finally, risk some glances into its future.

The Church Growth Movement in the Past
The Lord has granted Donald McGavran sixty years of Christian ministry. The first thirty of them were spent as a missionary to India. They were fruitful years and a great deal was accomplished both in evangelism and in social work. But they were also years of learning, of shaping his character, and of "the making of a missiologist," to borrow the title of a Ph.D. dissertation being completed at Fuller by Vern Middleton. One of the important transitions in this period was theological. McGavran had been trained in the liberalism of the day at Yale University Divinity School. But the realities of missionary field experience steadily turned him into a staunch evangelical. Apart from the subtle working of the Holy Spirit, it is doubtful whether the Church Growth Movement would enjoy its current stature.

In 1955 McGavran published a summary of what he had learned during that formative period under the title *The Bridges of God* (rev. ed., Friendship Press, 1981), and the Church Growth

Movement was born. He expressed deep frustration about the progress of the missionary enterprise of the time. He was appalled, for example, at what he saw while serving as secretary-treasurer of his mission, the India Mission of the United Christian Missionary Society. In reviewing the records one year, he became disturbed to find that his organization had spent $125,000 but had added only a total of fifty-two members to the churches. McGavran began to think that there must be a better way to do missionary work.

Back when *The Bridges of God* was published, liberal Christianity was having a heyday. The social gospel was in, and a massive effort had been mounted to redefine the terms "mission" and "evangelism." Mission meant fulfilling the cultural mandate. Evangelism meant giving a cup of cold water in the name of Jesus and helping Muslims or Buddhists become better people. Advocating conversion to Christianity was regarded as distasteful, something akin to coersion or manipulation. The World Council of Churches had been organized, and this kind of thinking had already begun to surface in its theological outlook. Donald McGavran, who himself had once advocated these positions, now saw their spiritual emptiness. He launched a thirty-year crusade to bring the meanings of mission and evangelism back to their classic, biblical moorings.

The Bridges of God became the *Magna Carta* of the Church Growth Movement. It's empirical background had been provided through Methodist Bishop Wascom Pickett's research on Christian mass movements in India. With characteristic and exaggerated modesty, McGavran says, "I lit my candle at Bishop Pickett's fire." But this flame was the beginning development of a new paradigm for understanding the dynamics of the worldwide spread of the Christian faith. McGavran's label for the paradigm was simply "church growth," and the new movement had been christened.

From that point it took McGavran fifteen years to solidify the Church Growth Movement. He did it by using four vehicles.

The first vehicle was voluminous correspondence. Dialogue through the mail was McGavran's stock in trade. Christian leaders all over the world have files bulging with McGavran's extensive and well-developed epistles. Some of McGavran's best writing is not in books, but in those files of correspondence. Many of the exchanges were heated, and McGavran's radical ideas were steadily becoming known.

The second vehicle was publication. Three foundational works were produced. *The Bridges of God* has already been mentioned. Then in 1959 came *How Churches Grow* (Friendship Press). In preparing for that work, McGavran did field research on church growth in Puerto Rico, the Philippines, Thailand, Taiwan, Japan, Jamaica, and several countries of Africa in order to broaden what he had already learned from India. *Understanding Church Growth* (rev. ed., Eerdmans, 1980) was published in 1970. It remains an irreplaceable textbook for any serious study in the field of church growth, and it is already acclaimed as a missions classic. All Fuller Theological Seminary programs in church growth— missiology, cross-cultural studies, and doctor of ministry—begin with a thorough study of *Understanding Church Growth,*[1] as do programs in many other seminaries and Bible schools.

The third vehicle was personal appearances. McGavran traveled far and wide advocating church growth principles as a way of becoming more faithful to God in carrying out the missionary task of the church. For many years it was a tiring and lonesome task, but eventually supporters began to come. One of the early supporters was Wade Coggins, executive secretary of the Evangelical Foreign Missions Association, who provided McGavran a platform with a series of annual church growth conferences held in Winona Lake, Indiana. Another was Norman Cummings, general director of Overseas Crusades. Overseas Crusades became the publisher of what was then called *Church Growth Bulletin* and is now called *Global Church Growth*, the chief publication of the Church Growth Movement. A combination of McGavran's winsome personality and his rock-hard conviction that the lost must be found struck a responsive chord, especially among evangelicals.

McGavran's fourth vehicle for solidifying the Church Growth Movement was education. If anything, McGavran has been an inveterate educator. His Ph.D. from Columbia is in education. He ran schools in India. He knew that freestanding ideas would make relatively little long-term impact apart from an institutional structure. So he founded the Institute of Church Growth in 1961 at Northwest Christian College in Eugene, Oregon. The physical holdings of the Institute consisted of a large oak table in a remote corner of the third floor of library stacks. Humble as it was, an institution was born.

By 1965 McGavran and his ideas had become so well known that he was invited to become the founding dean of a new school of missions at Fuller Theological Seminary in Pasadena, California. As already mentioned, he accepted on the condition that he bring his institute with him, and it was called the Fuller School of World Mission and Institute of Church Growth. McGavran invited his Australian research assistant, Alan R. Tippett, formerly a Methodist missionary to Fiji, to come with him to teach anthropology. Soon afterward, J. Edwin Orr became a visiting professor. Ralph D. Winter, a Presbyterian missionary to Guatemala, became the third full-time professor in 1967.

In a recently published book, McGavran looks back on almost thirty years of the Church Growth Movement and selects what he perceives to be its ten major emphases. What is at the top of the list? "The Church Growth School of Thought," says McGavran, "is deeply theological. If you would understand the church growth position at all, you must see it cradled in theological concepts—doctrines—which have been common to all denominations from Baptist to Roman Catholic." And what is the bedrock doctrine? "Only an unshakable conviction that God wants His lost children found produces or long maintains biblical mission."[2]

The Church Growth Movement in the Present

Over the past thirty years, the Church Growth Movement has undergone a process of molding and refining to emerge with a fairly discernible shape. It is mature enough to have passed through the tests of critical evaluation, but still young enough to have maintained recognizable boundaries. Unlike students in older academic pursuits, students of church growth can still feel the excitement and satisfaction of being able to master the whole field if they so desire.

Here are five of the more important facets of this new school of thought:

1. Church growth has expanded to include the Western world. For the first fifteen years of its thirty-year history, as has been mentioned, church growth was promoted almost exclusively from the perspective of the Third World. Donald McGavran had riveted his attention on the propagation of the gospel "on new ground." He, like the Apostle Paul, was not interested in building on another person's foundation, but in preaching the gospel where Christ had not yet been named.

In 1972 I invited McGavran to team teach an experimental course in church growth for American pastors. Our classes were held at Lake Avenue Congregational Church in Pasadena, California. The course was well received and the ideas began to catch on among American churches. This volume itself is a reflection of the maturity that has developed in American church-growth thinking. Other Western nations that have strong advocates of church growth principles include Australia, Canada, Norway, Sweden, and particularly England.

2. Church growth is now widely recognized as a movement. A chief way to know whether what one is promoting is regarded as a movement is to test the unsolicited feedback from outsiders. For some time now, many expressions of affirmation have been coming both from those whose focus is worldwide missiology and those who are dealing more specifically with American churches.

J. Herbert Kane, one of America's ranking missiologists and director emeritus of the School of World Mission and Evangelism at Trinity Evangelical Divinity School, writes the following in his textbook *The Christian World Mission Today and Tomorrow:*

> During the last decade a great deal has been written about church growth. This is understandable since it has been the most dynamic movement in mission circles in recent years. Evangelicals owe a debt of gratitude to Donald McGavran, father of the Church Growth Movement, and to the Fuller School of World Mission, which has majored in church growth.[3]

26

Roger C. Bassham, an Australian Methodist, makes the following statement in his recent book *Mission Theology:*

> The most persuasive and extensive evangelical contribution to mission theology has come through the Church Growth Movement, with Donald McGavran as its chief spokesman, in the period following 1960. Based upon a belief that evangelism leading to church growth is an essential dimension of Christian mission, McGavran and his colleagues have developed an extensive research and teaching facility in the Institute of Church Growth, located first at Northwest Christian College, Oregon, and since 1965, as a part of the Fuller Theological Seminary.[4]

And closer to home, Lyle E. Schaller, widely recognized as the dean of church consultants in the U.S., says that the Church Growth Movement was "the most influential development of the 1970s" on the American religious scene.[5] It might be noted that while Schaller's research and writing have made substantial contributions toward understanding American church growth, he himself does not choose to be identified with the movement.

One of the predictable outcomes of such popularity as this movement seems to be enjoying is a fuzziness of definition. There is something of a trend to make "church growth" mean anything good that the church might be doing. Some stewardship campaigns are called "church growth." Sunday school conventions are billed as "church growth." Some video satellite companies are selling their products under the "church growth" label. Many of us, understandably, are somewhat irritated with what we consider an illicit use of the term. I agree with Ebbie C. Smith, of Southwestern Baptist Theological Seminary, who said the following in 1984 in *Balanced Church Growth:*

> I use the terms, *Church Growth Movement* or *Church Growth Theory,* to refer to the body of teaching associated with the approach of Donald A. McGavran, Alan R. Tippett, C. Peter Wagner, Win Arn and others of the so-called "Fuller School."[6]

3. Church growth is now a discreet academic field. More and more Bible schools and theological seminaries are introducing courses in church growth into their curricula. I suppose that every month or two I get a letter from a professor who has been assigned the responsibility of teaching church growth and wants some hints as to how to proceed. This is one reason I have decided to make my basic church growth course, "Foundations of Church Growth," available to the academic community in general. I hope that this will help standardize what is taught in introductory church growth courses. The textbook, of course, is *Understanding Church Growth.*

One of the significant indicators as to whether church growth has become an academic field in its own right is the growing number of graduate theses and dissertations being written specifically on the movement. I am collecting these and would be glad to know of any others that have been written. I currently have nine: three on McGavran (one, incidentally, came from the Gregorian University in Rome), three on myself, and three on the Church Growth Movement in general.[7]

Church growth books continue to roll off the presses. I chuckle at the frustration reflected in the following statement by Professor Russell Staples, of the Department of World Religion at Andrews University:

> The line of books in my library dealing directly with church growth, all published during the last fifteen years, now threatens to reach the two-yard mark—and this in spite of considerable resistance to acquire new books on the topic. This sheer bulk of material is evidence of the high level of interest church growth theory has aroused and testifies to the perennial appeal of simply-stated practical strategies.[8]

Not all the works on the Church Growth Movement have been favorable to it. Church growth theory has been criticized in many articles and in many books. At least four book-length criticisms have been published: two by Mennonite Wilbert R. Shenk,[9] one by Presbyterian Harvie M. Conn,[10] and one by Baptist Ralph H. Elliott.[11] I myself have learned a great deal from these criticisms and have changed some of my positions as a result. I have responded to them to the best of my ability in my book *Church Growth and the Whole Gospel* (Harper & Row, 1981).

This kind of dialogue has helped to define the academic field of church growth. Church growth overlaps, but does not coincide with, such fields as theology, missiology, evangelism, history, pastoral theology, communication, and anthropology. Whereas some seminaries and Bible schools attempted to introduce church growth as a subsection of evangelism courses in the early days, many of them have since realized that offerings in church growth are best kept as discreet parts of the curriculum. Donald McGavran, of course, saw this from the outset and planned his school accordingly.

4. Church growth has made some significant contributions to Christian thought and ministry. Just a glance through this book will call attention to many of the areas of contemporary church life which have received direct contributions from church growth thinking. A separate chapter would be required to describe them all. Here I simply want to mention the two areas in which, in my personal judgment, the greatest contribution has been made.

The first area is theological. The Church Growth Movement has not been the only force for change, but it has been one of several instruments which God has been using to call a large segment of the church back to a more biblical view of mission. The legacy of liberal theology combined with the social upheavals of the sixties tended to overbalance theologies of mission toward what Arthur Glasser calls the cultural mandate, almost to the neglect of the evangelistic mandate. Experiments with this during the seventies generally failed either to produce vigorous church growth or, ironically, to bring about desired social change. In the eighties I perceive that we are now seeing a trend toward the more biblical position, articulated, for example, in the Lausanne Covenant, which prioritizes the evangelistic mandate without neglecting the concerns of Christian social responsibility in the cultural mandate.

I like what Pastor Jeffery Utter, of Pasadena's First Congregational Church, wrote in a church newsletter:

The age of liberal religion is past. The evangelical wave is upon us. In our church we need to learn—maybe relearn—the evangelical ways of thinking, feeling, imagining, reaching out to others. All without abandoning for a moment our commitment to pursue justice and peace, if necessary even against the powers that be.

The second area is methodological. The "people approach to world evangelization" originated in Donald McGavran's School of World Mission. It has now become a recognized starting point for the planning of missiological strategies. Ralph Winter, while yet a member of the Fuller faculty, gave the concept worldwide exposure through his plenary address at the International Congress on World Evangelization in Lausanne, Switzerland, in 1974. When the Lausanne Committee for World Evangelization (LCWE) was subsequently formed, unreached peoples became a prominent theme. I had the privilege of being named a charter member of the LCWE, and still serve. I presided over the Strategy Working Group for its initial five years before turning it over to Edward Dayton of World Vision. One result of that was the series of annual directories called *Unreached Peoples* which continues today, published by MARC of World Vision. Under the leadership of Ralph Winter, the influential U.S. Center for World Mission in Pasadena, California, was founded with the express purpose of reaching the unreached peoples of the world. On Christmas of 1982, *Time* magazine ran a cover story on Christian missions and commented, "The most important change in Protestant missionary strategy in the past 10 years has been to identify and seek to contact some 16,000 tribes and social groups around the world that have been beyond the reach of Christianity." The intellectual seed for all this can, of course, be traced to McGavran's *Understanding Church Growth*.

5. *Church growth delivery systems have been put in place.* Early in the Church Growth Movement it became obvious that the theories which were being developed eventually had to be translated into practical tools which could be delivered to churches and to mission fields.

The first major figure in this process was Vergil Gerber of the Evangelical Missions Information Service, who conducted pioneer intensive church growth workshops in over fifty nations of the world during the decade of the seventies. His book *God's Way to Keep a Church Going and Growing* (Regal, 1973), referred to as the "Gerber manual," was translated into over forty languages and has probably had more direct grass roots influence for church growth than any other book.

Here in the United States, retail agencies designed to provide practical resources for implementing church growth began to develop in the early seventies. They were pioneered by Win Arn, who became the Vergil Gerber of North America. He established the Institute for American Church Growth in Pasadena, California, and covered the United States and Canada with seminars, films, books, and many other resources. The Charles E. Fuller Institute for Evangelism and Church Growth was formed in the mid-seventies in response to the demand for church growth consultation. John Wimber founded it and later turned it over to Carl George. George's acclaimed Diagnosis with Impact program offers professional level training to church growth consultants.

Subsequently many other church growth agencies, each bringing slightly different emphases and expertise to the field, have emerged. They include Church Growth Designs of Nashville under Ron Lewis; Church Growth Center of Corunna, Indiana, under Kent Hunter; Church Growth Ministries of Atlanta under Mel Schell; Center for Church Growth of Houston under Joseph Schubert; Church Resource Ministries of Fullerton, California, under Sam Metcalf; and Church Growth Institute of Lynchburg, Virginia, under Elmer Towns. Besides these independent organizations, an increasing number of denominations have created departments of church growth and named national directors of church growth. One of them is Delmar Anderson of the Evangelical Covenant Church, who wrote a chapter in this book. Another is Bill Sullivan of the Church of the Nazarene.

The Church Growth Movement in the Future
While much has been accomplished in the Church Growth Movement, much more needs to be done. I regard four things as important for the church growth agenda in the near future. My

list by no means purports to be exhaustive. Win and Charles Arn, for example, are working on *oikos* evangelism, drawing out some implications of McGavran's people movement theory. Kent Hunter is developing new insights into philosophy of ministry and how it influences church growth. George Hunter is wrestling with the relationship of organizational management principles with church growth. Archie Parrish is blending church growth principles with an expertly designed personal evangelism approach. Many others are joining in to develop new horizons for church growth.

Here are my four concerns:

1. Church growth research methodology needs to be systematized and standardized. For thirty years an enormous amount of church growth research has been carried out. It has been extremely valuable. We know a vast amount more about why some churches grow and some do not than we did twenty years ago. But the research has been somewhat haphazard. Its quality has been spotty. I hope that in the very near future we can distill what has been most helpful in the past and come up with transferrable concepts which will enhance courses and seminars in church growth research methodology all over the country and the world. It would be mutually beneficial if we all agreed to use the same categories in analyzing and reporting church growth. I feel that *The Church Growth Survey Handbook* is a start, but many church growth practitioners do not even know it exists. Even that is not the final word and more input is needed.

2. The church growth theological methodology needs to be clarified, developed, and communicated to others. I mentioned previously that Donald McGavran feels that "church growth" is first and foremost a theological statement. If so, not only do the theological ideas themselves need to be verbalized, but so also does the methodology used to derive them. This is doubly important because the theological methodology has been considerably different from the one traditionally employed in seminaries and theological textbooks. Much of the criticism directed toward the theological ideas of church growth comes from individuals who are operating out of a different methodological paradigm. These differences must be surfaced and mutually understood if we are to be able to talk to each other intelligently, let alone ever agree.

Suffice it to say that the differences are not those of the well-worn debates between Calvinism and Arminianism or covenant theology and dispensationalism or evangelicalism and liberalism. All sides in those discussions have usually agreed on a theological methodology which adopts philosophy as a cognate discipline. Church growth, however, looks to social science as a cognate discipline and emerges with a phenomenological methodology which may appear altogether too subjective to many traditional theologians.

As a starting point, church growth often looks to the "is" previous to the "ought." Its epistemology tends to be centered-set rather than bounded-set, as Paul Hiebert of the Fuller School of Missions would put it. What Christians experience about God's work in the world and in their lives is not always preceded by careful theological rationalizations. Many times the sequence is just the opposite: theology is shaped by Christian experience.

To the traditionalist, philosophy of religion is an important body of teaching for proper theologizing. For church growth, sociology of knowledge is a key. I like the way Robert J. Schreiter puts it:

> Theology does not develop in a social vacuum or dwell within some abstract history of ideas. What issues get taken up, which methods are used to address them, and what solutions are considered acceptable reflect at least obliquely the social conditions in which the discussion takes place.[12]

Later on Schreiter adds, "While theology is by no means unilaterally determined by historical circumstances, we are coming to realize how great a role environmental influences do indeed play in how our theologies develop." He then draws out an interesting implication by suggesting that if we take the incarnation seriously "our theology should reflect the same anti-Docetism as does our Christology."

Let me illustrate what I am saying with a personal anecdote. The reaction of many traditional theologians to the controversial homogeneous unit principle of church growth has been a case in point. Most of the critics have drawn from the traditional theological methodology. Notice that on the basis of an "ought" proposition derived from their understanding of the Scripture, they have decided to reject the simple phenomenological "is" observation of McGavran that "people like to become Christians without crossing racial, linguistic, or class barriers."[13] When pushed, many of them would feel comfortable in admitting that the principle has *sociological* validity, but that it cannot be defended *theologically*. Few of them would recognize how much they themselves have been influenced by the contemporary social mood of racial equality and the melting pot theory.

In 1979 I published my doctoral dissertation under the title *Our Kind of People* (John Knox). I included a chapter entitled "Church Growth in the New Testament Mosaic," in which I reexamined biblical evidence and found that New Testament church growth generally followed homogeneous unit lines. Because I used a phenomenologically-informed hermeneutical methodology, my conclusions were unacceptable to the traditionalists. They called "foul!" and accused me of practicing eisegesis rather than exegesis. They told me I should stick to sociology and leave the theology to them. One was so incensed that he wrote an article-length review in *Sojourners* under the headlines, "Evangelism without the Gospel." We were passing like ships in the night because we were using different methodologies.

3. We need to develop ways to measure church quality as well as measuring membership growth. Many church leaders, when discussing church growth, will say, "Yes, so-and-so church is growing rapidly and they have a large worship attendance, but that's not the real question. The real question is: Are they truly preaching the gospel? Are they truly the church?" The implication is: Are Christians in growing churches of the same quality as those in churches which are not growing?

This is a valid question, even though the person who asks it is typically the pastor of a plateaued or declining church, hoping against hope that members of large growing churches will turn out to be low quality Christians compared to members of small nongrowing churches.

But while it is a valid question, it is, at this point in time, an

unanswerable one. Neither the questioner nor the questionee
has agreed how such church quality is to be measured. Back in
1980 I set in motion a process which I hope will eventually lead
to an instrument for measuring church quality and be widely
accepted internationally and interdenominationally. I hope that
soon we will objectively be able to say that such-and-such a church
at a given time is an 84 or a 69 or whatever on a scale of 100 in
church quality. I have enlisted the help of Richard Gorsuch of
the Fuller School of Psychology, an expert in research and statistics. *Leadership* magazine published our first findings in an article
called "The Quality Church" in 1983. Since then Fred Smith has
done a Ph.D. dissertation at Fuller School of World Mission on
the subject in which he developed a prototype instrument. It
may take several more years of field testing and revision before
we obtain satisfactory results, but I believe it will be worth the
effort.

4. We need to aim for biblical balance in evangelism and mission. I
previously mentioned the theological issue revolving around the
relationship between the evangelistic mandate and the cultural
mandate. In my opinion, this is the number one theological
question relating to mission and evangelism today. Over the past
few years much good work has been done on the matter in
various circles. The most outstanding, I think, took place in the
Consultation on the Relationship between Evangelism and Social
Responsibility held in Grand Rapids in 1982. It was jointly convened by the Lausanne Committee for World Evangelization and
the World Evangelical Fellowship. The resulting sixty-five-page
document was published as Lausanne Occasional Paper No. 21,
under the title *The Grand Rapids Report—Evangelism and Social
Responsibility, An Evangelical Commitment.*

I believe the *Grand Rapids Report* has gone a long way in bringing some biblical balance to the debate. Evangelicals across the
spectrum seem to be satisfied with it. One reason for this is that
it constitutes one of the strongest appeals for Christian ministry
to the poor and oppressed that has yet emerged from an evangelical conference. With that, it still follows the lead of the Lausanne
Covenant in legitimizing the conceptual separation of the two
mandates and the prioritization of the evangelistic mandate.

Much yet needs to be done, however, to translate this from the conceptual level to practical, grass roots ministry.

Signs and Wonders Today?

While there is a growing consensus among evangelicals that social ministry is an obligation for Christians, the exact shapes that ministry to the poor and oppressed should take are not yet clear. I increasingly believe that discovering the biblical balance involves, at least to some degree, doing social work as Jesus did it; namely, by healing the sick and casting out demons through direct, supernatural means. Let me explain.

Thirty years of research and field testing of church growth theories have contributed unprecedented technology to the implementation of Jesus' Great Commission. Substantial strides have been made in the integration of evangelical theological constructs with social sciences, with organizational management, with communication theory, with leadership development theory, and with many other contemporary fields of academic pursuit. A modern engine for completing the task of world evangelization has fairly well been assembled. But fuel is needed to make it run. The fuel, as I see it, is the power of the Holy Spirit of which we read in the New Testament.

Richard Lovelace of Gordon-Conwell Seminary sounds a legitimate warning: "Some evangelicals are reacting against an unbalanced reliance on statistics, church growth methods and human initiative, and moving back toward dependence on the sovereign initiative of God in renewing the church."[14]

It must be recognized that teaching on the Holy Spirit and God's initiative has not been absent from church growth theory. Donald McGavran and others have mentioned it frequently. J. Edwin Orr has been McGavran's teaching colleague for twenty years and has emphasized it strongly. These efforts have laid the groundwork for some new movements of the Holy Spirit, particularly in the area of supernatural signs and wonders.

The Grand Rapids Report, for example, does something that no similar evangelical document has done in recent years. It specifically recognizes supernatural signs and wonders as signs of the kingdom of God. The report lists seven signs of the kingdom, one of which is healing and another casting out demons. It affirms that "God is still free and powerful, and performs miracles today." Part of the true kingdom of God is "making the blind see, the deaf hear, the lame walk, the sick whole, raising the dead, stilling the storm, and multiplying the loaves and fishes."[15]

One of my personal research goals for the decade of the eighties is to discover just how supernatural signs and wonders have related to the growth of the church in the past and how they are likely to influence the church in the future. I am very much interested in examining models of power evangelism. Power evangelism reflects the New Testament pattern used by Jesus when he sent out his twelve disciples for the first time. He commanded them to preach the message: "The kingdom of heaven is near." Then he also commanded them to do the deeds: "Heal the sick, raise the dead, cleanse those who have leprosy, drive out demons" (Matt. 10:7-8, TLB). My initial findings indicate that while there are some cases of dramatic church growth without power evangelism, and while there are some cases of power evangelism with very little church growth, across the board power evangelism is clearly resulting in the most vigorous church growth.

The existence of an estimated 169 million Pentecostals/charismatics worldwide, with most of the growth coming since 1950, testifies to the results of power evangelism. In America the growth rate of Pentecostals is considerably higher than any other grouping of churches, and this is true in country after country. I personally am not advocating that we who have not been Pentecostals or charismatics need to become Pentecostal or charismatic in order to see strong church growth. While I am among the first to affirm their ministry, I am not, nor do I intend to become, either. But for some time now I have been seeing the supernatural power of the Holy Spirit operate through my own ministry as an evangelical Congregationalist in a way similar to Pentecostals and charismatics, but also somewhat differently. I call it the "third wave," and I write a monthly column under that title in *Christian Life* magazine. In Fuller Seminary we introduced it in 1982 with a course called "The Miraculous and Church Growth," taught jointly by John Wimber and myself.

A track record of thirty years has indicated that the Church Growth Movement is not a mere fad. It has had a fruitful past, it has gathered strength through the years, and its future looks bright. However, no church growth leader that I know believes the Church Growth Movement is an end in itself. It is only an instrument in God's hand to accomplish his purposes in the world. God's purposes, as Donald McGavran has well taught us, are to proclaim Jesus Christ as God and only Savior and to persuade men and women everywhere to become disciples of Jesus Christ and responsible members of his church.

1. Academically-oriented study materials on *Understanding Church Growth* are available. I have prepared a 25-hour self-study pack which involves reading the book, listening to six cassette tapes, and filling in note pages in a workbook under the title *Your Church and Church Growth*. Furthermore, my course "Foundations of Church Growth" is now available with 15 cassette tapes and a leader's syllabus for classroom preparation. Students' syllabi have also been published. For information on either of these resources, write or call the Charles E. Fuller Institute, Box 989, Pasadena, CA 91102 (818/449-0425).

2. Donald A. McGavran, "Ten Emphases of the Church Growth Movement," *Unto the Uttermost*, Doug Priest, Jr., ed. (Pasadena: William Carey Library, 1984), 248, 249.

3. J. Herbert Kane, *The Christian World Mission Today and Tomorrow* (Grand Rapids: Baker, 1981), 201.

4. Rodger C. Bassham, *Mission Theology, 1948-1975: Years of Worldwide Creative Tension—Ecumenical, Evangelical, and Roman Catholic* (Pasadena: William Carey Library, 1979), 198.

5. Lyle E. Schaller, Foreword to *Church Growth Strategies That Work*, by Donald McGavran and George G. Hunter III (Nashville: Abingdon, 1980), 7.

6. Ebbie C. Smith, *Balanced Church Growth* (Nashville: Broadman, 1984), 11.

7. The theses and dissertations alluded to include:

  John Bronnert, *The Value of Church Growth Thinking in Contemporary Britain* (M.A. diss., University of Manchester, England, 1983).

  Vern Middleton, *The Making of a Missiologist: The Life and Ministry of Donald A. McGavran to 1965* (Ph.D. diss., Fuller School of World Mission, Pasadena, in preparation).

  Moon Soo Park, *A Comparative Study of C. Peter Wagner's Church Growth Theory and Korean Church Growth* (Th.M. diss., General Assembly Theological Seminary, Seoul, Korea, 1984, written in Korean).

  Sakari Pinola, *The Missiology of Church Growth* (Th.D. diss., University of Helsinki, Finland, 1982).

  John J. Shane, *The Homogeneous Unit Principle in the Writings and Some Recorded Messages of C. Peter Wagner Applied to the Evangelism Strategies of Covenant Presbyterian Church, Columbia, South Carolina* (M.A. diss., Columbia Graduate School of Bible and Missions, Columbia, SC, 1983).

  James C. Smith, *Without Crossing Barriers: The Homogeneous Unit Concept in the Writings of Donald A. McGavran* (D.Miss. diss., Fuller School of World Mission, 1976).

  John E. Vawter, *A Critical Analysis of Peter Wagner's Seven Vital Signs As They Relate to Selected Evangelical Free Churches in the Twin Cities* (D.Min. diss., Bethel Theological Seminary, St. Paul, MN, 1983).

  Herbert M. Works, *The Church Growth Movement to 1965: An Historical Perspective* (D.Miss. diss., Fuller School of World Mission, Pasadena, 1974).

Donald M. Wodarz, *Church Growth: The Missiology of Donald Anderson McGavran* (Gregorian University, Rome, 1979).

8. Russell Staples, review of *Exploring Church Growth*, Wilbert R. Shenk, ed., *Missiology: An International Review*, July 1984, 382.

9. Wilbert R. Shenk, ed., *The Challenge of Church Growth* (Elkhart: Institute of Mennonite Studies, 1973) and *Exploring Church Growth* (Grand Rapids: Eerdmans, 1983).

10. Harvie M. Conn, ed., *Theological Perspectives on Church Growth* (Nutley, NJ: Presbyterian and Reformed, 1976).

11. Ralph H. Elliott, *Church Growth That Counts* (Valley Forge: Judson, 1982).

12. Robert J. Schreiter, "Culture, Society and Contextual Theologies," *Missiology: An International Review*, July 1984, 262.

13. Donald A. McGavran, *Understanding Church Growth* (Grand Rapids: Eerdmans, 1970; rev. ed., 1980), 223.

14. Richard Lovelace, *Renewal*, August 1984, 9.

15. Lausanne Occasional Paper No. 21, *Grand Rapids Report—Evangelism and Social Responsibility: An Evangelical Commitment*, n.p.: Lausanne Committee for World Evangelization and World Evangelical Fellowship, 1982, 31-32.

Part 2

CHURCH GROWTH
AND EVANGELISM

Through the years many have confused church growth and evangelism. They are not the same, unless . . . unless evangelism means not just sharing the gospel message, but actually bringing unbelievers to faith in Jesus Christ and into responsible church membership. Church growth insists that the evangelistic process does not end until the lost person becomes a disciple of Jesus, validated by responsible church membership. This is the bottom line.

In this section, Elmer Towns, who directs the Church Growth Institute in Lynchburg, Virginia, argues that clear goals are important in the kind of evangelism which leads to church growth. Vague goals bring vague results. W. Charles "Chip" Arn clearly explains the difference between traditional evangelism and disciple making. The difference is important.

George G. "Chuck" Hunter gets practical and shows how evangelism most naturally flows along social networks. McGavran calls these networks "bridges of God." Hunter also stresses that biblical evangelism moves beyond proclamation to making disciples. Then Win Arn, of the Institute for American Church Growth in Pasadena, California, brings it together conceptually in the "Church Growth Development Scale." If your church is going to be an evangelistic church that is truly making disciples, it must move, step by step, along the scale. By the time it reaches the stage of "innovation," evangelism will be happening in a vigorous way.

3
EVANGELISM:
THE WHY AND HOW
Elmer L. Towns

The word *evangelism* does not occur in the New Testament, although the word *evangelist (evangelistes)* occurs three times (Acts 21:8, Eph. 4:11, 2 Tim. 4:5). The evangelist is one who announces glad tidings or good news. Evangelism is both communicating the gospel so that a person understands it and persuading that person to respond to the message. Yet what seems so simple in explanation is misunderstood or misapplied by some and ignored by others.

Three Approaches
There are three approaches to evangelism that C. Peter Wagner, of Fuller Theological Seminary, has called Presence Evangelism (1-P), Proclamation Evangelism (2-P), and Persuasion Evangelism (3-P).

Presence Evangelism seems to stem from the biblical word *witness* or *testimony.* The presence of the Christian is an evangelizing factor, much like the presence of salt is a preserving factor. The Christian does evangelism by living the gospel before the lost, which involves being a positive testimony.

On the mission field, presence evangelism may occur through medical or agricultural work. In some Muslim countries where missionaries are not allowed to enter, Christian businessmen in secular employment become evangelists for Christ by their presence. When a person possesses the attitudes and character of Jesus Christ, he or she can witness the gospel by living an ideal life. Presence evangelism is reflected in what is usually called charity or social action. It is "giving a cup of cold water" in the name of Christ.

Some say that the Christian can do presence evangelism actively or anonymously. When the Christian is influencing others or standing for justice, it is presence evangelism, whether or not the unsaved realize the evangelist is a Christian.

Proclamation Evangelism is making the good news of Jesus Christ known so that the lost will hear it and understand it. J. I. Packer's book, *Evangelism and the Sovereignty of God,* advocates proclamation evangelism. This is usually interpreted to mean a positive proclamation of the gospel without persuasion by the evangelist. Packer, an Anglican theologian, changed the statement of evangelism written by the archbishops of the Church of England in 1918 to read, "To evangelize is so to present Christ Jesus in the power of the Holy Spirit that men *may come* to put their trust in God through Him, to accept Him as their Saviour, and serve Him as their King in the fellowship of His church." The original phrase *shall come* meant that evangelism implied positive results. The phrase *may come* relieves the evangelist from responsibility for the outcome. At the Lausanne, Switzerland, conference on evangelism, John R. W. Stott said that evangelism is "not to preach so something will happen, but to preach whether anything happens or not." When evangelists simply proclaim the gospel with no obligation to measure results, they have obeyed God and fulfilled their duty.

Persuasion Evangelism is not only proclaiming the gospel, but it also involves persuading or motivating the unsaved to respond. Persuasion evangelism is concerned with results. It is assumed that if the process of proclaiming the gospel is effective, then the evangelist should compel the lost to come to Christ. Persuasion evangelism is intentional preaching with a view of bringing men to Christ and into responsible church membership.

Those who believe in persuasion evangelism claim the command "Go therefore and make disciples . . ." (Matt. 28:19, NKJV) implies that the minister has an obligation to get results in evangelism. Disciples are countable, and their number can be expanded. Hence, disciples are the result of evangelism.

The term "make disciples" means to bring a person to Christ, but it includes more than getting a person to make a decision for Christ; it implies motivating the person to follow Christ as his disciple. This interpretation seems to fit persuasion evangelism.

The biblical basis of persuasion is found in the word *peitho*, "to persuade," which means "to bring another to a point of view." Paul states: "Knowing, therefore, the terror of the Lord, we persuade men" (2 Cor. 5:11). When Paul preached in Corinth, "He reasoned in the synagogue every Sabbath, and persuaded . . ." (Acts 18:4).

3-P EVANGELISM*

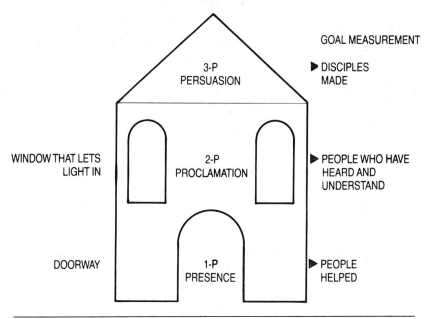

*From Church Growth Notes by C. Peter Wagner, Fuller Theological Seminary

Evangelists must begin with *presence* evangelism (1-P) by "winning a hearing." They must have a good testimony and be interested in meeting the needs of the lost. The godly life of the soul-winner will motivate some lost to seek Jesus Christ. Next, ministers must *proclaim* (2-P) the gospel to the unsaved. Before people can be saved, they must hear the gospel (see Rom. 10:14) and understand the message. Soul-winners must not add works to the gospel nor dilute its obligation. Finally, ministers must *persuade* (3-P) people to receive Christ. At times, Paul pleaded with great emotion (see Rom. 9:2; 10:1); at other times he persuaded with the rational arguments of a trial lawyer (see Acts 13:43).

Eight Words Define Evangelism

Another answer to the controversy regarding evangelism is to examine the words used in the New Testament that relate to evangelism. Note the progressive nature of these eight words that define evangelism, beginning at (1-P) and ending at (3-P).

8 WORDS RELATING TO EVANGELISM		
Witness	*martureo*	Acts 1:8
Speak	*laleo*	Acts 4:1
Evangelize	*evangelizo*	Acts 8:4
Teach	*didasko*	Matt. 28:20
Reason	*dialagomi*	Acts 17:2
Announce	*katangello*	Acts 17:3
Proclaim	*kerusso*	Acts 8:5
Make Disciples	*matheteusate*	Matt. 28:19

First, ministers are to *witness (martureo):* "ye shall be witnesses" (Acts 1:8). Witnesses share what they have seen and heard. Second, they are to *speak (laleo):* "As they spoke to the people" (Acts 4:1), which means to communicate a message. Third, they are to *evangelize (evangelizo):* "Therefore those who were scattered went everywhere preaching the word [evangelizing]" (Acts 8:4), which means "to gospelize," or "to give the gospel message." Fourth, they are to *teach (didasko):* "teaching them to observe all things that I have commanded" (Matt. 28:20), which is a systematic explanation of the gospel so people can understand and believe. Fifth, they are to *reason (dialagomi):* "and he reasoned in the synagogue every sabbath, and persuaded both Jews and Greeks" (Acts 18:4, also see 17:2), which involves answering objections to the message. Sixth, they are to *announce (katangello):*

"Jesus whom I preach to you is the Christ" (Acts 17:3), which is to call the gospel to people's attention. Seventh, they are to *proclaim (kerusso):* "preached Christ to them" (Acts 8:5), which is publicly to announce the gospel so that people can respond to it. Eighth, they are to *make disciples (matheteusate):* "Go therefore and make disciples" (Matt. 28:19), which is to bring people to a conversion experience and get them to follow Christ in the church.

Types of Evangelism
In the New Testament, evangelism was simple; it was a preacher preaching the gospel or a believer sharing Jesus Christ with a lost person. In an age of technology and marketing, especially with a desire for new labels and slogans, there have arisen a number of new titles to designate different types of evangelism, or at least perceived differences in evangelism.

1. Personal Evangelism. Many local churches and Bible colleges have a course entitled "personal evangelism" whereby students are given techniques, approaches, verses, and answers to objections so that they may win souls to Christ. Evangelical churches tend to label this as "evangelism," whereas fundamental churches call it "soul-winning." A high degree of motivation is included in personal evangelism classes.

There are various "plans" or "steps" which are taught to students on how they can present the gospel to the unsaved. Many churches use the "Roman Road of Salvation" which has four steps to salvation based on four verses in Romans. It establishes the person as a sinner and follows God's natural answer to the ultimate human need.

THE ROMAN ROAD OF SALVATION	
Human Need	Romans 3:23
Sin's Penalty	Romans 6:23
God's Provision	Romans 5:8
The Person's Response	Romans 10:9

Other churches use "The Four Spiritual Laws" developed by Campus Crusade International. This approach does not begin with an emphasis on sin, but the overriding motive is God's love. The thought is that soul-winners must have the same motive as God if they are going to reach people for Christ.

THE FOUR SPIRITUAL LAWS

- God loves you and has a wonderful plan for your life.

- Man is sinful and separated from God; thus, he cannot know and experience God's plan for his life.

- Jesus Christ is God's only provision for man's sin. Through Him, you can know and experience God's love and plan for your life.

- We must individually receive Him as Savior and Lord. Then we can know and experience God's love and plan for our lives.

Evangelism Explosion, developed by Dr. James Kennedy, is used in many churches. Teams of three are sent out to present the gospel. Their approach begins with an assumption that the person knows he or she will die and appear before God. The next step is to ask why God should allow the person to enter heaven. The lost person is then faced with the fact that he or she has not made preparation to enter into the presence of God.

EVANGELISM EXPLOSION

- Have you come to a place in your spiritual life where you know for certain that if you were to die today you would go to heaven?

- Suppose that you were to die tonight and stand before God and He were to say to you, "Why should I let you into my heaven?" What would you say?

The Bible teaches personal evangelism by the example of Jesus (the woman at the well, Nicodemus, Zacchaeus) and Philip (the Ethiopian eunuch). However, each time one person leads another to Christ is a clear example of personal evangelism. The examples of Paul evangelizing the Philippian jailer and Sergius Paulus grew out of situations where other circumstances drew the persons to Christ. In personal evangelism, the soul-winner makes an intentional effort to bring the unsaved person to Christ. Technically, personal evangelism is not a by-product of casual relationships, nor is it leading people to Christ after they respond to an invitation at the end of a gospel message. Granted, in both instances one person leads another to accept Christ. But in personal evangelism, the evangelist takes the initiative to present Christ privately so the other may respond.

Certain congregations are characterized as "soul-winning churches" because they plan programs for the intentional evangelization of the lost. This program of personal evangelism is carried out at a regular time. Sometimes this is done by visiting those whose names are supplied on a card, or by visiting all homes in a neighborhood. The evangelist goes door to door to witness for Christ (see Acts 5:42). Sometimes the evangelist goes to a public place such as a bus station with a view of attempting to win people to Christ. This is sometimes called "the fisherman's club" or "soul-winning visitation."

2. Crusade Evangelism. Churches conduct this method of evangelism by inviting an evangelist to come and conduct a series of meetings, usually called an evangelistic crusade. These have sometimes been presumptuously labeled "revival" meetings. (Many times, however, there is no outpouring of the Holy Spirit, so there is no indication of revival.) The meetings usually include special music (choir or soloist), an attempt to get the unsaved to attend, and organized prayer support. Historically, crusade evangelism in a church has attracted many unchurched people and has resulted in some of them coming to Christ.

City-wide crusades involve many churches in an urban area being responsible for attendance and financial and prayer support of an effort to evangelize an entire area. The rationale for a city-wide crusade is that a larger arena could be constructed or rented and a well-known evangelist and singer could be invited who are known for results; hence, the enterprise could be more successful than a crusade held in a single church. Dwight L. Moody and Billy Sunday held city-wide crusades in the past. Billy Graham does so today.

3. Mass Media Evangelism. With the growth of the influence of media, evangelists have used different aspects of media to preach the gospel to the masses. *Radio evangelism* has included the broadcasting of church services, Bible teaching programs, and evangelistic programs, such as the "Old-Fashioned Revival Hour" by Charles E. Fuller. Also included are Christian radio stations that broadcast the gospel twenty-four hours a day. Most believe radio evangelism is more effective among the lost outside the United States, whereas in the United States, Christian radio is more effective among church members.

Television evangelism is similar to radio evangelism, except that it visually presents evangelistic crusades and apparently has a greater response from non-Christians than does radio evangelism.

Literature evangelism involves printing the gospel in tracts (usually for free distribution), magazines and books (usually for sale), and Bibles (both free and for sale). Many foreign missionary agencies engage in colportage work, which is selling inexpensive Christian literature.

The media-coordinated evangelistic outreach of the "I FOUND IT" crusades of the mid-seventies combined a number of media—radio, television, billboards, newspaper advertisements, and others.

4. Saturation Evangelism, originally developed by Ken Strachan, director of the Latin American Mission, is a concept whereby a community is saturated with the gospel by Bible studies, visitation evangelism, media evangelism (usually Christian movies shown in public places), child evangelism, and large crusade evangelistic efforts to bring as many as possible to Christ. Strachan felt the efforts should not be tied to one evangelist, but rather should be the endeavors of the total church mobilizing its membership to use many avenues in evangelizing a community.

In 1971 Jerry Falwell, pastor of the Thomas Road Baptist Church in Lynchburg, Virginia, used the term *saturation evangelism* to mean "using every available means to reach every available person at every available time." Rather than applying it to city-wide crusades, Falwell said media evangelism was a twentieth century technique whereby one church could "capture its town" for Christ. Hence, Falwell adopted the term for local church evangelism. In this context, Jerry Falwell added telephone evangelism, cassette evangelism, and printing evangelism (every church purchasing a printing press and mailing its newspaper to its clientele). He also adopted the sociological principle of synergism, which is using multiple agencies for maximum evangelistic outreach, such as Christian schools, homes for unwed mothers, deaf ministries, camps, bookstores, and other local ministries to reach the church's "Jerusalem" by ministering to the various needs of individuals in the community.

The end product of Falwell's saturation evangelism was a large growing church that had multiple ministries, located on a massive campus, which became the focus of life for its members.

5. Super-aggressive Evangelism. This is a term the author coined to describe the attitudes of faith and optimistic fervor in evangelistic endeavors. The Christians in Jerusalem were enthusiastic in making contact with every person, presenting them with the gospel (Acts 5:28), and persuading them to be saved (2 Cor. 5:11), realizing that through faith the evangelist can accomplish unlimited results. (See *Church Aflame*, Impact Books, 1971.)

6. Life-style Evangelism. The Bible commands Christians to be witnesses (Acts 1:8), technically to be witnesses of the death and resurrection of Christ (Acts 5:30–32). Today Christians share their faith with lost people by witnessing what they have heard, seen, and experienced. Therefore, witnessing requires a Christian to have a good testimony so that he or she becomes an attractive advertisement to motivate lost people to want to have the same kind of life. When this is done, the Christian has built a bridge to the unsaved and has "won the right to be heard," or "earned the right to give the gospel."

Jim Petersen wrote *Evangelism as a Lifestyle* (NavPress, 1980) and contends that many Americans cannot identify with Christianity because of their secular presuppositions. If they simply accept the verbal formulas of the plan of salvation, they will not get saved; they must experience the life of Jesus Christ. To do this, a lost person must have a role model to give meaning to the words of Christianity before he or she can make a meaningful decision for salvation. Hence, the testimony of a believer is foundational in evangelism.

7. *Busing Evangelism.* There was an evangelistic explosion in soul-winning activity in the early 1970s. Many churches got into the bus ministry and experienced growth in attendance, decisions, baptisms and, as a result, built new buildings, added staff, and multiplied ministry. Busing evangelism includes canvassing a neighborhood (usually on Saturdays) to invite people to ride a bus to church (usually children). The worker is called a "bus pastor," and he usually has a driver to assist him. It is the worker's job to care for the children who ride his bus and to try to win their families and friends to Christ. Usually a church has a bus director who organizes all the workers, the route, the equipment, and provides a program to motivate workers to be effective in soul-winning.

During the late 1970s many churches that got into bus evangelism for the wrong reasons quickly got out when inflation caused the costs of gas, insurance, and equipment to spiral. Also, many churches were nurture-oriented, not evangelistically-oriented, and could not handle the unruly children brought in by the buses. Finally, other churches constructed buildings to care for the children but got into financial trouble when they discovered the children could not pay for the buildings. They got out of the bus ministry to stabilize themselves financially. In spite of the problems, many churches have continued a healthy evangelistic outreach through the use of buses.

8. *Front Door Evangelism* describes all the efforts a church makes to attract people through its front door where the lost will hear the gospel, respond, and be converted. Front door evangelism, also called "ingathering evangelism," depends on the corporate church activities to reach and win people to Christ. It is not personal evangelism, media evangelism, or any other phase of evangelism that attempts to win the unsaved outside

the church, then get them into church as a result of their conversion. A front door evangelist attempts to personally invite lost people to church where they will be converted. Also included is the use of advertisements to make the unsaved aware of the church and attract them to church.

Critics of front door evangelism maintain the church is designed for worship or Bible teaching of the saints; it is not an evangelistic crusade. They maintain there is no command in Scripture to bring the lost into the house of God, nor is there an illustration of unsaved coming into a church service. Yet the church is to preach to all people (Mark 16:15) and most preaching happens inside the front door of a church.

9. *Side Door Evangelism* describes the route that many take in coming to salvation. They do not come through a church service, rather they are reached by other agencies or ministries of the church. People attend a group Bible study, a recreational program, or other types of fellowship where they are confronted with the gospel by life-style evangelism or personal evangelism or *oikos* evangelism. Hence, they come to salvation through an agency in the church but not a regular preaching service. Side door evangelism is usually a result of Christians bringing their friends and relatives to Christ through a church ministry.

10. *Oikos Evangelism (Web Evangelism)*. Statistics reveal that most new converts are brought to Christ by friends and relatives.

HOW PEOPLE ARE BROUGHT INTO THE CHURCH	
By Advertisement	2%
By the Pastor	6%
By Organized Evangelistic Outreach	6%
By Friends and Relatives	86%

The Greek word *oikos* is translated *family, kindred, household* (including servants), or *own*. Many in the New Testament who were brought to Christ were the *oikos* of a new convert. Hence, *oikos* evangelism is when a new convert reaches friends and relatives for Christ. The Greek word *oikos* is associated with the outreach of New Testament personalities after they were saved: Lydia, the Philippian jailer, Matthew the tax collector, Zacchaeus, and Cornelius. Hence, the first evangelistic priority of a person after being saved is reaching relatives and friends.

Oikos evangelism is also called *web evangelism*. When applied to a church, it is the principle of the new convert reaching those closest to him or her. By working through web relationships, a church can evangelize its extended congregation (those who are responsive people) and guarantee a smaller dropout percentage of new converts and transfer members.

This chapter is not designed to train readers in evangelism nor to motivate them to win souls. It is designed to expose them to the types of evangelism that are available to today's church. I do not believe that one type of evangelism should be magnified over another. Evangelism, no matter what approach is used (see Phil. 1:14-18), brings glory to God when a sinner comes to God. However, some types of evangelism are more effective in certain circumstances, while others are more effective at other times. No matter what approach is taken, the church's mandate is to present the gospel so people will come to know Jesus Christ.

Type of Evangelism	Description
Personal Evangelism	*Presenting the gospel to one person and motivating him or her to respond.*
Crusade Evangelism	*A planned evangelistic meeting to present the gospel to the lost.*
Mass Media Evangelism	*Using various media to present the gospel*
Saturation Evangelism	*Using every available means to reach every available person at every available time.*
Super-aggressive Evangelism	*An aggressive outreach by faith to create the situation where the lost will be saved.*
Life-style Evangelism	*Living a good testimony before the lost so that an opportunity is gained to present the gospel.*
Busing Evangelism	*Canvassing the neighborhood to motivate people to ride a bus to Sunday school where they will hear the gospel.*
Front Door Evangelism	*Ingathering techniques and programs that motivate people to come into the church to hear the gospel.*
Side Door Evangelism	*Bringing people into various church activities through natural relationships with members where their felt needs are met, then presenting the gospel.*
Oikos Evangelism	*Motivating church members to use their various family and social relationships to present the gospel to their friends and relatives.*

4
EVANGELISM OR DISCIPLE MAKING?

W. Charles Arn

The careful study of growth and decline of American churches in recent years has led to a variety of important, helpful, and sometimes startling insights. And as a result, many, many churches today can testify to new effectiveness and ministry because of the "sanctified curiosity" (as Donald McGavran calls it) of church growth scholars committed to learning how God is blessing the growth of his churches.

Yet sometimes change comes hard. New insights rub against old ways of doing things. Traditions become sacred in their own right. New findings may, at first, be difficult to comprehend. Such may likely be the case with the discoveries about evangelism methods in the 1980s.

There is increasingly strong evidence in church growth literature, as well as in the practical experience of pastors and church leaders, to make the following, somewhat startling, observation: Today "evangelism"—as widely practiced in American churches —is inhibiting the fulfillment of the Great Commission!

Such a conclusion cannot be arrived upon without considerable forethought. Yet the evidence grows stronger with each new study of how people actually come to new faith, of how churches do and do not grow. In the process, these new insights create a rather bizarre dichotomy: many current evangelism methods at best are irrelevant to church growth and at worse are inhibiting the effective outreach of well-meaning Christians and churches.

Some instinctively disagree. At first I, too, rejected the suggestion as ludicrous. But after five years of extensive contact with laity and church professionals across the country, combined with a growing number of validating studies, I now believe such a conclusion frequently reflects reality. Today, the activities that comprise most churches' evangelism programs and the methods which most churches use to "do evangelism" are actually confining the Christian message within the walls of local churches. To go a step farther, I am finding that the very word *evangelism* is so closely associated with many ineffective and unproductive activities intended to Christianize the unconverted that even the use of the word creates obstacles in the minds of laity in most local churches. Perhaps a few generations from now the word can be reintroduced, when the inaccurate stigmas and stereotypes are gone. But for now, even the word is getting in the way of the process.

But all is not lost. Indeed, church growth analysis is intended to provide positive foundations for effective strategy, not tear apart old traditions for lack of a better endeavor. And so, in the constant search for effective disciple-making methodology, important new insights are indeed coming to the fore. And practical new models of effective outreach are being successfully integrated into growing numbers of churches.

In this brief chapter there is room to do little more than introduce some of these concepts and describe their implications. A more complete discussion of both the research and a proposed "church growth model of evangelism" is presented in the book *The Master's Plan for Making Disciples.*[1] Here I would like to highlight some important differences between "evangelism," as it is commonly practiced today, and "disciple making," a term which I believe should more correctly describe the church's efforts in response to the Great Commission.

What Is "Success"?

This question highlights one of the most significant differences between "evangelism" and "disciple making."

Evangelism. Success is achieved when a verbal response is given by the non-Christian, which indicates his/her personal endorsement of a new set of convictions reflective of the Christian faith.

Disciple Making. Success is achieved when a change is observed in the behavior of an individual, which indicates his/her personal integration of a new set of convictions reflective of the Christian faith.

It's a subtle, yet fundamental, distinction. But because the goals are different, the process employed in achieving each goal is different.

The church growth goal, in response to the Great Commission, is "to proclaim Jesus Christ as God and Savior, and to persuade persons to become responsible members of his Church."[2] A responsible church member is indicated through *behavioral* observations.

Evangelism, by contrast, is generally intended as a *decision-making* (not disciple-making) activity. Success is achieved when the person makes a verbal commitment. A "decision" centers around a point in time. A "disciple" centers around an ongoing life-style. Don't be lulled into believing that "decision making" and "disciple making" are synonymous. Nearly every pastor can testify that not all "decisions" produce "disciples" and responsible church members.

Because evangelism tends to define success in terms of a decision, many of its activities become, albeit inadvertently, counterproductive to a person becoming a disciple. Here are a few.

What Is a Method?
Evangelism. The method focuses on bringing a person to a verbal endorsement of Christian beliefs—the goal. It thus requires a *verbal presentation* of the content to which the person is expected to respond.

Disciple Making. The method focuses on bringing a person to a behavioral change—the goal. It thus requires the *experiential observation* of the behavior which the person is expected to imitate.

The question is whether a non-Christian's lifelong values, attitudes, and life-style are more likely to be changed on the basis of a verbal presentation of information, or the experiential observation of behavior.

Nearly every honest person will admit that there are things he or she should do, but does not—the things he intellectually believe but does not behaviorally act out. Paul said as much of himself (see Rom. 7:15). Even Christ spoke of the greater good of one who *acts* honorably though his words are contradictions, than the one who *speaks* properly while his acts are contradictions (see Matt. 21:28-31).

"Actions speak louder than words" is particularly true when it comes to bringing others to new faith and obedience. If the goal is a changed life, rather than repeated words, the method will make a difference in the result.

Effective disciple-making strategies should provide a variety of opportunities for non-Christians to be with other Christians to observe a variety of believers in a variety of situations. Research, in fact, bears this out. In comparing active and inactive members, it was found that those who continued as active church members had been exposed to an average of 5.79 different Christian influences prior to their commitment. Dropouts, by comparison, had seen or heard the Christian message only 2.16 times before their decision.[3] When enough opportunities have been presented for a non-believer to see the Christian faith demonstrated in the lives of others, the desire to affiliate with the church and the Christian faith is often initiated by the non-Christian who has seen Christ demonstrated, has experienced the love of Christian believers, and has determined it is a way of life he or she wants to have. Traditional "evangelism" strategy, however, usually considers any contact with the non-Christian as an opportunity to present the Christian message and ask for a response.

The more exposures a non-Christian has to Christ through his people, the more accurate his understanding of the real commitment he is making. The fewer exposures, the more incomplete his understanding and the greater the chance of the person dropping out.

Who Is Involved?

Evangelism. The assumption is that any individual can appropriately represent the person of Christ and provide sufficient evidence of the Christian faith to cause a non-Christian to accurately perceive the implications and meaning of being a Christian disciple.

Disciple Making. The assumption is that any individual Christian is an incomplete representation of the person of Christ, and that only through exposure to the body of Christ—the local church—can a non-Christian most accurately perceive the implications and meaning of being a Christian disciple.

The second assumption does not imply that no one Christian can bring another person to a new relationship with Christ and his church. Many individuals can and do. God uses any and all means to bring people to new life. Nor do either of these assumptions imply any limitation on God's sovereign ability to reach people in his own way.

What these assumptions do imply is that in our obedience to Christ's Great Commission, we should be aware that the local church—with its complementary assortment of spiritual gifts—more accurately reflects the body of Christ than any one individual member. And the local church provides the most accurate picture available in this earthly life of the complete body of Christ.

Understanding the unique function of spiritual gifts in the church today is an important step toward effective disciple making. According to the New Testament, there are some in your church (with the spiritual gift of evangelist) who are better able than others to lead individuals to new faith.

In the New Testament there are only three places where the word "evangelist" is used (the word "evangelism" is never used). In each case it refers to exercising the particular spiritual gift and/or performing a special activity only certain persons are expected to do. Acts 21:8 describes Philip—the evangelist. In 2 Timothy 4:5 Paul tells Timothy to "do the work of an evangelist." And in Ephesians 4:11 the spiritual gift of evangelist is introduced. The evangelists were those individuals responsible to "tell the good news of victory in battle" (the Greek meaning of *evangelist*). At the same time there are over a hundred references in the New Testament where followers of Christ are called upon to spread the good news of the Christian faith to others. The mistaken assumption of many evangelism approaches today is that "making disciples" means *telling* the good news.

Could a person have a role in making disciples if he or she does not have the gift of evangelist, but has, say, the gift of "hospitality?" Of course! This person's most effective witness may simply be in opening his or her home to non-Christian friends, or church visitors, or persons in need. Such an involvement in "making disciples" no longer requires every member to possess the characteristics required in traditional evangelism activities: extrovertive personality, verbal fluency, tenacity, a good memory for Bible verses, and answers to many theological questions. Making disciples simply means using your unique spiritual gift in the overall process of bringing others into the family of God. Win Arn and Donald McGavran make an important observation in their best-selling book *How to Grow a Church:*

> You would misuse Christ's gifts if you used them solely for the service of existing Christians. That is not why these gifts are given. As we see God's overwhelming concern for the salvation of mankind, we must assume that his gifts are given, at least in large part, that the lost may come to know Him, whom to know is life eternal.[4]

While each Christian is expected to be able to witness to the hope that is within him (1 Pet. 3:15), this does not mean that every Christian is a gifted evangelist. And it is a guilt-producing mistake to imply that every Christian should be. The most effective strategy for disciple making is to build on the unique gifts of each member of the body, and create a means of using those gifts—in concert—to reach others with God's love. As we say in the book *The Master's Plan for Making Disciples,* the more Christians a potential disciple knows, the more complete his or her understanding of God's love.

What Is the Process?

How Christians view the process of persuading the nonbeliever to come to a Christian commitment has a great deal to do with the eventual results of that endeavor.

Evangelism. There are two ways traditional evangelism has viewed this persuasion process. The first is a "content oriented" approach. This view sees the persuasion process as one of communicating certain facts which the hearer needs to know. When the content of the Christian message is presented correctly, an appropriate and positive decision can be expected. Any Christian can succeed if he or she learns how to present the content of the gospel accurately. The relationship between the Christian and non-Christian is characteristic of a teacher and student, the goal being to impart certain correct information.

A second traditional approach to the persuasion process is "confrontationally oriented." This view sees evangelism as a process of using the right technique. It could be an emotional appeal. It could be leading a person through a set of carefully prepared questions and answers. Learning the correct *method* is the most important requirement. Any Christian can succeed if he or she learns the right persuasive approach. The relationship between the Christian and the non-Christian is characteristic of a salesman to customer, the goal being to "close the sale."

Disciple Making. This approach to the persuasion process is "relationally oriented." It sees conversion as the result of a genuine relationship of caring, listening, sharing, and growing together through which God's love is personally experienced. The assumption behind this approach is that since people see things differently, a "canned approach" is not appropriate. Any Christian can succeed if he or she learns how to love. The relationship between the Christian and the non-Christian is characteristic of a friend to a friend, the goal being to love the person as God does.

A study was conducted to see if there was a relationship between how church members viewed the persuasion process and the outcome of their evangelistic endeavors.[5] The study identified three groups (240 people each) of "recipients" of an evangelistic presentation: (1) those who made a Christian commitment and are now actively involved in a local church; (2) those who made a commitment but soon dropped out; and (3) those who said "no thanks" in response to the evangelistic presentation.

There were startling results. It was found that 70 percent (169 of 240) of those persons who are now active church members came to their new faith and church through a member who saw the persuasion process as "relational." By contrast, 87 percent of those persons (209 of 240) who made a verbal commitment but soon became inactive came to that decision through a member whose view of evangelism was characterized as "confrontational." And, of those who said "no thanks," 75 percent (180) did so in response to a church member who saw evangelism as simply sharing certain content, facts, and theology. Interestingly, this study indicates that a confrontational or manipulative approach to evangelism actually results in a greater percentage of persons making a verbal commitment than does a relational approach. However, the dropout rate of such an approach is almost nine out of ten! As mentioned earlier, the goal affects the method. And sometimes the methods of evangelism can actually be counter-productive to the goal of making disciples.

What about Assimilation?

In a few evangelistic approaches today the question of a person's eventual involvement in a local church is not important. The fulfillment of the Great Commission will be reached when everyone has made a Christian decision. But in general, most evangelizers express a genuine desire that each of their converts find a place of involvement in a local congregation. Assuming this is the case, what are the differing assumptions as to how this process of assimilating new believers into a church will occur?

Evangelism. The assumption is that common *faith* between the new believer and the church member is the basis upon which active church membership can be established.

Disciple Making. The assumption is that a common *relationship* between the new believer and the church member is the basis upon which active membership can be established.

Numerous studies in the field of church growth indicate that the most important reason people are involved in their church today is their friendships and relationships. When people drop out of church, the reason most often given is not personal conflict in theology—it is that "I did not feel a sense of belonging. I did not feel needed, wanted, or loved." And when inactive members consider the possibility of a new church home, 75 percent tell researchers the most important thing they will look for is "the friendliness of the people."[6] Other studies indicate that persons who become active church members will have identified an average of seven new friends in the church within the first six months. The dropouts will have made less than two.[7]

The assimilation into the church actually begins before conversion. The friendships of non-Christians with other members of the church will be much more important to their eventual assimilation than commonality of belief. In fact, one of the most fruitful activities your evangelism committee could focus on in the coming year would be helping each church member build a close friendship with one or more non-Christians! It would have a far greater impact on your outreach and growth than training those same persons to verbally present the plan of salvation.

But, the response is sometimes, "If all we do is make friends with non-Christians, we'll have a church full of pagans—there will be no spiritual convictions at all."

Consider the strategy of one of the most productive disciple makers in recent history:

> Wesley had three ultimate objectives for people. (1) That they experience the grace of God and the gift of faith, and become conscious followers of Jesus Christ. (2) That they become united with others in a "class" or "society" (of Christians). (3) That upon achievement of 1 and 2, they experience growth toward Christian perfection. It is crucial to point out that the first two objectives could be achieved in a person's life-history in either order, and the more usual sequence was 2, 1. That is, most of the people who became Methodist converts first joined a class, and sometime later *became* conscious Christians! This helps to explain why Wesley, in his extensive open-air preaching, *never* invited people to accept Jesus Christ and become Christians on the spot! That statement must surely shock those of us whose assumptions about public evangelism have been carved out in the Billy Graham

era, as it would shock the evangelical Christians of any generation since Charles Finney began inviting responders to the "mourner's bench."[8]

Lyle Schaller makes a similar observation:

> The ones least likely to become inactive members are those who become part of a group, where membership in that face-to-face small group is meaningful *before* formally uniting with that congregation. They are assimilated before they join.[9]

Flavil Yeakley, a church growth researcher who closely studied the differences between dropouts and active church members, concluded in his doctoral dissertation:

> When a person has no meaningful personal contacts with the congregation in the process of his conversion, he is likely to feel no meaningful sense of identification with the congregation after his conversion and is therefore likely to drop out.[10]

The fact is that it would do many churches a world of good to have an abundance of pagans in their midst! Certainly Christ did not shrink from the prospect of sitting, eating, and talking with sinners. Yet some churches that pride themselves in their evangelistic fervor would have little tolerance for cigarette butts on the church property, dirty blue jeans in the sanctuary, or cuss words in the classes. I listened to the story of one pastor recently who had brought a teenage Christian rock group to the church for a Saturday night event. Seven hundred young people from the community had come, and over three dozen had indicated a desire to commit their lives to Christ. but the next morning, because the custodian had been out of town, members discovered empty beer bottles by the dozen scattered around the parking lot. Imagine, if you dare, the reaction of the church members! But it could have been a cause for celebration—the world had finally come to their church!

People today who respond to the Christian faith—its people and its message—are those who respond to the love and caring of Christ's people, not to a set of ideas or theological statements.

People are not talked into the kingdom. They are loved in. Reflecting God's unconditional love is the essence of the Christian gospel. And love is experienced, not verbalized. Or, to quote the Apostle John, "Love is not a matter of words or talk, it must be genuine and show itself in action" (1 John 3:18).

Each of these differences could be the basis of an entire book. Here I have only introduced the concepts. Hopefully it has stimulated your own thinking. I encourage you to examine your own church and its assumptions about outreach. If you disagree with some of these concepts, that's fine: research the process and results of evangelism in your situation. As you do, you'll discover the exciting rewards of becoming a church growth researcher. And that's what church growth is really all about—finding the right "growth mix" that will be effective in your church to reach the people in your community and see them discover the joy of fellowship and the fulfilling life in the body of Christ—your church.

1. Win Arn and Charles Arn, *The Master's Plan for Making Disciples* (Pasadena: Church Growth Press, 1982).
2. Win Arn, "Mass Evangelism: The Bottom Line" in *The Pastor's Church Growth Handbook, Vol. 1*, 98, Win Arn, ed. (Pasadena: Church Growth Press, 1979).
3. Flavil Yeakley, *Why Churches Grow* (Arvada, Colorado: Christian Communications, 1979), 65.
4. Donald McGavran and Win Arn, *How to Grow a Church* (Glendale, California: Regal Books, 1973), 36.
5. Flavil Yeakley, "Views of Evangelism" in *The Pastor's Church Growth Handbook, Vol. II*, Win Arn, ed. (Pasadena: Church Growth Press, 1982), 138.
6. Win Arn, "Relationships . . . The Glue That Holds Your Church Together" in *The Win Arn Growth Report #8*. (Pasadena, California: The Institute for American Church Growth, 1985).
7. Win Arn and Charles Arn, *The Master's Plan for Making Disciples*, op. cit.
8. George G. Hunter III, Unpublished manuscript on John Wesley's methods of evangelism.
9. Lyle Schaller, *Assimilating New Members* (Nashville: Abingdon Press, 1978), 76.
10. Flavil Yeakley, *Why Churches Grow*, op. cit.

5
THE BRIDGES OF CONTAGIOUS EVANGELISM: SOCIAL NETWORKS

George G. Hunter III

The modern Church Growth Movement and literature, launched by Donald McGavran's seminal research approach and discoveries, has in principle revolutionized the approach that future Christians will take to spread the faith. Evangelicals already possess an inherited collection of assumptions, approaches, and methods that "ought" to work. But church growth researchers have seen that many approaches and methods that ought to produce fruit do not, and some miss gathering an obvious harvest.

So, using the behavioral science research methods of observation—questionnaire, historical analysis, and (especially) interviews—church growth researchers have made remarkable progress in separating strategic fact from fiction, have sabotaged a number of entrenched evangelical myths, and have identified demonstrable ways forward.

For instance, Christians widely assume that the faith usually spreads (1) impersonally and (2) instantly. The first assumption is reflected in the methods that many sincere Christians employ—from pamphlet distribution, to radio and television broadcasting, to witnessing forms that primarily verbalize a rehearsed formula. Both assumptions are basic in the near-universal model of witnessing that is found, in interviews, to be present in most Christian minds: people usually become Christians when a Christian stranger on, say, a flight from Newark to Richmond, witnesses "cold-turkey" to a seatmate and, in one transaction, welcomes a new convert.

In fact, it almost never happens that way! Indeed, it is so unusual that, when it does occur, the story spreads like a prairie fire, makes the cover of *Guideposts*, and Gospel Films produces yet another winner that plays 20,000 Sunday evenings in as many congregations. Thus these stories of the unusual reinforce the myth that they are usual—or ought to be. But, in fact, the process of "adopting" the Christian faith (or any other significant life-change) usually takes place in stages, spread over weeks or months.[1]

Positively stated, the Christian faith spreads characteristically across the social networks of active credible Christians, especially new Christians. This was the earliest foundational strategic principle discovered by early church growth research, and is an important megastrategy today.

This principle was first perceived to be operating in the movements of some of India's depressed classes into the Christian faith. Bishop J. Wascom Pickett's landmark *Christian Mass Movements in India* reported the classic case of Ditt, a lame little man of the untouchable Chuhra caste in the 1870s. Upon his conversion at a mission station, Ditt—against the advice of the missionaries—immediately returned to his village, people, and trade, and experienced a period of ostracism. But he persevered and loved his people, and, as Pickett writes,

> Three months after his baptism he reappeared in Sialkot and presented his wife, his daughter, and two neighbors as candidates for baptism. He had taught them what he knew; they professed their faith and their purpose to follow Christ and had walked thirty miles to be baptized. After examining them, instructing them and praying with them, Mr. Martin administered the rite, whereupon they immediately started back to their village. Six months later Ditt brought four other men who were also adjudged ready for baptism. The missionaries were by now convinced that a work of God was in progress in Ditt's village. Ditt's humble occupation of buying and selling hides took him to many villages. Wherever he went he told his fellow Chuhras

of Christ. Many abused him, but an increasing number heard him patiently, and before long groups here and there began to follow his lead. In the eleventh year after Ditt's conversion more than five hundred Chuhras were received into the Church. By 1900, more than half of these lowly people—had been converted, and by 1915 all but a few hundred members of the caste professed the Christian faith.[2]

Pickett's account illustrates vividly the major principle that, when Christianity is spreading contagiously, it is spreading along the social networks of one or more active credible Christians. (It also illustrates another principle, that the faith spreads more easily within a social unit than across social units.)

Donald McGavran "lit his candle at Pickett's fire" and used Pickett's discovery as a hypothesis for wider testing. Through twenty years of research among growing and nongrowing churches in many languages and cultures of Latin America, Asia, and Africa, McGavran demonstrated that Pickett's discovery is universal. In every land and tribe and language and culture in which the faith has spread, the social networks composed of the relatives and friends of caring credible believers have made up *The Bridges of God*.[3] The faith is not usually spread between strangers, but between persons who know and trust each other. The social networks of the body of believers provide opportunity for a "web movement" of the Christian faith.

There are exceptional cases that fit the evangelical "myth." But some of the exceptions, upon examination, prove the rule! For instance, interviews with many apparently "instant" converts reveal that some stages toward faith had already been experienced in the person's recent life history, however unapparent to others. Typically, they report disillusionment with some idol, or a struggle with some unmet need, or a period of wondering and asking questions, or a period of observing the faces and lives of Christians. The evangelizer engaged them at a receptive period in their life history, gathering the harvest that was prepared but not necessarily obvious. Or, in cases where a person is won by a stranger, interviews reveal that first the person came to regard the Christian stranger as a trustworthy friend, permitting an apparent stranger to be the agent of his or her conversion. As in many areas of life, many examined "exceptions" prove the rule!

Actually, several types of networks are involved in the spread of faith. Sometimes neighborhood networks are potent. Frazier Memorial United Methodist Church in Montgomery, Alabama, has received over one hundred families from "Arrowhead"—a movement launched when one of the neighborhood's first four families joined Frazier and began inviting other new families. Sometimes collegial networks are potent, as one church in a city reaches many medical people, while another reaches teachers and their families.

More usually, the potent contagious bridges are along kinship networks or friendship networks. These two types of networks vary in their comparative evangelical power. For instance, in Mexico a large majority of new converts are brought across the bridges of kinship networks. In Anglo populations of the U.S.A., friendship networks are most potent. These two types of networks vary in number as well as potency. In tightly-knit societies, like tribes, there may be relatively few bridges between an unbeliever and Christians, but each bridge is strong. In looser-knit societies, like urban America, the bridges may be weaker but there are more of them to influence the undiscipled person toward faith.[4]

In the U.S.A., Lyle Schaller's twenty-five years of research show two-thirds to three-quarters of all new church members responding to the possibility from someone in their kinship or friendship network. In faster growing churches, the range is two-thirds to seven-eighths, and in very rapidly growing churches these two factors (especially friendship) account for over 90 percent of the new members.[5]

Of course, when any population of Christians is surveyed, some will not indicate a person as their major bridge into the faith. In Win Arn's research, some 10 to 25 percent indicate a first factor other than a friend or relative.[6] Occasionally the number attracted by other factors is somewhat larger. In 1983, some 8,000 Jewish believers responded to the question "What initially attracted you to the gospel, and what one agent most helped you to find the Lord?" *The Jews for Jesus Newsletter* published the results:

INITIAL ATTRACTION TO THE GOSPEL	
A person	47%
Search for truth	11%
Bible	8%
Book or other literature	8%
Supernatural intervention	6%
Group of believers	5%
Conviction/Holy Spirit	4%
Life crisis	3%
Radio/TV/Movies	2%
Curiosity	2%
Afterlife/Fear	1%
Ideals/World conditions	1%
No answer	4%

Of the 47 percent who reported "a person" as being their bridge, 62 percent reported that the person was a friend or family member.[7] This study, one of many similar studies of different Christian populations, shows perhaps the lowest percentage of conversions primarily due to relational human bridges of any such research project. Yet, even in this atypical ethnic population, the social networks of Christians are far more potent than any other single factor in evangelism. And interviews would reveal that a strong trust relation with one or more Christians was an indispensable factor in their evangelization, even if not recalled as the one agent that most helped. From all such research as this, we see additional ways in which some traditional evangelism approaches that "ought" to be prolific are not.

If the social networks of Christians are, indeed, the bridges of the seeking God of the biblical revelation, and if this is the first principle of informed church growth practice, how does one apply the principle and develop appropriate strategy? Explaining the principle is one thing, but making it work to make disciples is another.

A Mennonite church in Japan employs the following strategy: During the three month, one night per week, one-on-one post-conversion training for new members, the trainer and convert develop a list of all the person's names in the new convert's active social network. The trainer, near the end of the three months, asks the convert to underline all the names of persons thought not to be active disciples through any congregation. The trainer asks, "Which of these (underlined) people do you have some influence with?" Those names are circled, and the trainer and convert together reach out to each of those persons. As some of those persons are attracted into discipleship, the strategy is repeated.[8] Most churches could develop and execute a similar strategy, appropriately adapted to their culture and situation.

In a church growth manual developed for congregations bent on *Finding the Way Forward*,[9] I offer to church leaders a simple set of strategic guidelines that have helped other congregations:

1. Secure the names of all undiscipled persons within the social webs of your active credible Christians. Have some member of your evangelism committee visit, with each active member, the undiscipled persons he or she has listed.

2. As you win some of those target persons, secure the names of their undiscipled relatives and friends. Have an evangelism committee member visit, with the new believer, these people to be reached.

3. Survey each member each season to get the names of new undiscipled prospects. This will continually reveal a fertile harvest field for your church—undiscipled persons who are already linked to one or more persons in your congregation.

4. As you reach out, do not in every case attempt to gather Christ's prepared harvest in just one visit or conversation. Be prepared to visit with persons a half-dozen more times to help them work through what their response to the invitation might be.

5. As some of your people begin serving as new bridges for others, reinforce this action through appropriate public recognition. For instance when you receive new members into the church, invite members who served as bridges for them to stand with them, and pray both for new disciples and their human bridges.

Recognition, appropriately conferred, may be the most neglected and the most cost effective continuing strategy available in most churches today. Leaders completely control who they publicly say "thank you" to. It costs nothing except time—and precious little of that when well managed. Besides, our people have the impression that what gets recognition is most important in the organization and that which is not recognized is comparatively unimportant. So recognize your faith-bridges. As the importance of their outreach is perceived, as their ministry is modeled for others, as their stories get around, and as the people meet their converts, their tribe will increase!

Win and Charles Arn, in *The Master's Plan for Making Disciples*, have based an entire approach to evangelism essentially upon this one principle. They see the principle modeled in the New Testament *oikos*, that is, the extended household of family and friends that characterized an early Christian's sphere of intimates to whom the faith was likely to spread.

The Arns declare:

Webs of *common kinship* (the larger family), *common friendship* (friends and neighbors), and *common associates* (special interests, work relationships, and recreation) are still the paths most people follow in becoming Christians today.

And in America today, with some variation by region, culture, and class, between 75 and 90 percent of new members surveyed report a friend or relative as the one factor most responsible for their evangelization.[10]

The Arns support this church growth script for interpersonal evangelism with other church growth insights and a practical plan for helping Christians to perceive and reach across their web of influence. A number of churches have experienced renaissance through working "the Master's Plan." In one case, the Rev. Brad Dinsmore moved to the Lake Magdalen United Methodist Church in Tampa, Florida. He devoured *The Master's Plan*, had it studied in every class and group in the church, featured the film *For the Love of Pete*, and led Master's Plan workshops for other churches. In the last several years Lake Magdalen Church has experienced unprecedented growth and now leads Florida Methodism in net growth and new Christians received.

And yet most Christians (including self-designated evangelicals) do not share their faith—despite reading books, attending workshops, and discussing evangelism. Many Christians confess they would like to do evangelistic ministry—but "not now," or "I still don't know how," or "I'm just not the type."

Several years ago I began interviews with lay people (and pastors) who were already interested enough to attend an evangelism or church growth workshop or seminar but weren't yet doing evangelistic outreach. The interviews revealed that, in regard to *doing* evangelism, most of them harbored more hangups than the city art gallery! What was the source of this resistance to following the Great Commission? Gradually I came to realize that most Christians are immobilized by a stereotype of who "evangelists" are and what they do. Their mental state is ambiguous for they applaud the *goal* of the Great Commission—to find the lost and make disciples—but they feel negative toward what they perceive to be the necessary *means* to achieving that goal. Specifically, I have been able to identify four issues upon which most Christians flounder: (1) The type of persons who evangelize, (2) the feelings involved for the non-Christian, (3) the things evangelizers say, and (4) what they do.

Undoubtedly there are other issues, for the Evil One has strewn this path with many difficulties. I became confident of only those four issues, but what they enabled me to see was astonishing, as I pursued answers through more interviews. The research uncovered a nearly universal stereotype that triggers for Christians a dozen or more incapacitating connotations. When Christians reflect, they acknowledge this stereotype to be extreme and unfair, but nevertheless it is their mental image of evangelism.

When reluctant evangelical Christians describe their image of the type of people who most do evangelism, a clear caricature emerges. When they are asked to suggest adjectives, the following typically surface: aggressive, pushy, dogmatic, narrow-minded, hypocritical, ignorant, silver-tongued, moralistic, superconfident, bombastic, arrogant, naive, square, emotional, critical, insensitive, imposing, doctrinaire, closed-minded, won't take no for an answer.

Now that is a laundry list! People also mention some neutral words such as: bold, well-dressed, assured, outgoing, extroverted. And people offer occasional positive adjectives such as: authoritative, good speaker, scholarly, risk taking, positive. But over 90 percent of the adjectives are negative and alienating. That is their image of "the type of people who go in for evangelism." The problem is obvious. Most Christians do not see themselves reflected in that image, do not identify with it, and would not even want to be like it if they could be—though some believe that they "ought" to. As mentioned, upon reflection, almost everyone acknowledges the image to be an extreme and unfair stereotype. But, subconsciously, the image paralyzes most Christians, and it partly explains why they refrain from evangelizing.

When evangelical Christians are asked what feelings are involved for the receivers of stereotyped evangelism, the "feeling words" most often generated are: guilty, afraid, anxious, condemned, damned, inadequate, angry, hostile.

Interviews may not get to issues three and four: What do stereotypical evangelistic types *say?* and What do they *do?* because the answers to these last two questions are clearly implied in the discussion of the first two. The imaged behavior pattern pictures an unrequested and unnegotiated monologue, wherein the evangelizer controls the process, is not genuinely interested in nor open to the other person, gives the other no credit for knowing, believing, or having experienced anything worthwhile, and at the end demands premature response. Upon probing, a large majority of these people have never been personally submitted to such "evangelism," but they all know of people who have been! The message of the stereotype is authoritarian ("the only way to see things"), is a packaged presentation, and is steeped in the theological jargon of another era and cultural situation ("they don't talk like folks I know").

Many Christians refrain from doing evangelism because they do not know how to communicate in those ways, and do not desire to! So the church growth researcher, acknowledging this widespread image of evangelism, asks, "How does it *really* take place?" Specifically, what kind of people really help others find their way to faith and into the church? How do they make people feel? What messages do they communicate? What behaviors do they engage in that help make a difference?

For the past four years, while leading church growth seminars in many denominations across the U.S.A., and in Canada, Mexico, England, and South Africa, I have found one session of simple data gathering to be particularly instructive. Each participant writes the name of the one person most responsible for his or her involvement with Christ and the church. If several names come to mind, they identify the person involved in the most recent incident, or the one most vividly recalled.

Then they respond to four questions: (1) What was this person like for you? Write the adjective that best describes this "significant other" in your life. (2) How did the person make you feel, perhaps about yourself? Write a feeling word. (3) What, that you can recall more or less verbatim, did the person say that helped make a difference? Write a message statement. (4) What did the person do that helped make a difference? Write a behavior statement.

We spend the remainder of the session making a representative list of the responses to each of the four questions and we compare each list to the stereotype as described above. When each set of two lists are posted, the results are astounding.

When Christians report the chief characteristic of their human bridge into faith and the church, the two most cited adjectives are "caring" and "loving." Others frequently reported are somewhat synonymous: encouraging, concerned, accepting, understanding, supporting, warm, affirming, sensitive, kind. While different personalities with different needs respond to a wide variety of traits in other persons, there is always less than a 5 percent overlap between this list and the adjectives describing the stereotypical evangelist. A few adjectives reflective of the stereotype do surface, such as: persistent, confident, aggressive, winsome, persuasive, insistent. But the more extreme adjectives of the stereotype never surface in this data gathering, and about half of all training groups generate no adjectives that overlap with the stereotype. This contrast between myth and reality is remarkably consistent in each of the several countries where I have led this exercise, and is consistent in various denominational groups from Church of God and Southern Baptist to Presbyterian and Episcopal.

The degree of contrast continues with the other three sets of lists. The kinds of feelings allegedly involved in stereotypical evangelism, cited above, are probably the greatest inner barrier to evangelism today. That is, Christians have no interest in making people feel that way. The great news from contemporary research is that those feelings are not the key feelings that Christians report from the relationship with their human bridge into the faith. Indeed, it would be hard to imagine any greater contrast between myth and fact. In general, Christians reflecting upon their feelings at that time report feeling more secure rather than less, better about themselves rather than worse, and less pressured rather than more.

It is widely held that evangelism, whatever else it may be, is proclamation. To evangelize is to proclaim the glad tidings. Evangelism is the transmission of a message with accuracy and recall. But contemporary research qualifies that shibboleth. About half of all evangelical Christians have difficulty recalling *anything* their human bridge said that made the difference! Now undoubtedly the gospel was communicated to these people. They apprehended its meaning from a number of persons and experiences, through body language, words, and deeds. But their "significant other" was not basically "proclaiming." Much more is involved in the ministry of evangelism than verbalizing a message because people are much more than "souls with ears." Indeed, as Christians remember conversations that made a great difference, the evangelist was doing about 80 percent listening and 20 percent talking! Furthermore, many people report overhearing a significant message—in some context where they were free to listen and consider, with no eyes looking back and expecting an immediate response.

Nevertheless, effective evangelism frequently involves saying something faithful to another person. The variety of remembered messages that made a difference is vast. (1) Some messages, as one would expect, are theological affirmations: You are a child of God, created in his image. God accepts you and loves you just as you are. Jesus died for you. I guarantee that Christ can change your life. (2) Sometimes the message's main focus is the person being addressed: There is a purpose for you. Something good is going to happen to you. You have something to contribute to someone else. (3) Sometimes the message reflects the relationship between messenger and receiver: I am concerned about your salvation. I accept you as you are.

In summary, from established church growth research we learn that the gospel spreads along the social networks of living Christians. Now we are beginning to learn how it spreads, that is, the human relations dimension of the faith's expansion. At this level we encounter a stereotype about the kind of people who evangelize, how they make people feel, what they do, what they say. But most Christians are "not that type" and do not want to be. They resist the possibility of saying those things, doing those things, and making people feel that way.

The good news from this modern research is "that type" of evangelism does not have a widespread presence or impact in the world today. We have no evidence of any great reproductive work of that kind of evangelism in our churches. Indeed, Christians report from their own experiences a very different picture.

The good news is that the people of God are far more prepared and equipped to do the work of an evangelist than most have ever dreamed. And effective evangelism is not alien to those receiving the gospel, their style, their sensitivities, and their abilities. Indeed the kind of people who best spread the faith are the kind of people most others already are, or would love to become. Effective evangelists help people to feel in ways congruent with their good will. And effective evangelists say the kinds of things that are heard and do the kinds of things that are appreciated. This generation will see a vast sleeping army awakened, prepared, and equipped at a time when the church faces unprecedented opportunity in an increasingly receptive world.

1. See Everett M. Rogers, *Diffusion of Innovations*, 3rd ed. (New York: The Free Press, 1983).
2. J. Wascom Pickett, *Christian Mass Movements in India* (Lucknow: Lucknow Publishing House, 1933), 43-45.
3. Donald A. McGavran, *The Bridges of God* (New York: Friendship Press, 1955).
4. Donald A. McGavran, *Understanding Church Growth*, rev. ed. (Grand Rapids: Eerdmans, 1980), 403-404.
5. Lyle E. Schaller, "Six Targets for Growth," *The Lutheran*, September 3, 1975.
6. Win Arn and Charles Arn, *The Master's Plan for Making Disciples* (Pasadena, California: Church Growth Press, 1982), 43.
7. "We're Glad You Asked" in *The Jews for Jesus Newsletter*, Volume 6:5744, 1984, p. 4.
8. Donald McGavran and George G. Hunter III, *Church Growth Strategies That Work* (Nashville: Abingdon Press, 1980), 35-36.
9. George G. Hunter, *Finding the Way Forward* (Nashville: Discipleship Resources, 1980), fifth point added.
10. Arn and Arn, *The Master's Plan for Making Disciples*, 43.

6
UNDERSTANDING AND IMPLEMENTING GROWTH FOR YOUR CHURCH
Win Arn

After representatives from a number of churches attend the same church growth seminar and apply the same strategies, why do some churches see results, while others do not?

I have recently developed what I call the "Church Growth Development Scale" that, in many cases, helps to answer this question. It explains why an appropriate strategy of church growth depends on a number of factors; why a strategy may be highly successful for one church, and yet for another may cause a church split!

Locating your congregation on this scale can help you determine the appropriate steps you need to take to move your church forward in growth. As you study the Church Growth Development Scale, keep the following in mind: (1) Growth requires moving from one step on the scale to the next. A church cannot jump over a step, although sometimes leaders inadvertently try. When they do they encounter problems. (2) Individuals change before organizations change. Some church leaders try to change the organizational structure prior to changing individuals. When they do they encounter frustrations. (3) Correct strategy for growth will vary depending on where the church is presently located on the scale. (4) Movement on the scale may be forward or backward. (5) Leadership in a church may be at a different place on the scale than membership. This may create problems if it is assumed both groups are at the same point. (6) While I have drawn each step as distinctly separate, each step overlaps with the ones beside it.

Church Growth Development Scale[1]

1. Ignorance

   Congregation and leadership are uninformed of the mandate to make disciples. Church departments and ministries have no unified direction or sense of mission. The church tends to be self-centered and self-serving.

2. Information

   Church members have a general interest in learning more. Questions arise about what results "church growth" might have for the church. If no further action is taken, increased indifference and apathy toward the Great Commission develops.

3. Infusion

   Penetration of new ideas into the status quo may cause confrontation with apathy, prejudice, tradition. The tendency is to focus on problems. The need is for a *dream* to carry the church to the next step.

4. Individual Change

   "Church growth eyes" begin to develop in some leaders. A growing number of questions arise about whether present church activities are bringing satisfactory results. Little institutional reinforcement exists for members advocating change.

5. Organizational Change

   The church's goals are reviewed and clarified in light of the growing mission priority. New activities and ministries are introduced in response to the new focus. New committees and structures may be formed.

6. Awkward Application

   Some failures and some successes are experienced. Initially limited applications of church growth thinking are attempted. Some mistakes are made, but the learning process is rapid. The need for additional knowledge, training, resources becomes apparent.

7. Integration

   People grow more comfortable in understanding and applying church growth principles. Fewer dramatic changes, more refinement of previously initiated change. People feel a growing sense of accomplishment, and a secondary wave of results and successes occur.

8. Innovation

The base of support and involvement by members and the application of principles expands to other areas. Significant results are achieved, and growth begins to perpetuate itself.

Suggestions for Moving Forward on the Growth Scale

Knowing where your church is on the Church Growth Development Scale is only the first part. An equally important question is how to move from one step of the scale to the next. Here are a few beginning ideas. There are abundant resources available from the Institute for American Church Growth[2] to help you with practical and tested procedures to grow. Once you have located your church's position, consider the following.

Ignorance to Information. Show church growth films. Precede board and committee meetings with study of church growth books. Emphasize growth and outreach in sermons. Establish the biblical base that "God's will is that his church grows." Study growth and the early church in adult education classes.

Information to Infusion. Establish a church growth task force. Study the church's growth patterns. Formulate and communicate a dream for the church. Sponsor a church growth seminar. Conduct a diagnostic study of the church and community. Seek support of lay leadership. Expand reading and study in church growth.

Infusion to Individual Change. Share information from church diagnostic process. Ask what are appropriate responses to diagnostic information. Use church growth consultants. Give high visibility to the church's dream. Seek public commitment to growth by lay leadership. Conduct a survey to identify areas of need and opportunity for outreach.

Individual Change to Organizational Change. Establish a statement of purpose. Involve laity in setting growth goals and objectives. Identify needed new groups, new roles, new tasks. Provide continuing education for the task force. Keep the dream in front of the membership. Emphasize changes as additions not replacements. Use proven growth methods (for example, "The Master's Plan," "Caring Systems").

Organizational Change to Awkward Application. Publicly recognize and appreciate growth leaders. Closely monitor growth projects. Quickly recycle potential failures. Communicate early successes. Encourage the pastor and staff to model commitment.

Awkward Application to Integration. Encourage and inform "middle adopters" (see following definition). Provide growth events for the larger congregation to become involved. Expand the number of roles available in outward-focused areas. Sponsor a second church growth seminar for updating.

Integration to Innovation. Enlarge the staff with a director of evangelism/church growth. Celebrate God's blessing. Share credit with laity. Enlarge the dream. Build disciples and mature Christians from new members. Write a book to communicate your experiences!

Understanding and Encouraging Change in Your Church
When a proposal for change is introduced to move forward on the "Church Growth Development Scale" in your church, people will fall into one of five categories in terms of their response:

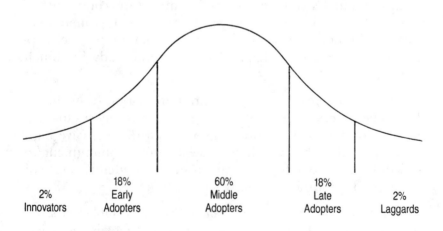

| 2% Innovators | 18% Early Adopters | 60% Middle Adopters | 18% Late Adopters | 2% Laggards |

Innovators. These are the dreamers, persons who are often responsible for new ideas but seldom receive the credit. Generally they are not acknowledged as leaders or policy makers. Many have the spiritual gift of faith.

Early Adopters. Those who know a good idea when they see it. Their opinions are generally respected in the church. They often receive credit for a new idea that may not have been theirs. Many have the gift of wisdom.

Middle Adopters. The majority who respond to proposals of others. They are generally reasonable in their analysis of new ideas, but are inclined to maintain the status quo. They are more easily influenced by those opposing change than those supporting it.

Late Adopters. These are the last in a church to endorse a new idea. They often speak against and vote against proposed changes or ideas or innovations. They may never verbally acknowledge acceptance, but they will generally adopt if the majority has demonstrated support.

Laggards. New ideas seldom, if ever, are adopted by this group. Their commitment is to the status quo and the past. They often sow discord after change. Often they are the leaders of division within the church.

An appropriate understanding of how churches grow—steps in church growth and necessary resources to see growth happen—can alleviate frustration on the part of the pastor and the church. By providing a measurable step-by-step process under the direction and guidance of the Holy Spirit, it is possible to overcome obstacles and find a sense of renewal, progress, and God's blessing in the life of the pastor, the people, and the church.

1. This "Church Growth Development Scale" was first introduced in Win Arn's *Growth Report,* a free publication sent on request from the Institute for American Church Growth, 709 E. Colorado Blvd., Suite #150, Pasadena, CA 91101 (818/ 449-4400).
2. Institute for American Church Growth, 709 E. Colorado Blvd., Suite #150, Pasadena, CA 91101 (818/449-4400).

Part 3

CHURCH GROWTH
AND THE BODY
OF CHRIST

The word church *in the phrase "church growth" is key. If the church is not healthy, God's goal of finding the lost and bringing them into the fold will not be accomplished very effectively. Since the church is so central, it is to be expected that the largest section of this book would deal with the church. Kent R. Hunter of the Church Growth Center in Corunna, Indiana, starts it off by answering the question: How important is church membership? He shows that it is extremely important, that it brings many benefits, and that the conditions of membership should be known up front when new people come to the church.*

Win Arn's chapter on key ratios surfaces some new and exciting research. It allows you to take quantitative measurements of important qualities of your church, just like the physician does in a physical examination. W. Charles Arn then probes deeply into the biblical and practical aspects of recruiting lay people as ministers in your church. In doing this, he elaborates on the 60:100 role/task ratio in Win Arn's chapter.

Charles B. "Chuck" Singletary of Church Resource Ministries reminds us of the growth triangle: quantity-quality-organic. He develops the organic side and shows how important the infrastructure can become if the church is to grow. Then Kent Hunter takes up the quality side and shows why only high quality churches really grow. John N. Vaughan, a recognized expert on the superchurch, takes the quantity side of the triangle and shows how some of the world's superchurches are serving their communities and meeting people's needs. Then Medford Jones concludes the section with some new research leading to practical church growth principles.

7
MEMBERSHIP INTEGRITY: THE BODY OF CHRIST WITH A BACKBONE

Kent R. Hunter

History shows many examples of the impotent church. People aren't growing in discipleship, the health of the church is poor, there is little effective outreach to the unchurched, and the vision of the Great Commission is clouded. It is not that Christ, the head of the body, is impotent. The all-powerful Ruler of the universe is resurrected, alive, and well! But the rest of his body is paralyzed. It's hard to talk about. It's hard to imagine. Yet everyone knows it's true.

The church becomes bureaucratic, institutionally fossilized, and static. Membership seems like a social club. The mission and ministry go around in circles like a carousel in a religious rut. Ecclesiastical atrophy permeates a structure that has become, in many cases, a political playground. It doesn't happen on purpose; most people never intend it to be that way. It happens because we humans—by our nature—are dead in sin. People dead in sin make for dead churches, at least from the neck of the body on down.

However, one of God's specialties is resurrection! He resurrected Jesus on that glorious Easter dawn. He resurrects the faith in people touched anew by the gospel. Even more, he resurrects churches! For an increasing number of churches on several continents, God is using the modern Church Growth Movement to perform this miracle.

The Church Growth Movement is many things. But above all, it is an ecclesiology. It gives focus to the nature, the function, and the health of the church as it relates to the effective implementation of the Lord's Great Commission. The historical growth axiom reflects the value of this focus: throughout history the church has shown signs of health and growth when it has known its identity. The identity crisis is prevalent in established churches that lose the excitement and zeal of the cutting edge of making disciples. We can easily become fat, lazy, self-centered, and maintenance-oriented: business as usual. But nothing is usual about the business of the church! We simply forget who we are. We forget whose we are—to whom we belong.

Christ has called us out of darkness into some marvelous light, Why? To reach out to all peoples. To grow. The Church Growth Movement helps the people of God look into the mirror of the Bible to see clearly. Among the results is the rebirth of self-esteem in that beautiful God-given privilege we call church membership.

Member of What?

The church is still bureaucratic in some ways. There are political and social aspects of the organization. But church growth proponents wave the banner that declares—as does Scripture—that first and foremost the church is a living organism. Utilizing the dynamic imagery of Scripture, the Church Growth Movement stresses the body of Christ, the vine and the branches, the shepherd and the sheep, the living temple of living stones, and the royal priesthood. Even more, church growth thinking focuses upon the church member as a living part of God's organism called the church. The connection is clear: As a part of the organism, each person has a vital part in the greatest adventure of all history—world evangelization, making disciples of all peoples.

In past decades some have said that the age of the church is gone, that the church is dead as a vital part of Christianity. On the contrary, says church growth thinking, the church is central. It is basic to God's unswerving purpose: the redemption of lost mankind. In a world of impersonalization, each person is a part of the body of Christ and has a ministry to perform. In an age of consumerism, the individual is seen as an important part of the body life in the Christian community, with responsibilities to Christ, to others, to the world.

All of this means that church membership means something.

92

It is not a fad. It is not just the fashionable thing to do. It is the privilege of those in fellowship with the King. That kind of integrity is reflected in at least five ways.

1. Each person in the church is important. Therefore, ministry in the body is important. Growing churches tend to develop formal and informal ways in which members can minister to one another. Core groups, cell groups, home Bible studies, prayer chains, service groups, and social action committees are just some of the ways that concern for members is structured. Unstructured ministry happens also, because people with church growth eyes believe that ministry—healing people's hurts—is everybody's business, not just the preacher's.

2. Since each person is important, sensitivity develops to people's felt needs. Felt needs are God-given channels for growth, especially across the natural bridges of friends and relatives, people with whom we work or go to school. People who live with a church growth mentality look for those needs and hurts that can be avenues for God's love and forgiveness.

3. Every Christian has at least one spiritual gift. A spiritual gift is a supernatural attribute given by God's grace to each member of the body of Christ. The gifts determine the function of ministry. God's way of looking at the different kinds of people in the church is not by intelligence, education, beauty, or social status. These categories divide; God unifies through the use of spiritual gifts. All Christians should use their gifts to build up the body.

4. Churches that get involved in church growth take on a new or renewed spirit of membership accountability. Membership is not a theoretical response to the gospel. A disciple is a responsible member of the body of Christ. Jesus said people will be known by their fruits. The activities, the involvement don't bring salvation—that happens by God's grace through faith in Jesus Christ. Yet the response is important because people are important. The spiritual activities of members can be monitored for the benefit of the church. Churches often monitor only one thing: money. In what area other than finances do people receive a quarterly statement or report? In growing churches, many are using the technology of the computer age to keep track of members' involvement in worship, communion, Sunday school, and

many other activities. Individuals are important, not as names on a roll or cash in the offering basket, but because Christ died for each one.

5. It should not surprise anyone, therefore, that membership conservation and reclamation are important church growth tasks. If members are that important to Christ, how can a church "file" people away in an "inactive file"? Like bodies in drawers at a spiritual morgue, many churches have piled and filed those they unaffectionately call "dead wood." A growing church must recognize that these important people are not dead wood but people for whom Jesus Christ died. Furthermore, an inactive Christian, in the view of Christian discipleship, is an oxymoron—a set of words that contradict one another. An inactive Christian is as impossible as a hot snowball!

Unwilling to allow such contradictions, many churches that want to grow begin to seek out those people on their inactive list. Some have moved away. Some are unwilling to respond. Some may even be dead. But churches that are caught in the momentum of church growth thinking begin to seek out and deal with each individual. They also want to be more accurate in their reporting methods. It is not uncommon, therefore, to see on a church report a membership figure much lower than previous years—because of a renewed commitment to seek out and care for every individual.

Skeletal Structure
If the body of Christ is a living organism, it needs a skeleton. If people are important, there needs to be a place for everyone. In fact, church growth thinking points to the various needs of people to belong on three levels.

First, people want a corporate identity. This is the celebration, the worship level where people look around and say, "This is our church." They worship, they praise, they celebrate together.

Second, people want to have their fellowship needs met. This can't happen in the celebration in many churches because the group is too large. Therefore, the congregation or subcongregation should be a smaller fellowship group with opportunities for Bible study and mutual care ministries.

Third, the small cell group allows people to be accountable

to one another, to pray for and encourage one another on an intimate level. Bible study and prayer also provide the spiritual power for care and concern through the love of Christ.

This structure is important to the growing church. It is part of the base that David Womack says is necessary to expand before the mass can be enlarged. He calls it the "pyramid principle." This and other structural expansion issues in church growth thinking result in growth, but are motivated out of high regard for the Christian disciple in the body of Christ.

Front-end Integrity
Dean Kelley, in his book *Why Conservative Churches Are Growing*, indicates that those churches with a high integrity toward explaining the meaning of life are churches that are showing numerical growth. The point is that churches grow when they provide for people in those areas for which churches are uniquely qualified. This is in contrast to churches that have gotten involved in many other issues due to poor focus and a lost sense of biblical priorities.

Church growth calls the local church to follow the priorities of Scripture: The Lord's will is that the lost be found and brought into the church. But how are these priorities communicated? How does the concern for quality discipleship get across to people who transfer in or to those who are "church shopping"? How does a church help people avoid joining the wrong local church—for them—and help them find a church that is best for their needs and gifts?

At first, front-end integrity may look like legalism or exclusion. But it is not exclusion when it is simply an honest acceptance of the fact that every church is different, has different expectations and priorities. It is not legalism because up-front integrity does not make statements that are prerequisite to salvation or even acceptance of Christian citizenship in the kingdom. Front-end integrity simply helps people decide whether *this* church is the right one for them.

The two most popular ways front-end integrity takes place are the application for church membership and the philosophy of ministry statement. An application for church membership simply asks for agreement on issues of doctrine and practice that are important to the particular congregation. It is regularly reviewed by some committee or board and can be used most effectively as a teaching device.

The philosophy of ministry statement is a document accepted by the church which states its uniqueness among area churches and its priorities for ministry. This type of document reflects the personality of a particular body of Christ. It helps to provide a mind-set for membership that is in harmony with the direction of the church.

For churches caught up in the Church Growth Movement, the concept of membership is important. As various methods are used to help strengthen that concept, the church is removing many obstacles for health and growth and establishing a backbone for the body of Christ. The end result is that people—by the hundreds of thousands—flock to these types of churches because they are sickened by spineless Christianity. They appreciate the love and integrity that parallels the ministry of Jesus Christ.

8
HOW TO USE RATIOS
TO EFFECT
CHURCH GROWTH
Win Arn

A church desiring to win and incorporate new people into its fellowship needs to have certain key ratios in order. As we have analyzed the information in the computer data file at the Institute of American Church Growth, where hundreds of different sizes and types of churches are monitored, certain minimum ratios seem to be essential for a church that is serious about effective outreach. Here are eight ratios. They are to be regarded as minimums. Hopefully your church will exceed these ratios. Check your church and find out.

1. Friendship Ratio—1:7. Each new convert or new member should be able to identify at least seven friends in the church within the first six months.

Friendships appear to be the strongest bond cementing new converts or members to their congregation. If new converts do not immediately develop meaningful friendships in their church, expect them to return to their old friendships—and ways— outside the church. Seven new friendships are a minimum; ten, fifteen, or more would be better.

There is an important time factor to this ratio, as well. The first six months are crucial. New converts or members not integrated into the body within that six-month time period are well on their way out the back door. The following chart clearly illustrates the importance of friendships established in the church during the first six months.[1] Note that all of the fifty "Converts—

Now Active Members" could name three or more friends in the church, with thirteen new members identifying seven friends, twelve identifying eight friends, and twelve listing nine friends or more. The "Dropouts" show almost the exact opposite pattern in the new friendships they established (or, more correctly, did not establish) in their church.

Number of New Friends Within Six Months	0	1	2	3	4	5	6	7	8	9+	Total
Converts—Now Active Members	0	0	0	1	2	2	8	13	12	12	50
Dropouts	8	13	14	8	4	2	1	0	0	0	50

2. Role/Task Ratio—60:100. There should be at least sixty roles and tasks available for every one hundred members in a church.

A role or task refers to a specific position or function or responsibility in the church (choir, committee member, teacher, officer, etc.). In typical churches of 300 members, there will be approximately eighty roles and tasks available. Of those eighty roles and tasks, sixty will be filled by 30 people (the willing workers who have more than one job). The remaining twenty roles and tasks are filled by an additional 20 people, thus involving 50 out of 300 members. In such a typical church would newcomers find a meaningful responsibility? Probably not.

The lack of variety and number of roles or tasks or ministries in most churches creates an environment which actually produces inactive members. Such a typical church of 300 members needs to open itself to newcomers by creating at least 100 new roles and tasks—roles and tasks that are not "busy work," but are "kingdom work," Great Commission work!—ministries that focus on meeting needs and changing lives. These roles are often called "Class II roles." Whereas "Class I roles" in a church focus primarily inward toward maintenance of the existing institution, Class II roles focus outward toward the surrounding community in an effort to reach persons for Christ and the church. Most plateaued or declining churches average fifteen Class I roles to every one Class II role. A more productive ratio would be 3:1, for every three Class I roles there should be at least one Class

II role. While this Class I/II ratio is more of an "outreach ratio" than an "assimilation ratio," it does give an important clue to the priority of the church and, thus, the probable reception given to the newcomer.

3. Group Ratio—7:100. There should be at least seven groups in a church for every 100 members.

In studying churches involved in the Two-Year Growth Process with the Institute for American Church Growth, we have found that plateaued and declining churches fall far short of this group to member ratio. The consequence of too few groups for members to build meaningful relationships is a high rate of inactives using the back door. A congregation would do well to analyze its own group ratio through such questions as: How many groups does our church have per 100 members? What percentage of the congregation is a regular part of one or more groups? How many new converts/new members have become a regular part of such groups in the last two years? How many have not?

Creating an effective group life is a fundamental building block upon which growth and incorporation depend. This important ratio is affirmed by other authorities. Lyle Schaller writes that "it usually is necessary to have six or seven of these groups . . . for each one hundred members who are thirteen or fourteen years of age or older."[2]

This ratio in a church will provide important answers to the question, How open is this church to newcomers?

4. New Group Ratio—1:5. Of the groups that now exist in a church, one of every five should have been started in the past two years.

The reason new groups are important is that established groups usually reach a "saturation point" sometime between nine and eighteen months following their formation. When a group has reached this saturation zone, it will, in most cases, stop growing and no longer be able to assimilate new people. Two or three members may leave and two or three may fill their places; but for all practical purposes, the group is, and will remain, plateaued.

How do you know when a group has reached the saturation point? Strongly suspect that, if a group has not grown in the last six months, it has reached the "saturation point."

The remedy—new groups! New groups, new growth, and new people involved. Maintaining this new group ratio will provide for a continued freshness in the group life of a congregation. It will provide opportunities for new converts/members to be involved. It will decrease the number of inactives. It will help close the "evangelistic back door."

5. *Board Ratio—1:5.* One of every five board members should have joined the church within the last two years.

In conversation with the pastor of an old-line denominational church in the Pacific Northwest, I asked, "How long would I need to be a member of this church before I might be elected to office?" He studied my question for a moment and then asked, "Would you attend regularly, give faithfully, and exemplify the Christian life?" "Yes," I responded. "Then you would be elected to office in this church sometime between the twelfth and fourteenth year after you joined."

What ingrownness! What self-centeredness! It is no wonder this church has a terminal illness. New board and committee members bring fresh and exciting ideas; they bring vitality; they are positive and enthusiastic about their new church; they are ready to earn their sense of belonging; they provide the best source of volunteers. Regularly review the board and committee structure in a church to assure the 1:5 relationship. Doing this will encourage an openness in the power structure and help assure that the church never forgets its real mission.

6. *Staff ratio—1:150.* A church should have one full-time staff member for every 150 persons in worship.

This ratio is a good indicator of a church committed to growth. By contrast, a plateaued church will often have a staffing ratio which is actually inhibiting growth. If the ratio reaches 1:225-250, it is unusual to see any significant increase in active membership. While more persons may join the church, the evangelistic back door will open wider and wider. Adding a staff person before this point is reached will help a church anticipate the influx of new people and provide a church environment that can accommodate them. Here is a rule of thumb:

AVERAGE WORSHIP ATTENDANCE	FULL-TIME STAFF	PART-TIME STAFF
0-150	1	0
150-200	1	1
200-300	2	0
300-400	2	1
400-500	3	0
500-600	3	1
etc.		

The second person a church should add to its staff should be a person ministering full-time in the area of evangelism/church growth, including the incorporation of new members into the fellowship. This person will normally pay for himself or herself through new giving units added to the church within the first year and a half. In some churches we have worked with, the new staff person's salary was paid within nine months.

7. *Visitor Ratio—3:10.* Of the first-time visitors who live in the church's ministry area, three of every ten should be actively involved within a year.

Calculating the visitor ratio provides three insights into a church's attitude toward newcomers: (1) it indicates the present members' openness toward visitors; (2) it indicates the priority of visitors in the functioning of the church; and (3) the ratio indicates the effectiveness of the church's follow-up strategy.

Whether persons are transferring to a new church or are looking for their first church, they always visit before joining. Visitors are the only source of church growth (except for biological growth—children of the believers). If visitors do not feel genuinely welcome, needed, or wanted, they seldom return. Studies from our computer analysis center indicate that through an effective strategy, churches are seeing four of every ten local visitors come back a second time. An incorporation strategy that focuses on these second-time visitors specifically will result in 70 to 75 percent of these visitors joining within a year (hence the 1:4 ratio of first-time visitors). Our studies indicate that typical nongrowing churches see only 10 to 12 percent of their first-time visitors join. Such a percentage, it turns out, is almost the exact number a church can expect to lose each year through transfer, death, and falling away. We are seeing some churches with an effective follow-up/incorporation strategy experience as many as 40 percent of first-time local visitors joining within a year.[3]

8. *"Great Commission Conscience" Ratio—3:5.* At least three of every five elected officers (a voting majority) should have a "Great Commission conscience."

What is a "Great Commission conscience"? It is an attitude which permeates the thinking and the decision-making process of a church. It is an attitude which sees people outside of Christ as lost. It is an attitude which causes rejoicing when new people join the church, especially if they are new converts. It is an attitude which prioritizes disciple making. It is an attitude which resonates with the Great Commission, found in its various forms, throughout Scripture. It is an attitude which sees missions as both "over there" and "right here." It is an attitude which motivates both corporate and personal action in prayer, giving, and service for Great Commission results.

How do you determine whether leaders in a congregation have a "Great Commission conscience"? You ask them! Here are ten simple "Yes/No" questions which will give you a clue. (Seven affirmative answers are an indication of a reasonably strong "Great Commission conscience.")

- I see the primary purpose of our church as   Yes/No
  responding to the Great Commission.

- I have participated in an outreach training   Yes/No
  event in the last year.

- I have invited an unchurched friend or   Yes/No
  relative to a church event in the past
  six months.

- I would support a motion to designate at   Yes/No
  least 10 percent of our church budget
  to outreach events/training/activities.

- I would prefer the pastor call on non-   Yes/No
  members more often than members.

- I would be willing to take a new member or   Yes/No
  visitor home for dinner once every six
  months.

- I have intentionally introduced myself to   Yes/No
  a new member or visitor in the past month.

- I have talked with an unchurched person   Yes/No
  about my faith in the past three months.

- I have prayed for a specific unchurched   Yes/No
  person in the past month.

- I would be willing to be a pioneer in a new   Yes/No
  group or new church fellowship to help
  reach people.

A congregational ratio for a "Great Commission conscience" should also be determined, and should be at least 1:5; which means at least one of every five members in a congregation must also have such an attitude. This 20 percent minimum reflects the research of social scientists studying innovation and diffusion, who have found that this is the critical number of members in any group which must endorse a new idea before the majority will accept it. The more members in a church with a "Great Commission conscience," the more likely that church will be open and receptive. Twenty percent of the membership can make a difference, but 100 percent is the ideal!

Effective ratios can be a guideline for continued growth and incorporation of new (and sometimes older) church members. A church which takes its ratios seriously will, in most cases, evidence health, vitality, and growth. God's command to go and make disciples implies "winning" and "nurturing." Ratios can help a church be more intentional and efficient in actualizing the Great Commission.

---

1. Win Arn and Charles Arn, *The Master's Plan for Making Disciples* (Pasadena: Church Growth Press, 1982), 156.
2. Lyle Schaller, *Assimilating New Members* (Nashville: Abingdon Press, 1978), 95.
3. One such evangelism training strategy which typifies this approach is "The Master's Plan for Making Disciples," which has been developed by the Institute for American Church Growth, 709 E. Colorado Blvd., Suite #150, Pasadena, CA 91101.

9
LAY MINISTRY:
A CLOSER LOOK
W. Charles Arn

"Hello, Jim? This is Bill Carlson on the deacon board from church. How're you doin'? . . . Good. Say, listen, Jim, the board came up with the idea last week that we need to let more people in our community know about the church. Well, we were brainstorming ideas, and finally settled on one. Listen to this: We're going to sell Easter lilies at the grocery store the whole month before Easter. But that's not the best part. You know Mary Wilson on the board is a florist. She thinks she can fix up the lily buds with a little note inside so that when the flower opens up, there will be a sign that says, GO TO CHURCH THIS EASTER. Great idea, huh? We're hoping the flowers bloom just a couple days before Easter. Can you imagine all those people with signs in their lilies? . . . What? When's Easter? Well, I'm not sure, let me check. Yeah, it's March 30. Say, that doesn't give us much time does it? Well, anyway, the board asked if you would coordinate the project. This is obviously a very important job and a real chance for ministry. They thought that since you always seem to be willing to work, you'd be the perfect one for the job. . . . Well, that doesn't matter if you don't know anything about flowers. I'm sure Mary Wilson can find some time to answer questions for you. . . . What do you mean 'you don't know'? Jim, this is a *very* important job. It's one that will have a major impact on the community. It's really what Christ commanded us to do, you know, to evangelize. I can't think of a better time than Easter to do that, can you, Jim? Listen, I already told the deacons that you would say 'yes.' You've never said 'no' before. You're not going to start now, I hope. The church needs you. And think of the ministry! Plus, there's no one else that will do it. And, anyway, it probably won't take much work. Just a little oversight, recruitment, and all that. . . . You will? Hey, that's great. Thanks again. The church really appreciates this." (click) "Hey, Martha, I finally found someone to take that job. Boy, that's a load off my shoulders!"

Have any members in your church ever felt like Jim in this story? Not sure whether they have been complimented by being asked to take another job, or railroaded because they've never said no? How many of your members really feel like ministers?

And what about "ministry"? What really is it? When are members doing ministry, and when are they not?

Paul talked about his own ministry, and that of every Christian, in his letters to the early churches. Toward the end of his life he said, "However, I consider my life worth nothing to me, if only I may finish the race and complete the task the Lord Jesus has given me—the task of testifying to the gospel of God's grace" (Acts 20:24, NIV).

Notice the assumption Paul makes about the ministry God gave him: "testifying to the gospel of God's grace."

Paul speaks of "the ministry" and this singleness of purpose in other letters to the first believers: "Therefore, if anyone is in Christ, he is a new creation; the old has gone, the new has come! All this is from God, who reconciled us to himself through Christ and gave us the ministry of reconciliation. We are therefore Christ's ambassadors, as though God were making his appeal through us" (2 Cor. 5:17-20).

And again: "So then, men ought to regard us as ministers of Christ and as those entrusted with the secret things of God. Now it is required that those who have been given a trust must prove faithful" (1 Cor. 4:1, 2).

"Therefore, since through God's mercy we have this ministry, we do not lose heart" (2 Cor. 4:1).

Paul encouraged early Christians to be true to their ministry of personifying God's love through their lives. To Timothy he said, "Keep your head in all situations, endure hardship, do the work of an evangelist, discharge all the duties of your ministry" (2 Tim. 4:5). To Archippus he said, "Take heed to the ministry which thou hast received in the Lord, that thou fulfill it" (Col. 4:17).

Every believer has a part in Christ's ministry. In fact, Paul frequently associates "the ministry" with the work of all of God's people: "We put no stumbling block in anyone's path, so that our ministry will not be discredited. Rather, as servants of God we commend ourselves in every way" (2 Cor. 6:3-4a). To the Ephesians Paul speaks of the work of God's people being "to prepare God's people for works of service, so that the body of Christ may be built up until we all reach unity in the faith and in the knowledge of the Son of God and become mature, attaining to the whole measure of the fullness of Christ" (Eph. 4:12-13).

Clearly there is a ministry to which Christ's body is called. Christ himself set the precedent for that ministry, and stated it simply: ". . . the Son of Man did not come to be served, but to serve, and to give his life as a ransom for many" (Matt. 20:28). Ministry means bringing the grace and love of Jesus Christ to people. It's as simple, yet as profound, as that. Ministry is reflecting the love of the shepherd for those sheep who have wandered away from the flock. Or, as Paul put it, the "ministry of reconciliation."

The ministry and purpose of the local church today must reflect the ministry and purpose of Christ. If "ministry" for laypersons in the church today is defined outside of this basic purpose, it is either substantially incomplete or simply inaccurate.

Who Are the Ministers?

In studying the Scripture, scholars have noted a fascinating change in terminology between the Old Testament and the New Testament concerning the word which describes the activities of God's ordained people. The word *sarat* is used in the Old Testament to describe the activities of the professional Jewish priests. Another word, *abad*, referred to the activities of the Jewish congregation. However, in the New Testament, the word which had previously been used only to describe the activities of the ordained priests is now used to describe the activities of the entire body of Christian believers (see 1 Pet. 2:9).

And in the New Testament, the Greek word used in references

to the Jewish priests, *leitourgia,* is also applied to the ministry of Christ (see Heb. 8:6). The obvious inference is that now Christ is the high priest (see Heb. 4:14–5:10), and each follower is a part of the holy priesthood (1 Peter 2:4-5).

Another fascinating insight can be found in studying the intent of the original writers from the Greek language. In its original use, the word *laos* (from which our modern word "laity" comes) never described a group of persons in the church set apart from professional leaders. The word *laos* was rather a description of the total body of believers. It appears in such places as 2 Corinthians 6:16 and 1 Peter 2:9, 10. There never appears, in the view of the New Testament church, a distinction between church members and clergy. The word *kleros* (from which the word "clergy" comes) referred not to a separate group of persons in the church, but to all who had received the inheritance of God's redemption (see Acts 26:18; Col. 1:11, 12). Certainly there were appointed elders and deacons. However, their value and status seemed to be no different than any other member's concerning the importance or expectation of their ministry. Every believer was—and still is—a minister!

How Do We Minister?
Ministry, and how we do it, is often associated with unfortunate misconceptions in the church today. Many lay people have been given the idea that ministry occurs only while doing "church work," and that it is a duty which inevitably comes with being a church member. As a result, many members have come to believe the term "lay ministry" is nothing more than a spiritualized catch phrase for their time and energy to be taxed by the church.

So, how do laypersons minister? And when is a Christian really ministering? Christ was asked a similar question and answered in the following way:

> Then the King will say to those on his right, "Come, you who are blessed by the Father; take your inheritance *[kleros]*, the kingdom prepared for you since the creation of the world. For I was hungry and you gave me something to eat, I was thirsty and you gave me

108

something to drink, I was a stranger and you invited me in, I needed clothes and you clothed me, I was sick and you looked after me, I was in prison and you came to visit me."

Then the righteous will answer him, "Lord, when did we see you hungry and feed you, or thirsty and give you something to drink? When did we see you a stranger and invite you in, or needing clothes and clothe you? When did we see you sick or in prison and go to visit you?"

The King will reply, "I tell you the truth, whatever you did for one of the least of these brothers of mine, you did for me" (Matt. 25:34-40).

Ministry in its purest and simplest form is touching other people's lives with love. It is showing and sharing God's love for his people through our intentional, specific love and caring. The entire message and ministry of Christ on earth was that of giving love. The ministry of Christ's followers is nothing different. Christ emphasized the importance of *intentional love* time and time again:

Greater love has no one than this, that one lay down his life for his friends (John 15:13).

Love your neighbor as yourself (Matt. 19:19).

"Love the Lord your God with all your heart and with all your soul and with all your mind." This is the first and greatest commandment. And the second is like it: "Love your neighbor as yourself." All the law and the Prophets hang on these two commandments (Matt. 22:37-39).

Love your enemies, do good to them (Luke 6:35).

A new command I give you: Love one another. As I have loved you, so you must love one another (John 13:34).

This is my command: Love each other (John 15:17).

Ministry is love in action. Throughout the New Testament the constant admonition to the Christian believer is to love. How is love actualized? Through ministry. Ministry is, in fact, doing love!

How many opportunities are there in your church for members to genuinely minister, in this definition of the word?

Two Approaches to Ministry

Local churches committed to encouraging their members in ministry will generally take one of two approaches: the "Institutional Approach" or the "Individual Approach."

The Institutional Approach. This approach to lay ministry centers around the institution of the church. People are seen as resources to service the needs of the organization. Members are seen as means to an end, the end being to perpetuate the church institution. When there is a job to be done in the church, the task is to find a person to do it. If the job is harder to fill, it simply means starting earlier and using a bit more pressure. Successful recruiting, from an institutional view of lay ministry, is finding a person willing to do the job, as Jim found out in the story which introduced this chapter.

This view of lay ministry has the following negative results:

- It lowers the self-esteem of laity in the church.
- It increases the likelihood of members working in a job rather than a ministry.
- It stunts the creation of new ministry opportunities.
- It decreases the chances of the church responding to changing needs.
- It emphasizes the status quo and inhibits change.
- It perpetuates a limited "power circle" in the church.
- It limits "ownership" of the task by members.

The Individual Approach. The other approach to ministry is centered around people, not organizations. Members are motivated for involvement because the ministry opportunities are focused around their interests and needs. In this view, the church exists to enhance the ministry of the people, rather than the people for the ministry of the organization.

An individual approach to ministry in the church means much more frequent change in ministry functions. As the gifts, skills, interests, and concerns found in the membership change, the ministries of the church reflect this change. This fluidity of ministry is in contrast to the institutional approach to lay ministry where the tendency is to maintain roles from one generation of church members to the next. As a result, what may have been an important ministry and appropriate use of the spiritual gifts of some member years ago may have lost its value and meaning to the people who are asked to take over.

An individual approach to ministry will seek to identify the special gifts, skills, background, and concerns of the members and match them with appropriate ministry positions in the church. If there are none which fit, a new ministry position is created rather than forcing the "round peg into the square hole." In the process, old church positions may well be dropped if they become difficult to fill because no one in the church is willing or qualified to assume them.

There is a fascinating insight from the New Testament church into finding the "right" person for the "right" position. It is in Acts 6, concerning a dispute which arose in the church between the Greek widows and the Jewish widows over who was receiving more food at the expense of the other. It seemed to be a silly dispute, but it was one that could potentially have been divisive in those tentative first years of the new church.

How would the problem be handled? Would it divert the outward-focus of the early church and consume the energies of its leaders? Would the mission priority be lost in internal bickering? Could the spiritual gifts in the early church be used? Listen . . .

> So the Twelve [apostles] gathered all the disciples together and said, "It would not be right for us to neglect the ministry of the word of God in order to wait on tables. Brothers, choose seven men from among you who are known to be full of the Spirit and wisdom. We will turn this responsibility over to them and will give our attention to prayer and the ministry of the word" (Acts 6:2-4).

Of course . . . the gift of wisdom! This petty dispute could quickly have become a diversion from "the ministry of the word" for the apostles. But it became a creative use of gifts in ministry for others. What an important lesson about a healthy, growing body: one person's problem may be another person's ministry!

How many of your members are really ministering? And is your church committed to providing an opportunity for members to be "servants of Christ" (1 Cor. 4:1) to the people so much in need of that ministry?[1]

---

1. A helpful "Church Action Kit" has been designed by Dr. Charles Arn to help congregations enhance the ministry of their lay members. The *Mobilizing Laity for Ministry Kit* is available from the Institute for American Church Growth, 709 E. Colorado Blvd., Suite 150, Pasadena, CA 91101.

10
ORGANIC GROWTH:
A CRITICAL DIMENSION
FOR THE CHURCH
Charles B. Singletary

My introduction to the Church Growth Movement came in 1976 as a student at Fuller Seminary's School of World Mission. I began my training with a course entitled "Principles of Church Growth," taught by C. Peter Wagner. As a Navigator staff man working in community ministries, I had become quite concerned with how we might best help local churches incorporate solid principles of Christian discipleship into the lives of their people. Up until this point, most church members I had met had not been well trained in Christian discipleship.

Much of that first course on church growth was consumed by either verbal or silent debate with Peter Wagner on the question of quality versus quantity in church growth. After much patient discussion, Wagner was finally able to convince me that the quality versus quantity issue was actually a false issue. One of the things that turned the tide was an article by Alan Tippett in which he pointed out that the real key to healthy church growth was to achieve somewhat of an equilibrium between quality, quantity, and organic growth. (See figure 1.)

Ever since that light turned on, I have become an avid student and an enthusiastic promoter of the Church Growth Movement. The quality, quantity, organic growth triangle has appeared on overhead projectors and blackboards in church classrooms all over America since that time. I rarely speak or teach on the subject of church growth without at least alluding to it.

Almost invariably, in trying to help churches incorporate solid principles of Christian discipleship and church growth, the "nut

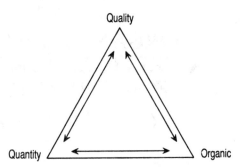

Figure 1

to crack" is how to achieve good organic growth. Organic growth has been defined in many different ways and has been given a number of different names. For the sake of this discussion, we will say that organic growth pertains to the infrastructure or cellular growth within churches. It consists of all sorts of sub-groups, small groups, and networks so vital to the assimilation, nurture, and mobilization of the membership. Organic growth involves the leadership and shepherding network of a church. Its health is normally a function of the number and quality of well-trained leaders or workers which are able to be mobilized in a local church context.

In highlighting the need for increased emphasis upon this critical dimension of growth, I would like to make four rather strong comments born out of my experience in working with churches. Organic growth is:

1. The single greatest area of need in the health of churches.
2. A direct reflection of the philosophy of ministry of a church.
3. A direct reflection of the leadership's vision for the church.
4. Crucial to the task of world evangelization.

Briarwood Presbyterian Church in Birmingham, Alabama, is a classic example of a healthy church deriving great benefit from strong organic growth. Briarwood's membership of 3,000 may not be that impressive by superchurch standards, but it is one of the most effectively mobilized churches I know of. It is also one of the most influential.

Briarwood's strength in organic growth is facilitated by three major factors. First, Briarwood has a *strong pastoral example.* From the beginning Pastor Frank Barker has set the pace in commitment to small groups, informal networks, heavy involvement of lay leadership in shepherding the flock. Week by week, Pastor

Barker has led the way in early morning discipleship groups, home Bible studies, visitation evangelism teams, ladies' discipleship training, cottage prayer meetings, covered dish suppers promoting interest in missions, and all kinds of other efforts to strengthen the "church scattered." He has personally led or participated in thousands of small group situations with the membership in Briarwood's twenty-five-year history. Until recently, when multiplication has accelerated so extensively, it would have been a rare individual, from the smallest child to the oldest senior citizen, who had not been involved in a small group experience with the pastor.

Second, an *environment* has been created in which one of the shared values of the congregation is to be significantly involved beyond the major worship services of the church. The church scattered is considered just as important as the church gathered. A comprehensive shepherding network has been established to help make sure that each member and visitor is given numerous attractive opportunities to be in discipling relationships and other nurture/outreach situations. Leaders are trained to provide constant surveillance and shepherding care. Leaders are mobilized continuously and are given the training, freedom, and encouragement to form new groups in their individual spheres of influence.

Third, Briarwood has adequate *staffing* to facilitate the proliferation of all types of prayer, discipleship, Bible study, fellowship groups, and evangelistic teams. Staff members each follow the model set by the pastor. Each major subgroup of the church has a well-defined, smoothly functioning leadership team. These teams are trained to concentrate on the various aspects of organic growth so as to give a greater opportunity to effectively assimilate and nurture the membership. This, in turn, facilitates the overall healthy, balanced growth of the church.

What are the indicators of healthy organic growth in a local church?

1. A strong emphasis on prayer. The congregation is highly committed to prayer—corporately, individually, and in all types of small group settings. The atmosphere is charged with the understanding that God is at work in the midst of his people and that prayer is vital to that process. People literally "pray at the drop of a hat."

2. An obvious ministry of the Holy Spirit. The gifts and fruit of the Spirit are evident and expressed throughout the membership. Although there is structure and organization, there is much freedom and spontaneity as the Holy Spirit freely ministers. The high trust level which must characterize such an atmosphere is attributable to the confidence placed in the power of the Holy Spirit to orchestrate the ministry.

3. Biblical balance. Biblical teaching and biblical styles of worship and ministry set the stage for healthy organic growth. Spiritual maturity causes spiritual reproduction. (Babies don't multiply!) There is good ecclesiology; good understanding and application of body life.

4. Individual and organic reproduction. The body is multiplying individually and corporately. Members are discipled to the point of spiritual reproduction. This type of spiritual maturity causes them to bear much fruit. As the individuals and cells multiply, there is ultimately both spontaneous and deliberate church planting.

5. High level of lay mobilization. A relatively small percentage of the membership are simply spectators. Growth is not the result of high-powered promotion or entertainment-oriented programs. Growth is not dependent upon strong, dynamic personalities. Most members have discovered, developed, and are using their spiritual gifts.

6. Qualitative and quantitative growth of the membership. When organic growth is healthy, the growth in the number and spiritual maturity of church members is a natural (supernatural!) by-product. Admittedly, heavy numerical growth can occur without good organic growth, but this type of growth is always precarious and frequently short-lived. As mentioned above, this heavy numerical growth is normally the result of heavy promotional activities and is very dependent on these activities to be maintained.

7. Healthy body life. A loving, caring fellowship is thriving with healthy interaction among members. The membership has a high sense of belonging. People are ministering to one another and to the surrounding community. A strong emphasis is placed on people being mobilized in their areas of giftedness.

For any church seriously interested in healthy, balanced, sustained growth (as opposed to simply growing numerically with little specific concern for organic growth), I have seven practical suggestions:

1. Pray specifically for organic growth. Jesus' admonition to his disciples to pray for laborers can be directly applied to this type of growth. Ask God to create an atmosphere with a strong emphasis on praying for and training laborers. Ask him to give the current leaders the vision and dedication needed to produce this type of growth. It is very costly as indicated in John 12:24.

2. Make a deep commitment to organic growth. Initially, it's the most difficult way to grow. Just as in the physical realm, the difference between comfortable marriage and costly marriage is reproduction, so the difference between comfortable Christianity and costly Christianity is spiritual reproduction. You must start small, go deep, and *then* think big—something very difficult for most Americans to do with consistent progression.

3. Take stock. Get a growth-oriented diagnosis done on your church by a well-qualified church growth consultant. Make sure there is specific emphasis on infrastructure analysis. Form a church growth committee using the most mature, visionary leaders in your church. Ensure that the committee is capable of influencing and monitoring the health of organic growth in the church.

4. Commit to train leaders. This type of growth requires many, many leaders at every level. Make a long-range, continuous commitment to identifying, recruiting, training, and mobilizing leaders. The more you have, the more you need.

5. Fight the temptation to be efficient but not effective. Jesus' model during his earthly ministry should be indelibly imprinted on our hearts and minds. He spoke to thousands, he healed hundreds, but he only trained twelve with intensity. Keep decentralizing. Keep an emphasis on unity without uniformity.

6. *Think of God's kingdom.* Allow your ministries to flow freely into the community and into all spheres of life. Don't be possessive, but keep everything in an open hand. Be careful to give God the glory. Rejoice that Acts 1:8 is being fulfilled.

7. *Trust God for results.* Organic growth requires a high level of trust—particularly in the ministry of the Holy Spirit. It can't be programmed or orchestrated. Risks must be taken. Ministries proliferate until they can't begin to be counted or controlled. Freedom and autonomy must be given. Out of structure flows spontaneity.

The acid test of healthy organic growth is: Are well-trained and well-qualified laborers being produced who will go to the uttermost parts of the world to make disciples? Are ministries being proliferated? Is the church big and strong or just big and fat? Is there momentum for sustained growth or is there a precarious situation where one leadership crisis will result in decline? Organic growth produces healthy, sustained, balanced growth.

The critical nature of organic growth is of such importance that all church leaders seriously interested in their church reaching its full potential in Christ should give it highest priority. God will bless since organic growth is simply the fruit of careful application of the biblical patterns of church growth.

11
THE QUALITY SIDE
OF CHURCH GROWTH
Kent R. Hunter

At first glance the Church Growth Movement appears to have a hyper-concern for numbers. There is a great deal of emphasis on growth, fulfilling the Great Commission, graphing and monitoring growth trends, and measuring effectiveness. The neophyte might conclude that this is indeed a "numbers game."

Further investigation into the principles of the Church Growth Movement, however, lead one to the conclusion that this discipline of Christian thought carries with it one of the strongest emphases on quality growth in the New Testament church since the book of Acts. A study of church growth thinking leads beyond numbers to people. These are not just people at whom someone has preached. They are people who have responded. The goal is disciples.

The Discipleship Goal

One of the central themes in the church growth literature is making disciples as the goal of evangelism. Helping people, meeting their needs, is important—essential to a genuine Christian ministry. But it is not enough. Preaching the good news about Jesus Christ and the power of the cross for forgiveness of sins is necessary. It is the gospel that the Spirit uses to call people to repentance and faith. But a person is not evangelized until he or she becomes a responsible member of the body of Christ. Folded into the sheepfold, the new Christian takes on a lifelong life-style of following Jesus Christ, learning, growing, and interacting with fellow members of Christ's body.

This goal for evangelism has a focusing effect on evangelistic strategy. It goes further than "planting the seed and cultivating." This goal means more care and more responsibility for those who work with young Christians in the faith.

God builds the church. In 1 Corinthians, chapter 3, the Apostle Paul clearly indicates that it is God who "brings the increase." Only God can make the plant grow. Yet, Christians with church growth eyes see clearly that God does not do this in a vacuum. He uses people. It is indeed a great "*co*-mission" as we are co-laborers with Christ. God uses people to reach people.

The responsibility for Christian nurture is strong when the goal is discipleship. The value of the Sunday school is resurrected to its rightful place. The opportunities for Christian day schools are obvious. Christian parenting leads to nothing less than the lofty goal of discipleship. Christians in the body minister to others who are also growing. Adult Sunday school is a regular part of life—because the Christian life is not being a "church member" but a disciple. Pew sitting is unthinkable when discipleship is seen as the life-style of the Christian.

More Than Numbers
The discipleship goal clearly is the beginning point for the Church Growth Movement's emphasis that growth is more than numbers. It is not ironic at all, therefore, that *More Than Numbers* is the title of one of the books written by Paul Yonggi Cho, the pastor of several hundred thousand people who belong to the largest church in the world in Seoul, Korea.

The comprehensive growth that church growth people have in mind is a four-part growth.

1. Growing up. The Scripture says that we are to grow in the grace and knowledge of Jesus Christ. This is an essential prerequisite for all other growth. This aspect of quality growth focuses on the study and internalization of the Word. Churches don't grow unless people grow. People don't grow unless they are involved in God's Word. This aspect of quality growth is so important that when there is the lack of biblical growth in a church, church growth people consider the church sick. The disease, known as "arrested spiritual development," was first coined by

C. Peter Wagner and is described in his book *Your Church Can Be Healthy* (Abingdon). It is a malady which roadblocks health and growth in the local church.

2. Growing together. This is another aspect of comprehensive growth. In the New Testament the concept of *koinonia*—fellowship—is strong. This is the glue that makes the Christian community unlike any other social group. It's the supernatural dynamic of a forgiving, loving, accepting group of people who themselves have been forgiven, loved, and accepted by God through Jesus Christ. Paul, in his letter to the Ephesians, writes about the building up of the body. This activity of building up one another has a reflection on numerical growth. The word "to edify" or "to build up" in the Greek comes from a word that means "to mend a net." Since Jesus called his people to be fishers of men, and the church is called a net in the Scripture, it stands to reason that a net that is torn and full of holes is not going to be effective in catching fish. However, as the net is mended—the building up, the edifying of one another—the quality of the church allows it to be a more effective tool in God's hands for the building of his kingdom. Down through the centuries when the church has been what it ought to be, outsiders have stood in awe, exclaiming, "My, how they love one another!" Quality growth leads to quantity growth because unbelievers are drawn to the Christian community like bees to a beautiful flower.

3. Growing out. Since making disciples is the goal of evangelism, evangelism is the activity of the whole church. Someone plants; someone waters; God brings the increase. Then others nurture, serve, help, model, and teach. The goal is not a dead-end road. The goal is not church membership. The end result is not a name on the church rolls. The discipleship goal is to build people who are equipped to be part of the process of kingdom growth. Disciples are reborn to multiply.

It is this multiplication factor that God will use to fulfill the Great Commission. It will not happen by addition. Consequently, true quantity growth depends on quality growth. The two are inseparable. The priesthood of all believers is an aspect of quality growth that church growth people emphasize as essential for the fulfillment of the Great Commission. Everyone is a minister. Everyone has a ministry. Each Christian has a part in the body of Christ.

The emphasis on spiritual gifts in church growth avoids the Corinthian confusion described in the New Testament. It appears that Paul wrote to the people in the church at Corinth to help them to see, among other things, that spiritual gifts were not an end in themselves. They were a means to an end. They were the means that God used for the work of ministry that would lead to bodily growth.

When a local church gets involved in a good, solid, biblical study of gifts for growth, lay people begin to realize that they have a ministry. They are part of the team—God's team—with Christ as the head of the body and each part functioning with a different gift. Envy, jealousy, and false humility (the "I can't do anything" attitude) are put away with a healthy attitude concerning the diversity of gifts. This leads the local church to a beautiful quality of ministry as described in the New Testament. This effectiveness, in turn, leads to growth as the church reaches out.

4. Growing more. The multiplication factor also includes churches. Parenthood is part of God's plan for churches. Sometimes the goal of church growth has been represented as superchurches with thousands of members. That's fine because those churches are important. But church growth thinking challenges churches not to just grow larger and larger. It calls for churches to start other churches through planting ministries. Bigger is not necessarily better in church growth. Quality must be maintained. Often, the fastest way God's kingdom has grown is by the starting of new churches: new, healthy, growing churches. Actually, upon investigation we find that large churches are often planting new churches as part of a comprehensive strategy. The Church Growth Movement, in all the aspects of comprehensive growth, stresses the importance of quality.

A Mind-set of Scrutiny
Church growth thinking fosters a worldview of accountability. It's a stewardship of mission that says, "How can we be most

effective in employing our limited resources toward the fulfillment of the Great Commission?" This permeating mind-set for quality ministry impacts the work of the church in at least five major areas.

1. The assimilation of new members is very important. Follow-up to evangelism and follow-through for church membership are essential elements on the road to discipleship. The Lord's will is that not one be lost. Often we have blamed people for hardness of heart, when in reality they have been newborn babes in the faith, and we have expected them to care for themselves on the doorstep of church entry. The Church Growth Movement has done much to reevaluate the value of the church as God's dynamic organism for the growth of his kingdom. Assimilation into the body of Christ is an important aspect of a person's own growth and the ultimate fulfillment of the Great Commission.

2. The desire for quality Christians in quality churches is reflected in the much celebrated and frequently debated homogeneous unit principle. This important church growth principle is often wrongly seen as a membership policy. It is not that. It is an evangelistic strategy built on a deep desire that we become all things to everyone that by any means—save compromising the gospel—some might be saved. It is the people group approach to world evangelization that has a high view of and sensitivity to culture. It also carries the very important theological premise that Christianity is transcultural. This is quality growth that refuses to be culturally chauvinistic. It refuses to make Western Anglos out of Australian aborigines. Instead, the quest for biblical quality in missions calls for a ministry used by God to make them disciples of Jesus Christ—Australian aborigine Christians. The homogeneous unit principle calls for disciple making without foreign roadblocks to the reception of the gospel.

3. The quality concerns of church growth are reflected in the areas of communication. The desire to be on target to get the gospel to people unhindered is called a receptor-oriented communication. The gospel is not changed. Theology remains the same. But the communication of the gospel changes in style, language, and form. Since language is alive, it changes. If the gospel isn't communicated in the "heart language" of the recipient, it affects theology in a negative way. The hearer can get

the idea that God is "foreign" if a language is used from an outside culture. The biblical fact of the incarnation demands that using language that is out of date, burdened by tradition, or loaded with unnecessary baggage is cultural idolatry and counterproductive to quality church growth.

4. The concern in the Church Growth Movement for maximum effectiveness is also reflected in the harvest principle. Church growth helps Christians to go where the crop is ripe. The concern is directed to the most receptive peoples.

The issue is not: Who will we seek to evangelize, and who will we forget about? The issue is: Who will we evangelize first? Where will we pour most of our resources now? Where will we only cultivate and wait for God's *kairos*—his time, for *his* harvest? This is one of the central issues which motivated Donald McGavran to develop some of his foundational work in India—the work that led eventually to the modern Church Growth Movement.

The issue of resistance and receptivity is ultimately a question of priorities and intelligent choices. It is grounded, however, on a deep desire for quality outreach. How can we make disciples with most efficiency now so that the most can be won so that they can help us turn to others who are most receptive next, and so on.

5. One of the plagues of a second generation church is mediocrity. It infects churches to the point where apathy is entrenched and attitudes are lethargic. Church growth teaching has an amazing effect on poor attitudes. Its desire for effective ministry toward the Great Commission calls for people to measure, monitor, and evaluate the performance of their church—of themselves as Christians. To the apathetic, the effect is one of discomfort and, as they develop, an openness to learn and grow. To the lethargic, it is challenging as new avenues of insight open up vistas of exciting opportunities. In church growth thinking the local church is important. The individual is important. The Great Commission is important. The lost are important. God's work is important. In this sense the qualitative desire for effectiveness has a renewal dynamic that touches churches and individuals within them. To that end, the Church Growth Movement is providing renewal to the Christian church worldwide and new impetus to the fulfillment of the Great Commission.

Quality and quantity growth are inseparable. Quantity without quality is false growth. It's short term; it can't last. Quality without quantity is self-centered and suffers in the stagnancy of arthritic religion. Church growth brings a balance that, by the power of the resurrected Christ, brings life to Christians and churches who, in turn, will bring life to the unevangelized and unchurched around the globe.

12
TRENDS AMONG THE WORLD'S TWENTY LARGEST CHURCHES
John N. Vaughan

The decade of the 1980s has brought a significant increase in information about large churches of the world. While several of these churches are in the United States, other megachurches averaging over 3,000 in attendance each week are beyond our borders. As attention continues to be placed on these churches, others that are now unknown to church growth leaders and researchers will be discovered.

Meaning of the Term "Largest"
Large means different things to different people. To some it means seating capacity of buildings and to others it means Sunday school attendance, cell group attendance, or even attendance at worship services. A growing trend among some church groups is to count adherents. An adherent is considered a person who identifies a specific church as his church in his city or community. The individual may attend services with some regularity even without officially joining the congregation. Finally, state churches tend to view membership by baptism in a family and parish context. This last form may include hundreds or thousands of unconfirmed members within the ministry area of the congregation.

While some churches are able to assemble a large attendance for worship services in a cathedral setting that maintains no formal membership, other churches are, with membership, able to mobilize and involve the congregation in a variety of other training and evangelism ministries on a weekly basis.

St. Peter's in Rome, for example, with a seating capacity of 40,000 to 50,000, is able to assemble 20,000 people for the annual worldwide telecast of the mass on Christmas Eve. The largest mass each week, among the other hourly services each Sunday morning and afternoon, will average 8,000 in attendance at 10:00 A.M. Likewise, Paris' Cathedral of Notre Dame, with a seating capacity of approximately 1,900, will average 6,000 to 7,000 in attendance during its seven masses each Saturday evening and all day Sunday.

In contrast, however, Korea's Yoido Full Gospel Church in Seoul has an auditorium that seats an estimated 25,000 people. Total membership of the congregation surpassed the 400,000 mark in 1984. Even as early as January 1984, the church reported 316 pastoral staff, 20,805 deacons and deaconesses, 19,839 cell groups with a weekly attendance of more than 297,000, and a Sunday school enrollment of 12,120 people from birth through the university age group.

Charles Mylander's "composite membership" formula, described in his book *Secrets of Growing Churches* (Harper and Row, 1979), provides an equitable method of measuring participant involvement among diverse churches. Since fewer churches, across denominational and church group lines, have masses or cell groups, the three most common activities selected among churches are worship attendance, membership, and Sunday school attendance. Because participant involvement varies widely even among these three areas, the sum of the three is divided by three to provide an overall picture of people involvement.

A significant dimension of large churches meriting special attention is the large Pentecostal congregational model found throughout Brazil. At least a dozen churches, mostly Assemblies of God, range in membership from 18,400 to 120,000 members. Rather than schedule the meeting of participants through multiple worship services at various times in the same auditorium, these churches have created a network of smaller satellite chapels. These chapels are often viewed as annexes or extension ministries, like Sunday school departments or classes, reaching out to a multitude of communities by the mother or sponsoring church. Each chapel is able to reach the masses in its own community in a homogeneous context. This requires that the people being reached within these various communities cross religious barriers while having to cross few unnecessary social and economic barriers.

The chapels are owned and operated totally by a sovereign mother church that may be located in another city or even another state. Both the mother congregation and its extension ministries function as church planting agencies due to their high priority on evangelism and missions.

Each church has a right to focus on the specific category of largeness in which it excels. Hopefully, someone will always be at work identifying these various dimensions of growing churches.

Identification of the Largest Churches

The largest churches as congregations are listed in four different categories and are described in detail in my book *The World's Twenty Largest Churches* (Grand Rapids: Baker Book House, 1984). The four categories include composite membership, total membership, worship attendance, and Sunday school attendance. Each listing, by design, may include churches not included in the composite membership listing.

Europe. The largest churches, St. Peter's in Rome and Paris' Cathedral of Notre Dame, have already been briefly mentioned. Additional confirmation is still needed on other European churches since the Vatican has not released confirmation.

Soviet Union. Moscow Baptist Church in three Sunday services averages 5,000 in weekly attendance. This is possible since religious freedom is severely limited and many competing churches have been closed to public gatherings and worship restricted. Sunday school teaching of children is prohibited by law.

Mainland China. P. Richard Bohr, in his July 1983 article, "State Religion in China Today" in *Missiology,* reported the Mo'en Church in Shanghai, People's Republic of China, as having a combined weekly worship attendance of more than 6,000 in three Sunday services. This is reported to be the largest Christian congregation in this city of twelve million people.

Africa. Until the death of pastor John F. Rowlands in recent years, Bethesdaland, a Church of God movement in the Indian community of South Africa begun in 1931, was probably the largest Christian congregation in Africa. Known since its conception as Natal's International Revival Center and organized around Bethesda Temple of Durban, membership included an estimated 36,000 members. This group grew as a result of an Indian people movement.

Today, however, the largest known congregation is the Miracle Center of Benin City, Nigeria. Pastor Benson Idahosa reports worship attendance of 10,000 weekly, with thirty satellite branches in Benin City and a total of 600 branches throughout Nigeria. The main worship center seats 6,000 worshipers. Crusade and television evangelism serve as the major means of evangelism.

Asia. Six of the world's largest churches are in Korea. Five of the churches are in Seoul and one is in Inchon. Among these churches you will find the largest congregation in recorded Christian history (Yoido Full Gospel Church, Seoul); the world's two largest Presbyterian churches (Young Nak Presbyterian Church and Chung-Kyeon Presbyterian Church, both in Seoul); the world's two largest Methodist churches (Kwang Lim Methodist Church of Seoul and Inchon's Soong-Eui Methodist Church); and Asia's largest Baptist church (Sungrak Baptist Church in Seoul). The use of small groups, called cells, composed of groups of twelve to sixteen members each is the most common strategy for church growth in Korea.

South and Central America. The world's second largest congregation is the more than 80,000-member Jotabeche Methodist Pentecostal Church of Santiago, Chile. Central America's giants include San Salvador's Evangelistic Center and Mexico's Faith, Hope and Love Ministry Center with five satellite locations. Another major congregation of importance is Brazil for Christ located in São Paulo. Street evangelism and electronic media are major growth strategies used in these churches.

North America. By composite membership, the largest churches include three Independent Baptist Churches (First Baptist Church of Hammond, Indiana; Highland Park Baptist Church of Chattanooga, Tennessee; and Thomas Road Baptist Church of Lynchburg, Virginia). Six of the largest churches in North America are affiliated with the Southern Baptist Convention (First Baptist Church of Dallas, Texas; First Baptist Church of Jacksonville, Florida; North Phoenix Baptist Church of Phoenix, Arizona; First Southern Baptist Church of Del City, Oklahoma; and Bellevue Baptist Church of Memphis, Tennessee). Finally, two independent churches included among these churches are Calvary Chapel of Costa Mesa in Santa Ana, California, and Melodyland Christian Center of Anaheim, California.

The first three churches have established reputations for their experience with bus evangelism as a major strategy, while all eleven U.S. churches are heavily committed to involvement in electronic media. Most are actively involved in mass evangelism through television and/or radio. Several have nationwide ministries. The major growth structure used for both evangelism and assimilation of new converts is the small group. The small group design is usually in the form of Sunday school classes that meet at the main church center accompanied with large outreach ministries outside the walls of the church. Others, especially the independent churches of the non-Baptist variety, tend to develop small groups that meet in homes and restaurants throughout the city.

Trends among the Churches

Among the observable trends common to these churches are the role of the founding pastor, pastoral tenure, boldness about bigness, intentional use of small groups, diversity in the design of small groups, the active commitment to planting new congregations, widespread use of electronic media for citywide and even national evangelism, saturation evangelism strategies, and the ability to identify masses and groups of people receptive to the gospel and near the point of conversion.

The pastor is unquestionably a key to the growth of the churches. He is usually a person who has either founded the congregation or is the one responsible for the historic movement of the church toward growth. Average tenure among pastors of these churches is twenty years. None of the present pastors have served their present church less than ten years.

There are more large churches today and they are growing even larger and faster than in recent decades. The ten largest churches of the world alone have among themselves nearly 650,000 members. The large church is uniquely suited as a force for evangelism in the urban centers of the world. It possesses financial resources, manpower, and webs of influence to penetrate entire communities within the city. Also, the size of the large church tends to be the catalyst that attracts the attendance of even more people.

The twenty largest churches tend to structure small as they have grown larger. This does not mean that some do not have a few large classes, but it does mean that even those with large groups usually have many more groups with less than fifty people attending than groups larger than fifty members. A study of both Yoido Full Gospel Church and Young Nak Presbyterian Church, both in Seoul, also indicates that, as teacher-pupil ratios are relaxed and small groups become larger, the growth plateaued. When, however, the ratio was reduced, growth continued. The teacher-pupil ratios tend never to exceed 1:25, and most average 1:14 or even smaller for the individual congregations.

Some of the churches consist of multiple congregations staggered in their use of the same space at different times on the same day. Others organize numerous mini-churches scattered across the city in more than one location. The single location model tends to be used in the United States, Europe, and in communist bloc countries. Latin American countries tend to prefer multiple locations. Asian churches have developed a combination of both models through multiple services and the use of hundreds, even thousands, of cell groups composed of eight to sixteen members each. These cell groups are usually centered in homes rather than at the main church campus. Through the influence of Yoido Full Gospel Church of Seoul, churches on other continents have begun experimenting with the satellite approach of using cell groups. Seven of the twenty largest churches report a combined total of nearly 25,000 cell groups being operated among themselves.

Church planting has proved to be the most effective and fastest method of generating great evangelization of the masses. Seven of the twenty largest churches mentioned earlier have collectively begun a total of at least 1,400 new congregations. The major difference between churches in the United States and those in other countries is in the manner and number of churches started. American churches tend to plant one or two new churches at a time, while churches outside the United States tend to begin several churches simultaneously. American churches usually release their offspring as sovereign, autonomous congregations as soon as possible, while Latin American churches often maintain control of their new churches.

The widespread use of electronic media to reach the multitudes with the gospel has already been mentioned.

Saturation evangelism is a term popularized by Jerry Falwell's effort to preach the gospel to every available person, at every available time, by every available means. This concept becomes reality among some churches in their major investments of time, money, energy, and human resources in electronic media, printed media, street evangelism, day schools, colleges, and even seminaries.

People movement evangelism is the strategy, either knowingly or unknowingly, used to reach receptive groups with the gospel. This method of growth often involves a church or churches keenly alert to and in sympathy with regional or national issues, moods, and movements of the time. In Chile and Brazil it took the form of mass migrations of farmers into urban centers such as Santiago and São Paulo. In Korea it was the migration of tens of thousands of people from North to South Korea due to military invasion. In California it happened as Calvary Chapel of Costa Mesa responded to the national "Jesus People" youth movement. A similar occurrence happened with First Baptist Church of Houston, Texas. Both media evangelism and bus evangelism have aided the rapid reaching of large groups of people with the gospel.

Finally, the dynamic of prayer and recognition of the Holy Spirit as the energizer for growth by these churches is significant. Faith, as the biblical ability to see the unseen, is nurtured in the basic love for and saturation in the Bible, prayer, and reliance upon the guiding work of the Holy Spirit.

For further reading, see John N. Vaughan, *The World's Twenty Largest Churches* (Grand Rapids: Baker Book House, 1984) and *The Large Church: A Twentieth Century Expression of the First Century Church* (Grand Rapids: Baker Book House, 1985).

13
DYNAMIC CHURCHES COME IN ALL SIZES
Medford H. Jones

American churches have been characterized by identification with a variety of concerns. These concerns have included being prestigious, being a denominational witness, being the community conscience, keeping traditions and cultural mores, being a character builder, being a symbol of history, being a movement, being evangelistic, advocating social action, advocating ecumenism, and being committed to church growth.

This chapter advocates the central concern that every congregation be biblically dynamic in its own circumstance. The dynamic church effectively works out the challenge of its situational environment within New Testament norms. If it can grow in numbers of loving obedient children of the Father, it will do whatever is necessary to grow. If it cannot grow in numbers, it will carefully and prayerfully analyze alternatives compatible with the New Testament mandate. If its only choice is to die, it will arrange for its demise with dignity. It will conserve its assets and distribute them wisely. To avoid the aberrant power of subjectivity, professional counsel should confirm any decision that a church cannot grow and should close.

Complexity characterizes any congregation's nature, challenge, and ministry. Intelligent, prayerful programing must be based upon thoughtful assessment and planning. Most dynamic churches are becoming more sophisticated in diagnosis and prognosis. Increasing numbers are using professional consultants to improve growth and outreach. Dynamic churches determine cause and effect relationships and establish objectives consistent with their resources and the environmental challenge.

This chapter arbitrarily categorizes those congregations as "dynamic" that have had both a net membership gain in the past three years and have received new members equivalent to 10 percent of their membership in the past year. No case is made for this particular categorization. However, congregations in this category demonstrate identifiable differences from the churches that have not experienced a net membership gain in the past three years. The information presented here is based largely upon a survey done by the author in cooperation with the North American Christian Convention. Twenty-four hundred congregations responded from a communion of 5,500 American churches surveyed. This brotherhood of 5,500 churches is growing at a 2 percent annual rate and is reasonably analogous to other communions with a strong mission orientation.

No one church fully displays all the characteristics found among dynamic congregations. Frequently congregations may not be aware of the specific factors in their success. The characteristics of dynamism vary by size of congregation although size has very little influence upon a church's being dynamic. As far as possible, this treatment avoids the peculiarities of short-term pastorates with their usual "boom and bust" nature. Here are the general characteristics of the dynamic church.

Preeminence of the Gospel and the Word

In dynamic congregations, preaching is the "Word" as proclamation. The pastor usually reminds one of the New Testament preacher who was famous for the gospel among all the churches (see 2 Cor. 8:18). The preaching is biblically centered and generally perceived as expository. It gives practical guidance for putting faith into practice in daily living. It leads to biblical commitment and demands Christ-like verdicts.

In dynamic congregations, teaching and Bible study are the "Word" at the participative level. People usually carry their Bibles, follow sermons and lessons in them, and are personally getting into the Word. Many individuals "share" or teach others personally. A higher percentage of the membership is involved in classes and group Bible studies. Nurture, caring, and shepherding are a natural part of these developing relationships.

These groups tend to recruit and to encourage people to serve.

A higher percentage of membership involvement in Bible study is a direct result of programs that provide increasing opportunities for group involvement in terms of felt needs and personal preference. Nationally, the survey shows dynamic churches having 21 percent more in Bible school. Dynamic churches more aggressively increase group experience opportunities, providing 14 percent more classes and groups. Dynamic churches are more effective in involving people in productive study of the Scriptures. Dynamic churches average 11 percent more in worship although many large older churches are among the nongrowing segment.

Worship and Devotional Life
Intentionally Support Purpose and Mission

Worship in dynamic congregations focuses on the presence of God and the living Word. Love for Jesus and God is focused and praise is an integral part of worship. A spirit of freedom, spontaneity and even exuberance is usually apparent in contrast to more formality in the nongrowing churches. Audience participation is prevalent. The ordinances are usually observed in a manner that focuses upon unity and mission.

Worship is more "first day" oriented than "Sabbath day." It is more beginning than end, more resurrection than rest, and looks predominantly forward. It leads people to serve rather than to be served.

Worship in dynamic churches encourages those forms of service biblically described as "sacrifices" and "offerings" that are "acceptable to God" (1 Pet. 2:5). The dedicated bodily service of Romans 12:1, 2 is stressed. Praise, witness, converts, and good deeds are typical offerings by members and leaders of dynamic churches. (See Hebrews 13:15, 16 and Romans 15–16.)

As a result, worship attendance is 13 percent larger in dynamic compared to nongrowing churches. The percentage of members in attendance is higher. Forty percent more are in prayer and Bible study groups. The ministry of reconciliation through the Word, service, and love is vital to the worship programming and the life-style of the active members.

Music that "speaks to the heart" is carefully planned to reinforce the content of worship and to motivate the worshipers for committed service. Their larger music programming recruits, converts, nurtures, and assimilates people into "bodily relationship" within dynamic congregations.

Most dynamic churches have variety in their services, including "planned spontaneity" to minister to the needs of all. To provide comfort, convenience, and room for growth, twice as many dynamic churches have two or three worship services compared to nongrowing churches. Service and reconciliation are the central criteria for their worship programming.

Worship in the dynamic church informs, convicts, motivates, and commissions. In a real sense, the closing benediction says, "As you go, make disciples." Thus, a divine partnership with God for witness and service is implanted within the worshiper. Nationally, 12 percent more members of dynamic churches do evangelistic calling than in other churches; 11 percent more do formal shepherding; 30 percent more are in training for service; and 20 percent more work in Sunday school. Worship enhances the mission effectiveness in the dynamic church.

The Ministry of the "Priesthood" of Believers
Leadership in the dynamic congregation is a combination of volunteer and paid leaders maintained in an effective servant mode. Dynamic churches have 50 percent longer pastorates, permitting the leadership team to become more indigenous or "of" the congregation. Thus, they are the congregation's "own." They are respected for their integrity and partnership with God in mission.

Both the leadership and the congregation have come to terms with the reality of being humble and powerful at the same time, being both servants and leaders. They have forged, out of disparate personalities, one team to wage one war against the one enemy. In this climate the membership readily accepts and supports the church's goals. The paid staff is accorded strong influence and leadership. They have earned the right to lead because over time they have demonstrated their faith and good judgment.

The leadership team leads. They accept the onus of leadership and bear its responsibility. They take charge with a "can do" attitude depending upon God and his people. They do not wait for legalistic voted approval but usually assume permission and proceed. They communicate well and tend to seek concensus rather than risk dividing the house by formal voting. Feedback channels are kept open and planning is continuous. The leadership team is determined and purposeful, but flexible enough to change when a shift will enhance effectiveness. They force resources to serve rather than permitting them to dominate. By faith and commitment dynamic churches are more mobile and acquisitive. Their properties are 43 percent larger. They maintain more multiple services. They are planning 50 percent more enlargement of programs and facilities in the next year than are the nongrowing churches. They manage conflict frontally in truth and love believing that conflicts eliminated are better than festering tension. They report 21 percent less tension between elders and deacons. They are outward and goal oriented in the belief that obedience requires both faithfulness and fruitfulness.

A primary priority of the leadership is the equipping and deploying of additional workers. They fully recognize that prepared workers precede vigorous growth. The leadership team is fully committed and willing to pay whatever price is necessary for the church to achieve its purposes. Their example elicits sacrificial service from the members.

Priestly servant followers are the ultimate foundation of the dynamic church. It is sensed among the members that true Christian worth is in service even as "the Son of Man did not come to be served, but to serve" (Matt. 20:28). They understand that serving requires them to follow their leaders. These priestly servant followers espouse the goals of their church and support them. They have had opportunity for input and thoughtful prayer. They exercise initiative and imagination in their service utilizing the program and structures provided for their use. As a direct product of the leadership's example, a high percentage of the membership serves. Strong intuitive leaders multiply happy productive workers, especially when they model good stewardship of time, talent, and wealth.

Warm Fellowship
Fellowship in dynamic churches is nurtured by the Word, the Holy Spirit, prayer, service, and the mutual support of fellow

members. It is heart-to-heart and has the substance of reality. Honest, loving care is so rich that people often refuse to accept promotions if it requires moving away from their church.

Because of the tendency in dynamic churches to provide more kinds of opportunity for involvement, the group and fellowship life is more open, accepting, and seeking. It brings people in and holds them. It minimizes the outsider syndrome and reduces membership attrition. Shepherding, caring, and nurturing are a natural result of the character of this fellowship. The key to such effective fellowship is abundant acceptable opportunities for group life involvement couched in meeting needs.

People Centeredness
Dynamic churches are up-to-date, informed, conditioned to their cultural environment, and able to address the people with a non-judgmental attitude. They are aware of people's needs and seek to fill those needs as a direct ministry in a variety of ways. Such service is freely and graciously given. An essential characteristic of most dynamic churches is the spirit and attitude that comes from broad genuine service to people and their resulting response in witness.

Any church, regardless of size or environment, can and should be vitally dynamic in its own specific situation. Some churches that are truly dynamic in their own situation would be excluded by the arbitrary formula used here to indicate dynamism. However, the conclusions we have drawn remain valid. Building a dynamic church requires faith, intentionality, and purposiveness. It requires honest partnering with God in the achievement of his will. It requires honest assessment of the available resources and the challenge. It requires willingness to pay the specific price necessary within each specific situation. If any kind of growth is possible, the dynamic church will do whatever is necessary to grow. If death is its only alternative, it dies with Christian dignity leaving a wholesome legacy. Regardless of the circumstance, dynamic churches are exciting to observe because the power and presence of God are refreshingly present.

Part 4

CHURCH GROWTH
AND CHURCH PLANTING

If reaching the lost is the chief imperative for the Church Growth Movement, what is the most efficient way of reaching them? Elmer Towns and Thomas Younger reply with no hesitation: planting new churches. Research has clearly shown that this is true. Towns goes to the heart of the matter—the Great Commission of Jesus—to show how it relates to church planting. His chapter is a fresh challenge for effective evangelism. Then Younger contributes one of the most practical chapters in the book. He tells how he, as the pastor of a church in Fort Wayne, Indiana, supervised the planting of twelve daughter churches from one congregation.

14
THE GREAT COMMISSION AND CHURCH PLANTING

Elmer L. Towns

Most people recognize that the Great Commission commands Christians to evangelize lost people. Few realize the implied method to carry out this commission. The Great Commission implies that church planting is the primary method to evangelize the world. To reach lost people in every culture of the world, a church must be established in every culture to communicate the gospel and nurture those who are saved. In a simplistic observation, one of the reasons why so much foreign missions work is fruitless is because great effort is spent on winning people to Christ apart from identifying them with a New Testament church. All methods of evangelism have their place: radio evangelism, television evangelism, medical evangelism, mass evangelism, personal evangelism, educational evangelism, presence evangelism. But God's primary method of evangelizing a new community is by planting a New Testament church to reach the area with the gospel.

Many are ignorant of the role of church planting in evangelism. Others dissent because they do not really understand God's program of evangelism. They have never understood the role of church planting in the Great Commission. A careful study of the Great Commission reveals the complex and divergent nature under which the command was given and the difficult task that Jesus wanted accomplished.

The Great Commission was given at five different times in separate locations. On each occasion the Lord added to the previous command, and the reader must see the total picture to understand the full implication of the Great Commission.

The Great Commission was initially given on the afternoon of the resurrection to ten disciples. Jesus said, "As the Father has sent Me, I also send you" (John 20:21, NKJV). Jesus was simply giving his perplexed disciples a commission to represent him. At this place the message, destination, and task were not given to them. Perhaps they were not ready to receive it.

A week later in the upper room Thomas was present, making eleven disciples. Jesus told them, "Go into all the world and preach the gospel to every creature" (Mark 16:15). Two aspects were added to the commission. First, they were not just to minister to Israel but to the world, and second, they were to preach the gospel to every person in the world.

The next time the Great Commission was repeated was at least two weeks later. The disciples were no longer in Jerusalem but on a mountain in Galilee approximately one hundred miles away. He assumed they would eventually obey, for he used the participle "as you are going" (Matt. 28:19). This is based on the previous command to go and preach the gospel to every person. Here Jesus added two aspects to the Great Commission. First, they were to disciple (imperative), which involves a command to get results. Secondly, they were to center on nations, *ethne,* "people groups." This concern with social groups has vast implications that we shall see later.

The fourth giving of the Great Commission (Luke 24:46-48) stated that the gospel message must include repentance and belief. The last reiteration was given the same day at the ascension. This included the power of the Holy Spirit to indwell them and also the geographical scope: Jerusalem, Judea, Samaria, and the uttermost parts (Acts 1:8).

Strategy in Matthew 28:19, 20

The giving of the Great Commission in Matthew 28:19, 20 includes strategy. The church is to go to different nations or groups of people and evangelize them. This is best done by planting indigenous churches where people can be saved, baptized, and continually discipled in the Word of God. It is with this in mind that Vergil Gerber concludes that "the ultimate evangelistic goal in the New Testament, therefore, is twofold: (1) to make respon-

THE GREAT COMMISSION

	WHERE	WHEN	TO WHOM	WHAT	KEY
1. John 20:21	Upper room, Jerusalem	Resurrection Day	10 disciples	I am sending you	Commission
2. Mark 16:15	Upper room, Jerusalem	One week later	11 disciples	Go to all the world and preach to every person	Recipients
3. Matthew 28:19, 20	Mountain in Galilee	At least two weeks later	11 disciples	Disciple all "peoples," then baptize and teach	Strategy
4. Luke 24: 46-48	Jerusalem	40th day	11 disciples	Preach repentance and forgiveness of sins, based on resurrection of Christ	Content
5. Acts 1:8	Mt. of Olives	40th day	11 disciples	Jerusalem to uttermost part of earth	Geography

sible, reproducing Christians, (2) to make responsible, reproducing congregations."[1]

Matthew 28:19, 20 states: "Go therefore and make disciples of all nations, baptizing them in the name of the Father and of the Son and of the Holy Spirit, teaching them to observe all things that I have commanded you." This Great Commission includes church planting for the following reasons:

1. To "make disciples of" people in all nations is best fulfilled by an indigenous church in every culture.

2. "Baptizing" identifies a new believer with Christ and with the church. The result of baptizing is to plant a church to carry on this process.

3. The focus of discipling is *ethne* ("nations"), which has three meanings: (1) ethnic groups, (2) gentiles, (3) nations. In all three, the target is not individuals but groups of people. The best means of evangelizing a group of people is through a ministering assembly of saved people—the church.

4. "Teaching them to observe all things that I have commanded you" means instructing believers to obey the words of

Christ (including the Great Commission). This command was carried out in the New Testament church by "teaching the apostles' doctrine" (Acts 2:49). The continuous teaching in the church became the basis of the church's growth and fellowship. When new areas were evangelized, the result was new churches with new believers who had to be taught the words of Christ.

5. By illustration, the New Testament records stories of believers going everywhere establishing churches (see Acts 9:31). Wherever the gospel was successfully presented, a church sprang into existence.

Beginning with the great dispersion of the Jerusalem believers (Acts 8:1), the disciples successfully multiplied congregations and planted additional churches. In fact "new congregations were planted in every pagan center of the then-known world in less than four decades."[2] As the believers were scattered, so was the seed of the gospel that would take root in various national soils. In Acts 9:31 a geographical broadening had taken place so that believers are placed "throughout all Judea, Galilee, and Samaria" (as directed in Acts 1:8). Based on the understanding of the eleven disciples and the success that resulted from their obedience, it is evident that planting local churches throughout the world is God's plan.

The dynamic church-planting efforts of the Apostle Paul, Barnabas, Silas, Timothy, and others who were all early disciples verifies the concept of local church expansion to which Jesus Christ is committed. Surely they would have done no less than he commanded and no more than he empowered.

6. By analogy each produces after its kind so a church sends out missionaries who should plant churches like those that sent them out.

> From the day God said to Adam and Eve, "Be fruitful, multiply, replenish the earth," multiplication has been the secret of the growth of the human race, until this geometric progression has reached the staggering proportions of a population explosion.
>
> Even when we grasp the simple fact that multiplication is the secret of the growth of the church, we need to ask—a multiplication of what? Not committees, not

146

high offices, not even individual believers as such. We must apply our secret at the level of the local church. To start rapid growth by multiplication, we must encourage our own local church (be we pastor, layman, or missionary) to reproduce itself in another part of the city or in a neighboring town or village.[3]

Engel and Norton believe that one believer winning another is not enough. They state that "it is a demonstrated principle of church growth that Christianity gains in a society only to the extent that the number of existing churches is multiplied. Multiplication of new congregations of believers, then, is the normal and expected output of a healthy body."[4]

Several authors, including Weld, McGavran, Michael Green, Roland Allen, and others, refer to the strategy that the Apostle Paul used in his church planting endeavors. The Apostle Paul concentrated his efforts on cities, which were centers of communication, transportation, and commerce. Paul planned to evangelize these areas by planting churches. He would often go to the synagogue seeking first to win his Jewish countrymen (Acts 13:5, Salamis; Acts 13:14, Pisidian Antioch; Acts 14:1, Iconium; Acts 17:1, Thessalonica; Acts 18:1, 4, Corinth). Paul gained a hearing with the Jews who attended the synagogues and later continued with the gentiles (God-fearers) who also had heard of him and his message. As the Scripture indicates, before Paul reached Thessalonica he had been practicing his plan for starting churches to the point where Acts 17:2 records; "Paul, as was his *custom*, went in to them, and for three Sabbaths reasoned with them from the Scriptures" (emphasis added).

Referring to the rapid and wide expansion of the early church, Roland Allen emphasizes "spontaneous expansion," although he does explain the issue of organization as well.

The Church expanded simply by organizing these little groups of early disciples as they were converted, handing on to them the organization which she had received from her first founders. It was itself a unity composed for a multitude of little churches, any one of which could propagate itself, and consequently the reception

147

of any new group of Christians was a simple matter. By a simple act the new group was brought into the unity of the Church, and equipped, as its predecessors had been equipped, not only with all the spiritual power and authority necessary for its own life as an organized unity, but also with all the authority needed to repeat the same process whenever one of its members might convert men in any new village or town.[5]

Donald McGavran, whose concern and interest is clearly the multiplication of new churches, believes the sequence of the Great Commission to "make disciples of all nations" precedes "teaching them to observe all things." McGavran argues:

> Only churches which exist can be perfected. Only babies who have been born can be educated. Only where practicing Christians form sizable minorities of their societies can they expect their presence seriously to influence the social, economic, and political structures. The Church must, indeed, "teach them all things," but first she must have at least some Christians and some congregations.[6]

Since the purpose of the Great Commission is finalized when a New Testament church is planted, those church planters who establish a church are not doing something that is spectacular or overwhelmingly unique. They are simply carrying out the command of Jesus Christ. Also, church planters should not be thought of as divisive (sapping strength from existing churches) or selfish (wanting to control a church so they plant their own) nor independent (unwilling to take an existing pulpit). They should be thought of as those who are employing the most biblical methods to reach the developing areas of the world.

1. Vergil Gerber, *God's Way to Keep a Church Going and Growing* (Glendale, California: Regal Books, 1973), 18.
2. Ibid., 17.
3. Paul David, "Church Multiplication," *Church Growth Bulletin*, Vol. 2, No. 1 (September 1965), 92.
4. James F. Engel and H. Wilbert Norton, *What's Gone Wrong with the Harvest? A Communication Strategy for the Church and World Evangelism* (Grand Rapids: Zondervan, 1975), 143, 144.

5. Roland Allen, *The Spontaneous Expansion of the Church* (Grand Rapids: Eerdmans, 1962), 143.

6. Donald A. McGavran, *Understanding Church Growth* (Grand Rapids: Eerdmans, 1970), 359.

15
THE LOCAL CHURCH
AS A CHURCH
PLANTING BASE

W. Thomas Younger

It was late in September after a Sunday of preaching. I lay awake most of the night, sensing that God was speaking to me. When was I going to get on with the task of planting churches? That was in Fort Wayne, Indiana, where, after that night, almost half my ministry involved church planting. During the seventeen years at Immanuel Baptist Church we planted twelve new churches.

However, my interest in church extension did not begin in Fort Wayne, but dates back to the time of my conversion in the Glen Park Baptist Church in Gary, Indiana. Central Baptist had mothered Glen Park among others, first, under the vision of William Ward Ayer and then of Robert T. Ketcham. Early in my Christian experience and call to the ministry, I dreamed about the day when I too could become involved in this kind of ministry.

Our first opportunity came in July 1951 when my wife, Davi, and I were called to help plant Immanuel Baptist Church in Arcanum, Ohio. We assumed responsibility for seven families in southwest Darke County with approximately 2,000 people in the extended community. God blessed the church with growth. Several young people were called into the ministry from Immanuel during the five years we pastored there.

During that time one of our young men, Don Worch, asked if I would help him become established as a pastor in a Baptist church. We agreed to meet in Fort Wayne, a city of 150,000 people at that time, and inquire of another church named Immanuel about the possibility of planting a daughter church. Don and I looked over that city one day and visited the pastor, Carl

Brown. Nothing came of the venture. Little did I realize, however, that God had a ministry for me in Fort Wayne—but it was to be a year or so later.

I learned about it first from Lyle Jessup, a missionary whose home church, Immanuel, Fort Wayne, was without a pastor. Would I allow him to submit my name for consideration? My interest was keen because of the dreams for church planting and the recent survey of the city. Within four months I was called to Fort Wayne. The people became aware of some vague ideas I had for church extension. They didn't know I already had a commitment from a friend, Earl Umbaugh, to become pastor of our first branch church—not yet born.

Davi and I arrived in Fort Wayne in July 1956, eager to lead Immanuel into greater growth and also in a new ministry of church planting. We had approximately 400 members with 350 in Sunday school and 280 in morning worship. We had a delightful time getting acquainted those first two months, but all the while I was stirred up about where and when we would give birth to our first church. As I mentioned in the beginning of this chapter, on the last Sunday in September I lay awake most of the night, sensing that God was speaking to me, asking when I was going to get on with the task of planting churches. I told the Lord I would get on with the task first thing in the morning, and it was then I found rest.

Early Monday morning I met Sidney Peek, retired railroader and chairman of our board, at the Methodist cemetery in northeast Fort Wayne. "What's up?" asked Sidney. I told him we were going to look for a building to rent for a new church. "Where?" asked Sidney. I replied that I didn't know, but we'd find out. Sidney responded: "Let's go, brother." We drove out St. Joe Center Road about three miles to the corner of Lahmeyer Road, and saw the Bojrab Clubhouse in the middle of a cornfield—a meeting place for occasions such as weddings, dances and assorted parties. To get to the clubhouse, we drove down a long, narrow lane, with tall corn in the harvest stage standing like sentinels on either side. One of the Bojrab brothers was busy cleaning up after a party the night before. We asked about costs for renting his club. We explained our intent was to start a Baptist church that coming Sunday. He said he would let us know that evening at five o'clock after talking it over with his brothers. I gave him five dollars showing good faith; he gave me his address.

On the way back to the cemetery to pick up his car, Sidney asked, "Do you think people will come to a church out in the middle of a cornfield? Who will we get for a nucleus of people? Who will pastor?" I talked about the population of this end of the city; that it showed strong signs of future growth; that we had seven families who lived here; and that Sidney could preach until we found someone to pastor full time. Sidney warmed to the idea. He was a Moody Bible Institute alumnus. Moody people take pride in living by the maxim: "Always prepared."

Later, I asked my secretary to phone the other deacons to meet us at the clubhouse that evening at six o'clock.

I met the Bojrabs at 5:00 P.M., shared dinner with them—my first introduction to fried eggplant—agreed on a contract to rent the building, paid the first month's rent, and hurried to the clubhouse to meet my deacons.

We explained to them that we were going to use the clubhouse for Sunday school and worship on Sunday, then proceeded to show them around. We entertained questions: Who would come to a place out in the middle of a cornfield? How did we know this community would support a Baptist church? Can we start a church at this time?

I had invited Bill Eidson, a young businessman, to meet with us. He lived in that area and had already agreed to be part of the nucleus for the new church. The Eidsons, from a Southern Baptist background, joined our church the same Sunday as Davi and I. I asked Bill how he felt about starting a church. Bill was like his father, a long time deacon in another church, whose stance was usually against any proposal his pastor presented. But Bill said: "As for following our pastor, that's what we pay him to do—lead. We ought to follow his leadership until his mistakes prove he can't lead. Then fire him!" Bill's support carried the day. We were in business. Church services were set for Sunday! We phoned six other families immediately, asking them to meet in Bill's home Friday evening. They all agreed.

Wednesday evening at Immanuel I shared the news about the new church starting. Then I explained a philosophy and method that we used for years: We would plant churches where there was potential for growth; provide as large a nucleus of people as we could from our own church; secure a good leader-pastor; give all financial help possible; provide needed encouragement and help; and not interfere with the new church once it was planted. We prayed that God would bless the new church and keep the old one, Immanuel, from dying: after all, we stood to lose 10 percent of our people.

Friday evening we met with the seven families in Bill's home. We appointed all of them to some task or ministry for which they were equipped, fervently praying for God's blessing on this new venture. On that Sunday in October, twenty-nine adults and children arrived with a box of hymnals, offering plates, and bottles of Airwick to conduct their first service (the Airwick to purge the air from Saturday night revelry at the clubhouse). Soon after I phoned Earl and Sergie Umbaugh, inviting them to Fort Wayne to consider the possibility of shepherding this new church. The Umbaughs met with our seven families. They accepted Earl as pastor; he accepted them as his flock. We had a great time of fellowship, getting acquainted with one another and praying together.

Months later I was dreaming about how we could start another church, wondering how many new works we could trust God for. It seemed imperative that we set goals. About that time a copy of the *Sunday School Builder,* a Southern Baptist publication, crossed my desk explaining that the Southern Baptists had a goal of planting 30,000 new churches by 1965.

I figured how many churches that would mean for Fort Wayne were they to come there. The number was fifteen. I shared this with my pastor friend, Earl. We prayed about the faith projection of fifteen new churches by 1965. We felt it good to make the goal public knowledge. A strange thing happened about that goal-setting exercise.

When Earl's church building was dedicated, we had a sign made with Shoaff Park Baptist Church printed on it, across the bottom in bold print our goal: "The first of fifteen new Regular Baptist Churches to be planted in Fort Wayne by 1965." The sign was placed in the ground just before dedication, but we got cold feet about the bold declaration of how many churches we hoped to plant. We brought meat wrapping paper from a supermarket and covered the bottom of the sign.

However, God had something to do with the goal, for the next day there was a cold, strong wind whipping along the ground. I was shocked when we drove up to the new property and saw in bold letters—larger than life—"The first of fifteen new Regular Baptist Churches to be planted in Fort Wayne by 1965." I became convinced it was a goal to be adopted publicly, and we lived with it before us for years.

Making the goal public was more important than I realized. My own congregation became fearful hearing me talk about church number two: where it would be located, when it would be started, how many families the mother church would lose. Also, after Earl and I surveyed southeast Fort Wayne and determined that this was the place for our next church, we just weren't able to pull the trigger of faith to start it. Two years went by. One day we drove up and down the streets of Waynedale asking God to give us the courage to trust him. It was then that I learned the lesson that circumstances are not always favorable when it comes time to step out by faith.

We decided to plant the church. It appeared we had only two families living in that part of the city. So we called for God to raise up someone in our congregation to drive over to this area— as missionaries. Two more families came to the front. We secured a pastor and we were off and running. The church was born.

Then, in a period of fourteen months, we planted three more churches in other areas. One day we got our pastors together with the challenge to plant four churches simultaneously; two were born. Now with a decade of experience and ten churches on the scene, we were developing more patience and planning in the process. We purchased a five-acre tract of land in northeast Fort Wayne, where we already had planted our first church. This area had exploded with growth. Twenty of our families at Immanuel lived in the area. Immanuel began praying that God would raise up ten families to form the nucleus for this new work. We prayed for a year. During that time we contracted a mobile home manufacturer to build a mobile church to accommodate 125 in Sunday school and church services.

Once our nucleus was selected, the property paid for, and mobile church ready, we called David Jeremiah to pastor the new

Blackhawk Baptist Church. It was thrilling to see the church surpass Immanuel in size. Blackhawk is now fifteen years old with an average attendance of 1,200 on Sunday and a budget more than a million dollars in 1984. Plans are imminent to build a sanctuary to accommodate 2,200 people.

Looking back thirty years, there are lessons I learned that still remain with me. I mention seven:

1. We lived by scriptural principles like the one in Proverbs 11:24: "There is one who scatters yet increases more; and there is one who withholds more than is right, but it leads to poverty." We took God literally in scattering our resources.

2. We walked by faith; our prayers were often with desperation. We sent away over one hundred families in starting churches. Many times we were on our faces before God to replenish our own force of workers. One Sunday evening we bid good-bye to nineteen people leaving to start the Wallen Church; the next Sunday we had nineteen new faces in our morning service.

3. God is debtor to no one. Immanuel prospered. Right in the midpoint of new church ministry, we relocated our own facilities.

4. We never found the perfect time to start a church. There were always enough negative circumstances to test our faith.

5. We learned that there were people resources available when we needed a nucleus for another church. Charles Jefferson said it well: "Christian men and women are filled with energy, but in many cases the energy turns no wheels. There is in every church a Niagara of force which creates neither heat nor light. There is in every church desert land which would blossom as a rose if it were irrigated by an engineer's skill. There are swamps which could be drained if only the necessary knowledge and genius were at hand" *(The Minister as Shepherd,* p. 95).

6. Vision was indispensable. Skeptics, critics, and second guessers abounded, especially in the early years. I insisted on following my earlier vision and goal, treating dissenters as well as I could, but continuing on. Most of them joined with me in time. I am thankful to God for each of them.

7. Good things take time. In the tenth year at Immanuel, I almost left. It wasn't until the twelfth year that Blackhawk, our largest church, was born.

Part 5

CHURCH GROWTH
AND TECHNOLOGY

Insights into modern church growth technology permeate all the previous chapters. Church growth research and development is moving ahead on all fronts. This section deals basically with two specialized areas of church growth technology: consultation and use of computers. Carl George has gained a superb reputation as a church growth consultant over the past half dozen years. He did much of the pioneering work in the field and developed the first professional level consultation training program called "Diagnosis with Impact." George writes on church growth consultation in general, while one of his protégés, Delmar Anderson, deals with how it can work within a denominational structure. Anderson, of the Evangelical Covenant Church, was, so far as is known, the first denominational executive with the title "Director of Church Growth."

You will enjoy Melvin Schell's computer-oriented mind in his chapter on total church growth. He is one of the first church growth leaders who came to the field with extensive background in computer science. His model is one that many will find helpful.

16
CHURCH GROWTH CONSULTATION
Carl F. George

Church growth consultation began at the Charles E. Fuller Institute in 1975, when it was still called Fuller Evangelistic Association, under C. Peter Wagner and John Wimber. I took over from Wimber in 1978. For seven years, I have examined large numbers of churches in North America. People who represent seventy denominations have studied with us and used materials provided at the Charles E. Fuller Institute (CEFI). Thousands of pastors and tens of thousands of lay persons have been guided toward growth in our training programs. With the experience we have now, we can better address seven key questions:
1. What makes church growth consulting necessary:
2. How is church growth consulting different from ordinary forms of church consulting?
3. Who provides help to churches?
4. How is church growth consultation helpful?
5. What forms does consulting help take?
6. What is CEFI doing to help consultants?
7. What is the future of church growth consulting?

What Makes Church Growth Consulting Necessary?
Church growth consulting is necessary because many congregations come to a place where some leaders want a church to grow larger and others are not sure it should or can. Those who want to see growth encouraged become frustrated by those who are satisfied with the current size and by other obstacles they must overcome to grow.

Because a consultant comes from the outside, both sides in a struggle can believe he or she will be able to "see it like it is" and "tell it like it is" without playing favorites. The hope is that the group will move past personalities and agree to deal with real issues that are blocking growth.

The next steps leading to growth may be beyond the group's ability or experience, such as: calling a pastor in a new church or in an older church following a long pastorate, building a larger facility, preparing to relocate, overcoming a schism, parenting a new mission congregation, planning to meet the different needs of a changing neighborhood, dismissing a key staff member, or raising a large capital fund.

How Is Church Growth Consulting Different from Ordinary Forms of Church Consulting?

Church growth brings with it a bias for the numerical expansion of the Christian movement. Church growth consultants draw on the biblical theology of the Church Growth Movement. That movement has a carefully crafted biblical rationale. It argues that the church in our age has a mandate to proclaim Christ's kingdom and to anticipate a positive response to that proclamation. Indeed, the movement insists that the manner of the proclamation should be strategically adjusted until a response is evident. The desired response is an increasing number of individuals who confess Jesus Christ as their personal Savior and obey him as their Lord. The minimum acceptable measure of obedience is defined as responsible membership in a local congregation. This must lead to numerical expansion of the Christian movement. It encourages membership enlargement of each congregation, as well as an increase in the number of viable congregations.

Church growth consultants also draw from the social sciences, including anthropology, sociology, social psychology, psychology, educational psychology, instructional technology, communications, organizational development, management, and marketing.

Church growth consultants bring a kingdom growth bias into their consultations. They are continually asking themselves and their clients: "How can this situation be helped to make more and better disciples of Jesus Christ?"

Some desperate organizations seek to enlarge their member-ships merely as a survival tactic. This is an inadequate motivation and lacks the attractiveness of the life-changing power of the gospel. Other church consultants may focus on organizational comfort, personal adjustment, problem-solving, fund-raising, and other worthwhile goals, but they often stop short of chal-lenging the church to live up to the mandates clearly given by the risen Christ to disciple all nations. We have been discovering that church growth consulting has a prophetic dimension—to awaken within a congregation a commitment to obey the Great Commission.

Of special interest to the consultant is Michael Harper's re-counting of a modern day prophet he learned about from the Bishop of Afghanistan. Apparently the bishop told Harper of an earlier visit from an African brother who carried the title of prophet, even to the point of listing it on his passport as his official occupation. The man had been sent to Afghanistan from a legitimate church in Africa, so the bishop authorized him to minister. The bishop confided to Harper that he had not been a very popular fellow, but he did more good than anyone else they could name who had visited the diocese. He had gone from church to church and just "sorted the people out," having the quality of insight and an ability to confront that stripped away masks of pretense, discerned intentions, and brought a much needed touch of reality to otherwise fruitless discussions.[1]

It is this capacity to deftly intervene, with the professional skills of the change agent and consultant, and the spiritual sen-sitivity and dependence of the prophet, that is needed by our churches today.

Who Provides Help to Churches?
Church growth consulting is usually a third party activity, prac-ticed by people who are outside of a local church. Most churches have denominational ties, and most denominations have area ministers or district superintendents who move among the churches and provide a great deal of the help that is needed. They serve as functional third parties.

To see how a third party may function, let me analyze a familiar church practice. In my own childhood in Independent Baptist churches in the Southeast, one of the most highly visible events of the year was the annual revival and evangelistic meetings. These meetings lasted from one to three weeks. The featured speaker was typically a colorful communicator with a head full of Texas cowboy stories. He would delight his audience with accounts of God's interventions in the lives of Christians elsewhere as he brought refreshment to a strife-weary congregation. The stories and the evangelist's manner served as more than a distraction to the humdrum, business-as-usual activities. In retrospect, a number of benefits to the congregation can be cited:

1. Because the evangelistic meeting could be seen as something special and out of the ordinary, it encouraged the mobilization of member attendance and helped to reset within them a priority for participation in local church activities. Levels of interest were raised and the people had an expectation of enjoying the experience, which they would celebrate in their own storytelling over the months to follow.

2. Where the evangelist had an especially interesting personality or manner of delivery, the church was able to offer "the best show in town" during the period of the revival, so that it had something to offer that it did not normally have. This ability to display value provided an incentive for the membership to invite friends and acquaintances to the meetings, introducing them to the congregation during a time when the outsiders would be able to see the congregation in a most favorable light.

3. The evangelist coming from the outside was not intimidated by the community. This meant that he had the ability to make the bold moves necessary to break through the stained-glass barrier and identify additional pools of likely candidates for church membership. Such moves to reach out bridged the acquaintance gap that had developed over time. The evangelist could frequently make contact with representatives of enough new nests of prospects or family units that the church could glean the benefits of those connections for months to come.

4. Various factions within the congregation would have an opportunity to turn their attention from picking at one another to enjoying the outsider, who was perceived as neutral and not a combatant in the ongoing struggles and strife of the clans. This provided a period of truce and gave time for individuals

to rethink their relationships. They would be able to come to a renewed sense of appreciation of one another. They could commit to mutually working out differences within a context where love and affirmation predominated over anger and demoralizing bickering.

5. The conflicts that had been developing between the professional minister and the lay leadership were also dealt with.

The way pastor-church conflicts usually worked became predictable after seeing several such crusades or conferences. Somewhere about two-thirds through a series of meetings, the evangelist would have sensed a way to appeal to the most cherished values of the group and cause the pastor and lay leadership to see that their continual power struggles were unhelpful to the health of the congregation.

He would then call for repentance on the part of one or both of the leadership elements so that some kind of public acknowledgment of wrongdoing would be seen as serving the highest purposes of the kingdom of God. The result would be a tearful meeting of the lay leaders and the pastor at the altar of the church with exchanges of forgiveness. It was common to see embraces, hear statements of remorse about wrongdoing, and witness pledges to affirm one another's ministry. They would resolve to plan together for a more fruitful future.

Frequently, these times of recommitment were accompanied by special offerings raised to give assistance to the pastor and his family, who in many cases had been systematically deprived of financial reward as resentments toward them had developed over a period of time.

The importance of this recommitment to work together among the various strong leaders of the church cannot be overestimated, and the absence of this form of itinerate ministry is a probable major feature in rapid pastoral turnover experienced in many denominations.

Without the help of the external consultant in the guise of evangelist, or if you prefer, the evangelist with spiritual and organizational consulting skills, churches develop a pattern of call, honeymoon, disenchantment, contention, and rejection of their leaders.

Ideally, denominational executives should be able to rescue

the ministry in such situations, and in many cases they do provide such help. However, our experience indicates that denominational executives are often handicapped in intervening for several of these reasons:

1. They are too busy with administrative and organizational maintenance to deal with special cases.

2. They may not be trained in consulting skills.

3. The majority of local churches are small, and the greater part of their experience is with the very small or very new church. Therefore, they may lack credibility with the leaders of larger churches.

4. They have the ability to pass judgment on the pastors and can negatively influence their careers; therefore, they may not be acceptable as confidants.

5. Many church executives do not have a theology of growth. They have adopted philosophies of ministry that are focused on maintenance rather than expansion.

6. Some situations are very thorny—a wrong move in an attempted conflict resolution can mean serious loss of financial or political support for district personnel or programs.

7. The kind of personalities typically installed as executives have more traits for soothing and smoothing than the kind of cutting edge discernment sometimes needed for effective treatment to produce growth in the local body.

This means there is a place for consultants who are not in the executive power structure of a denomination. There is also a place for trans-denominational consultants who have the capacity to affirm and celebrate the effective distinctives of a denomination's heritage. These outsiders can bring startling new perceptions to a group and spark a renewed appreciation of the group's own cherished traditions.

How Is Church Growth Consultation Helpful?

The effects of consulting vary with the myriad situations in the churches. Churches are planted, relocated, expanded dramatically, redirected to provide ministry to newly acknowledged target groups. New classes and programs are added. Staffs are enlarged; much money is raised. Pastors and staff are counseled, dismissed, and hired. Schism is averted; new facilities are built. Big plans for significantly greater future ministry are laid out. The people are motivated and instructed to improve pastoral care, communicate more helpfully, renovate facilities, raise staff salaries, resolve tensions between day school and church factions, advertise more effectively, discover new talent for lay workers, experience spiritual renewal, see new adult confirmations, and come alive to their potential.

One measure of the helpfulness of consulting is by reports of those who have been helped. Much of the consulting work done by associates of the Charles E. Fuller Institute is the result of word-of-mouth advertising—pastors telling pastors where they found help. Denominational executives, too, have often made referrals of special or difficult cases.

We have watched congregations break the 60 barrier, the 200 barrier, the 1,000 barrier, and the 3,000 barrier. Old congregations have relocated or retooled. Whole districts and entire denominations have opened themselves to Church Growth influence, including diagnostic, planning, and training help at every level. Congregations have practiced self-help through consultant-led church growth interventions.

What Forms Does Consulting Help Take?[2]
Consultants can assist pastors and lay persons through a variety of techniques.

1. Coaching pastors and lay task forces to do self studies. CEFI has developed a library of consultant-directed "Church Growth Training Modules" for individual church or cluster use. Task forces are organized and directed through several months of activity using prescribed modules.

2. Conducting clinics and workshop events at a local church on setting goals and discovering spiritual gifts.

3. Leadership retreats and staff team-building events.

4. Diagnostic analysis. A comprehensive service for examining most essential factors influencing a church's health and growth. This is especially helpful for churches facing profound dilemmas. It involves data gathering and careful field interviewing and surveying, leading to written recommendations.

5. Master planning. A customized interactive process leading to expertly guided recommendations for preparing a master

plan for achieving significant goals in a church's development.

6. The "Total Church Development Model." A three-year program of diagnosis, planning, and training with extensive participation by the local congregation leading to the formation and implementation of a "Priority Plan for Growth." The overall process and many of its components are directed by a local consultant, using CEFI tools and techniques. This is described fully in chapter 18 by Melvin Schell.

7. Casual or occasional consultation. Dealing with specific issues or areas of church growth, as needed, on a time and expenses basis.

What Is CEFI Doing to Help Consultants?

The basic consultant training programs offered by the Institute are entitled "Diagnosis with Impact." These courses are offered as professional training courses and have also been accepted as courses for credit within the Fuller Theological Seminary Doctor of Ministry program. "Diagnosis with Impact" was named because of the growing awareness of Fuller Institute staff that the various activities involved in diagnosis were being reported by client churches as having helpful effects, long before specific recommendations from the analyses had been formally acted upon by the churches.

Training in basic church growth consulting skills takes several forms:

"Diagnosis with Impact" is a one-and-a-half- or two-year internship on a continuing educational model. It consists of an opening week of classwork in Pasadena; four supervised cases spread over at least fifteen months, including at least one field case accompanied by an experienced consultant; readings; and an intensive closing week of classes. This internship is helpful in gaining the concepts and skills needed for the role of a church growth consultant.

Case panel events involve selected cases in progress being brought before a panel of experienced consultants with interns in attendance.

Training events/materials include:[3]
- Plant-a-church seminars, basic and advanced

- Planning and managing for growth in the local church
- Problem-solving workshops
- Church Growth training modules
- Multi-staff church conference

What Is the Future of Church Growth Consultation?
Effective role performance—whether as lay leaders, local pastoral leaders, church executives, parachurch workers, or church growth consultants—requires not only a role concept and a set of enabling skills, but also networking with other persons operating within those roles who can support and maintain role performance. The programs at Fuller Seminary, the Charles E. Fuller Institute, and to some extent the newly created North American Society for Church Growth are calculated to initiate and support practitioners who share this vision.

A closely affiliated network of over 200 practitioners is envisioned at the Charles E. Fuller Institute alone. The persons who have the potential for this kind of role either as third-party consultants or as executives in the churches probably number 10,000 in the United States. There will probably be full-time work available for one third-party or external consultant for every thousand or 1,200 churches in addition to the available denominational executives.

Parachurch organizations other than consulting groups have specific program agendas which require their perceiving the churches as financial sponsors. They cannot be reasonably expected to subvert their mission agendas to concentrate on the health of their donor churches because they would take on the character of denominations and thus would be less suitable as apostolic agents or sending arms of their constituent and supporting churches. A network of church growth consultants, however, has great potential for applying the insights of the Church Growth Movement to individual local churches.

1. Michael Harper, *Let My People Grow* (Hodder & Stoughton, 1977), 54.
2. For church leaders wishing to inquire further, write for *Catalogue of Services*, available from Charles E. Fuller Institute, Box 91990, Pasadena, CA 91109, or call 1-800-CFULLER.
3. Write CEFI for information on current programs.

17
CHURCH GROWTH CONSULTATION IN THE DENOMINATIONAL CONTEXT

Delmar L. Anderson

The Covenant Church has historical roots in the Lutheran Reformation in Sweden and was flavored by strong influence from the Moravians and Pietists of Germany. It was officially organized in America in 1885. At the beginning of 1985, its centennial year, the Covenant Church had 84,381 members. It has broken out of its Swedish mold and has a current decadal growth rate of 18 percent.

I was appointed as a church growth consultant for the Evangelical Covenant Church in September 1981. My consultant role has its roots in a proposal adopted by the denomination's Board of Church Growth and Evangelism, entitled *Proposal for Accelerating Church Growth in Some Churches of the Evangelical Covenant Church*. The concept behind the proposal is to have paid church growth consultants work with a limited number of churches on a contract/fee basis to meet churches where they are, not simply to produce canned programs to be disseminated to all of them. My main preparation for the task took place at Fuller Seminary in the Doctor of Ministry program and at the Charles E. Fuller Institute in the "Diagnosis with Impact" program. I also received training at the Robert H. Schuller Institute for Successful Church Leadership and by attending a Churches Alive training event.

The basic consultation approach that was developed is called "Church Growth and Evangelism Opportunity Assessment for Local Churches." It is designed to provide pastors and church leaders with a clear evaluation and recommendations for action. The cost to churches is $500. I am also certified to conduct twenty-three different Charles E. Fuller Institute modules of training in single churches and, in some instances, on a district basis with several churches. Modular training often follows an Opportunity Assessment. It falls into seven categories: introduction, analysis, planning, spiritual gifts, activity, assimilation, and evangelism. Modules generally comprise four sessions, with the consultant introducing the module at the first session and training the pastor to conduct the remaining three sessions.

God has used the Opportunity Assessment and the modular training to bring new perspective and change to about twelve to fourteen churches per year. In September 1983, James E. Persson joined the department as its second consultant. His training parallels mine. We service all types of churches: inner-urban, country town, outer-urban, metropolitan suburb, midtown, independent city, and rural. Jim and I are growing in our ability to help local churches identify strengths, solve problems, and determine options for growth.

The Opportunity Assessment Process
The format of the diagnostic report which is sent to the church is illustrated by the following abbreviation of a thirty-two-page report to a 260-member suburban church.

I. Introduction

A. *Purpose of Report*
This report will focus especially on future staffing needs, with a focus on staffing for growth. The report will help church leaders fine-tune the church's ministries for continued harvest and spiritual growth.

B. *Components of the Study*
The first phase was gathering pertinent data. Forms and questionnaires were sent to the church. When they were returned, they were carefully studied and summarized. The second phase was a visit to the church. The final meeting of the field visit was the presentation of an oral report to the church council.

C. *Assumptions*
1. That the pastor wants the church to grow and is willing to pay the price.

2. That the congregation wants the church to grow and is willing to pay the price.
3. That the church places evangelism as a high priority in its programs and ministries.
4. That the church has a mission field of unchurched persons to win for Jesus Christ.
5. That the church is planning to provide staff and space for growth.
6. That a mutual ministry of pastor to people and people to pastor is taking place.
7. That if the church can only get a clear sense, a clear conception, a clear vision of the road ahead, it will be able to accomplish, achieve, and fulfill the vision.

D. *Purpose and Philosophy of Ministry*

The pastor has a holistic view of the purpose of the local church. He wants the church to bear witness in every way to the reality of Christ's kingdom and to present before the heavenly Father every believer mature in Christ. His approach is to practice the presence of God.

II. Background and Typology

A. *Historical Sketch*

The church was born in 1963 with 22 charter members. The main reason the church was started at this time and place was that there was no Covenant Church in this rapidly growing area.

B. *Present Picture*

The church site comprises approximately three and one-half acres. There are 150 off-street parking spaces. During the peak hours, the parking lot is 80 percent full. At the time of my visit, the congregation was nearing completion of a new sanctuary to seat 450.

C. *General Church Typology*

The church is located in a suburb with residential neighborhoods interspersed with shopping centers, entertainment centers, and light industrial zones. Sixty-three percent of the members live within five miles of the church.

D. *Socio-Economic Typology*
Economically, the membership families are in the following income categories: lower (29%), lower-middle (28%), middle (32%) and upper-middle (11%).

E. *Facilities*
The nursery is bursting at the seams. Special attention needs to be given to providing adequate Christian education spaces for future classes and activities.

III. Leadership Characteristics

The senior pastor, the minister of evangelism and discipleship, and the office secretary completed the following leadership evaluation instruments: Personal Profile System, Leadership Style Questionnaire, Modified Houts Spiritual Gifts Questionnaire, and Staff Worksheet. A Volunteer Worker Analysis was also done.

IV. Congregational Assessment

A. *Growth History*
The decadal growth rate of active membership is 105 percent. For Sunday morning worship attendance it is 124 percent.

B. *Congregational Characteristics*
1. Sixty-eight percent have attended the church less than six years.
2. Most were attracted to the church by a friend or because they lived nearby.

C. *Evangelism Strategy*
While the evangelism and church growth strategy is multifaceted, the heart of it centers on worship.

D. *Finances*
The five year average annual percentage increase in giving is 18 percent.

V. Community Overview

Based on a survey of average Sunday morning attendance

in area churches, there are 37,224 people with some church connection. There are an additional 69,776 who could be classified as unchurched.

VI. Interpretation of Data

A. *Congregation's View*
The congregation sees itself as Christ-centered with a clear message of salvation. People orientation takes precedence over programs and there are lots of opportunities for fellowship.

B. *Consultant's View*
This church knows why it exists. There is a strong family emphasis that can be strengthened. Hurting persons find healing and help. People from a variety of backgrounds are growing together in Christ.

VII. Recommendations

A. *Staff for Growth, Not Maintenance*
Criteria for paid staff: depends on the church's philosophy of ministry. All staff should agree on philosophy of ministry. *The paid staff the church needs now and in the future* (other than the senior pastor):
1. Minister of evangelism and discipleship
2. Part-time youth pastor (youth and family ministry)
3. Director of Christian education
4. Director of music
5. Associate/assistant pastor
6. Business/manager/church administrator/executive minister

(In the actual report, these staff positions were placed on a time line and described in detail.)

B. *Training*
The church must not wait for additional staff before giving special attention to training needs. The church should sponsor special training events and underwrite expenses so teachers and leaders can attend district and national training events.

C. Evangelism

The church should intentionally anchor its evangelism outreach to growth groups with periodic outreach events. The "Body Evangelism" module of training offered by the Department of Church Growth and Evangelism would also be helpful in raising the witness level of the entire congregation.

D. Advertising

What God is doing in your church is too good to keep to yourself. This report includes resources to give you guidance in developing creative and effective advertising.

E. Communication

Hold a leadership retreat off the church campus and deal with communication: 1) with God, 2) with one another in the body of Christ, and 3) with the world. In the following Sunday morning worship service leaders should share what they have experienced, and the entire congregation should be invited to sign up for small communication groups, with weekly meetings for three to five weeks.

F. Church governance

A special committee or task force should be designated to study church governance. This report contains *A Resource to Strengthen Council Governance.*

Follow-up

A follow-up visit is made to the church after it has had a couple of weeks to read over the report. Four copies of the report are provided. While meeting with church leadership and congregation, the consultant explains the rationale for recommendations and seeks to help the church to begin to implement one or more of them.

Results

One church with growth potential printed copies of the Opportunity Assessment report for every member and held a congregational meeting to discuss it. Following that meeting, the consultant visited the church, and a large percentage of the membership attended the meeting. Since the consultant's assessment visit, a young couple had come to faith in Jesus Christ. A decision was made to contract for the "Body Evangelism" module of training. The church also proceeded with plans and funds for a much needed addition to their building.

In some churches, recommendations for additional staff have strengthened the church's outreach. In several churches, the "Purpose and Needs Oriented Planning" module has brought a new sense of direction and clear understanding of role and purpose. Spiritual gifts discovery clinics and modules have brought excitement to God's people as they match gifts and tasks. The consultation visits sometimes help a church confirm that it is on the right track or help it make growth-oriented decisions. Some consultants deal with sick churches, but more and more healthy churches have Opportunity Assessments with a view to maintaining growth momentum through proper strategies and programs. Sometimes blockage factors, long suppressed or unrecognized, are surfaced and handled so that the church can move on. Churches and pastors are realizing the value of a denominationally oriented outside consultant.

18
USING COMPUTERS TO SUPPORT TOTAL CHURCH GROWTH

Melvin F. Schell, Jr.

> Church Growth means all that is involved in bringing
> men and women who do not have a personal relation-
> ship to Jesus Christ into fellowship with Him and into
> responsible church membership.[1]

Early in the Church Growth Movement, it was necessary to almost
exclusively emphasize the evangelistic elements of the Great
Commission.

Nevertheless, the Great Commission has always been understood to be an organic system that reproduces and grows based
on total church involvement. This is what C. Peter Wagner implied by the phrase "all that is involved."

To focus attention on the importance of this idea, I have developed the technical concept of "Total Church Growth." In this
chapter, I discuss the ways computers can be used with Total
Church Growth to bring significant improvements to the
church—improvements that may even rival those made by the
printing press!

In order for this to happen, however, "Twelve Requirements"
must be fulfilled:

1. The formation, training, and guidance of Spirit-led ministers and lay persons who are committed to acquiring and
   using a factual base of information to lead their churches in
   growth.
2. A standardized, systematic way to classify all data about the
   church.

3. A standardized, systematic way to identify cause and effect relationships between the variables within the local church—especially those that relate to health and growth.
4. The collection and analysis of appropriate data from within a local church.
5. The collection and analysis of appropriate data from large numbers of local churches.
6. The communication of information among the members of a local church—especially information from the analyzed data.
7. The communication of information among a large network of local churches—especially information from the analyzed data.
8. The identification and classification of the types of churches in the network.
9. The identification and classification of the effectiveness of various methods being used by churches that are part of the network.
10. The feedback to the church leadership of specific recommendations for methods that have the best possibilities for meeting their priorities in their type of church.
11. The feedback to the church leadership on how effectively their plans are achieving their prioritized goals—with recommendations for corrections to improve goal achievement.
12. Continual research and publication of the results of this analyzed data with special attention given to the detection of trends, general needs, and workable programs.

The data that must be processed in order to meet these requirements is difficult to handle without computers. Of course, the computer does not directly affect every item, nor does it tell us how to implement the requirements. It just makes it much more practical!

This has always been important to the leaders of the Church Growth Movement. In fact, most of what I know about the principles behind the requirements were learned from such men as Donald McGavran, Peter Wagner, Ralph Winter, Win Arn, and Carl George.

Because of their influence, in 1976 I changed my organization—a branch of Evangelism Explosion—to Church Growth Ministries and began consulting with churches in the Atlanta area. And, due to my prior experience with IBM, I began using the computer for church analysis.

I soon found, however, that the lack of a good system for organizing our data made it difficult to use. I tried to write a manual to clarify the procedure, but was frustrated by the lack of system. Without it, I could not help a church assemble their own data and, on the basis of that data, develop an easy-to-follow plan that would help them grow.

Since we were committed to the concept that "plan ownership" is essential to "plan execution," we had to persist in developing a system that each church could use with minimum guidance. After weeks of intense prayer and effort, a new system of organizing the data emerged.

We called this new system "Total Church Growth" because it organized all of the data into four specific areas (see below). This, in turn, made it possible to write the *Church Growth Committee Guide*, a seven-volume set containing instructions on how to lead a church in developing a workable plan for Total Church Growth.[2] We field-tested this new material and found that it did indeed help the leaders of typical churches develop and sustain growth.[3]

But the manual methods we used to analyze the data and track the plan were inadequate. We saw these problems could only be overcome by the direct use of computers in the churches. As a result, Omega Information Systems, Inc., was formed in 1980 to supply this need.

It has since released Adam II software for larger churches, Adam Jr. for smaller churches, and dVELOP II for other types of ministry organizations. This has led to an international group of users who have added their feedback to our previous experience. This, in turn, has led to the development of the "Twelve Requirements for Total Church Growth."

It is this constant input from church leaders that has brought about the practical success of Total Church Growth. As a result, the Twelve Requirements start with the equipping of Spirit-led leaders—an essential ingredient if we are to help the majority of churches and not just those with extraordinary preachers.

In fact, the most successful businesses in the country have been shown to be those who ". . . are truly unusual in their ability to achieve extraordinary results through ordinary people." In their best-selling book *In Search of Excellence*, Thomas Peters and Robert Waterman devote two chapters to illustrating this point. In summary, they say:

> These companies give people control over their own destinies; they make meaning for people. They turn the average Joe and the average Jane into winners.[4]

People in the church must also be in control of their own destinies if the church is to have real meaning in their lives. There must be a ". . . plethora of structural devices, systems, styles, and values, all reinforcing one another" if this is to take place.[5]

But how, you might reason, is this all going to happen if we are working with ordinary people in ordinary churches? In most cases, it will take an outside consultant or ministry organization to stimulate and guide these efforts.[6]

Even with this support, however, the success of any program will require the leadership of a committed minister. On the other hand, the approach we use does not require that the minister or the laypeople be able to make things happen by sheer force of personality. Instead, it gives them the tools to develop simple, workable solutions for the complex needs of today's church.

This avoids the danger of ignoring the complexity—as so many do—by insisting that it is enough to be sincere, trust the Holy Spirit, and let God take care of everything. Sincerity is not enough. The Bible says, "The Lord is a God of knowledge, and with Him actions are weighed" (1 Sam. 2:3, NASB). Growth helps provide that knowledge by grouping all data into one of four major areas.

Area I: External Growth and Development
This area focuses outside of the church on those who are not part of the active church. They can be separated into two sub-categories.

A. Transfer growth prospects are committed Christians not active in a local church.

B. Conversion growth prospects are unconverted persons who need to receive Christ and become active in church.

Area II: Internal Growth and Development

This area focuses on the people who are part of the organized church. They also can be separated into two subcategories.

A. Discipleship growth prospects are committed Christians who need to grow in a holistic way.

B. Renewal growth prospects are insiders who are not committed, confident Christians. They need to receive Christ and become active disciples (children in this category are prospects for biological growth).

Area III: Organizational Growth and Development

This area, also called the operational center, focuses on the administration and coordination of external and internal ministries. It also has two subcategories.

A. Hardware and firmware (structures and strategies) are the more permanent elements of the church. Structure refers both to buildings and group organization within the church (which are quite dependent on buildings). There are six types of groups.[7]

   1. Membership groups   4. Cell groups
   2. Worship groups   5. Discipleship groups
   3. Fellowship groups   6. Stewardship groups

   Buildings, lands, and other more permanent parts of the church are called hardware. Creeds, organizations, policies, and official programs also tend to be quite permanent and are therefore referred to as firmware.

B. Software is the more informal and generally less permanent elements of staff, systems, style, skills, and shared values of the church.

   (Note: The terms hardware, firmware, and software are borrowed from the computer science field. In the discussion above, however, they do not refer directly to computers.)

Area IV: Foundational Factors

These are the unseen forces which exert a powerful influence on the entire church. There are two subcategories in this area:

THE TOTAL CHURCH MODEL

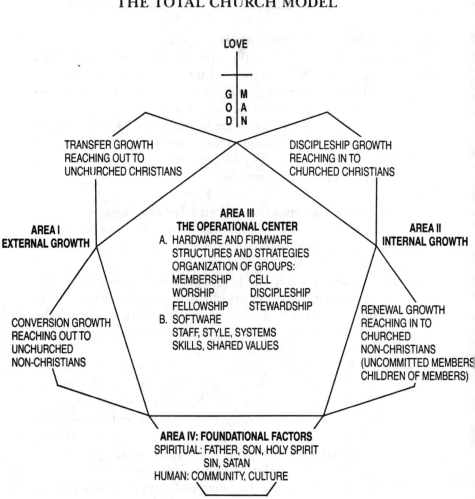

A. Spiritual factors include the direct influence of Father, Son, and Holy Spirit. They also include God's indirect influence through our understanding of him as he is revealed through his creation, his Spirit, his church, and his written Word. And, we must also consider the direct influence of sin as it operates both in the people of the church and in satanic and other demonic forces.

B. Human factors include the community and culture of the people involved in the church. Community refers to the sociological influences of the geographical neighborhood in which the church ministers. Culture refers to the more remote forces that influence the people, especially the religious affiliations.

The Total Church Model provides a fairly accurate way of relating the four major areas within the church.

Using the Total Church Model as a guide, it is possible to develop a profile analysis of the entire church. To do this, it is necessary to combine data from interviews, observations, questionnaires, and direct measurement of participation. This provides a starting point against which change can be measured, and this is essential if we are to determine what really happens as a result of our plans.

To illustrate, let us do a hypothetical analysis of a personal evangelism program. We assume the program used a highly-structured method in which one skilled person leads two others through a rigorous on-the-job technique of learning evangelism. Here is a sampling of what our computer-aided profile analysis might reveal if it had been processed regularly.

The analysis reveals that the annual growth rate went up in the first year, but declined sharply thereafter. The key reason was an almost immediate decline in the rate of transfer growth (item 9) and an eventual decline in the rate of conversion growth (item 10). Transfer growth probably suffered from an overemphasis on "decisions" by the evangelist.

The lack of an assimilation group for new converts probably led to their dropping out, as well as to the declining number of members who felt they belonged to a small group (items 4 and 5). The dwindling number involved in the evangelism program was likely due to "evangelist burnout," while the visibility of the program probably reduced the overall number of members who witnessed and won others to Christ outside of the program (items 1, 2, and 8).

On the other hand, the members incorrectly perceived they were doing more evangelism (item 5), and the number of members who experienced either personal growth or a renewal growth conversion experience through the evangelism training probably

HYPOTHETICAL PROFILE ANALYSIS OF A CHURCH EVANGELISM PROGRAM	Before	1 Year	2 Years	3 Years
1. Members who witness regularly	45%	46%	43%	41%
2. Won at least one person to Christ per year, outside of family members . . .	25%	27%%	25%	22%
3. Opinion of members about how well church does evangelism	25%	35%	36%	37%
4. Members who feel like they really belong to a group within the church	65%	62%	58%	55%
5. Groups with sharp external assimilation focus	0%	0%	0%	0%
6. Members who feel they are growing spiritually	64%	66%	70%	66%
7. Members who made deep commitment to Christ *after* joining church	5%	9%	10%	7%
8. Members participating in personal evangelism program	0%	4%	12%	8%
9. Members who transferred into church	7%	5%	3%	1%
10. Members who came into church . . . by conversion process	5%	8%	7%	5%
11. Membership annual growth rate . . .	12%	13%	10%	6%

led to the increases shown in items 6 and 7 (which were the major long-term benefits from the program).

If this had been a real church using a computer to apply the principles of Total Church Growth, they might have corrected the problems that caused a good program to do so much harm. And, it's not just evangelism programs that run into these types of problems. Most of the really important church ministries are being frustrated by a lack of knowledge.

We can know the truth, and the truth can set us free from the gloom of unsuccessful programs and defeated leaders. It is thrilling to see the change in churches which are applying these principles and experiencing the sweet smell of successful programs and triumphant leaders.

Some may criticize these ideas because they sound like a worldly intrusion into the mystery of God. The fact is, the Bible is filled with examples of God's diagnosis and planning. Perhaps the best example is in Revelation 2 and 3, where the Holy Spirit did a "total church profile" for the seven representative churches of Asia Minor.

And, most importantly for us, he closed each diagnostic session with this command: ". . . he who has an ear, let him hear what the Spirit says to the churches." I believe this command is just as important as the Great Commission or the Great Commandment, for even they were first heard by those who had ears to hear what the Spirit spoke to the churches!

God still speaks to us through his voice in the local churches that make up his body, and we must get his instruction and guidance through that voice. But how is that possible when we have millions of churches sown among billions of people? God never gives a command without also giving the power to fulfill that command, and I believe that the breakthroughs in computers and communications are a major part of the resources God has given to us to hear his voice.

Coupling these technologies with the Total Church System can give us a more accurate way to hear what the Spirit is saying and doing among the churches. That objective knowledge, carefully gathered, analyzed, and communicated, could have tremendous impact on the church. It could even shift the decision-making powers from a rather small number of influence brokers to the grass roots of the church.

If the "megatrends" of secular society can be accurately predicted from computer analysis of newspapers, can the megatrends of God be detected by local church analysis?[8] What would it mean if the movements of the Holy Spirit could be detected in time for church leaders to get in step with him before the opportunity passes?[9]

Furthermore, programs and methods can be analyzed on a widespread basis and more precisely matched with the needs of local churches. This can lead to significant improvements in ministry as the church moves from wasteful trial and error techniques to empirical analysis.

Of course, for all of this to happen, a very large number of churches would have to be committed to the Twelve Requirements. In order to promote that, more immediate incentives would have to be offered to members of a network, such as financial planning help, sermon preparation help, and numerous other generally needed aids to ministry. Once churches have tied into such a Christian source, they would be more likely to make a full commitment to Total Church Growth, and that alone makes the effort worthwhile.

Therefore, whether in the local church or in the worldwide church, the possibilities of the Twelve Requirements are great! The development of systems like Total Church Growth, coupled with low cost computers and communications equipment, now make these benefits available to almost every church.

---

1. C. Peter Wagner, *Your Church Can Grow* (Glendale, California: Regal Books, 1976), 12.
2. This guide is available from the Charles E. Fuller Institute of Evangelism and Church Growth, Box 91990, Pasadena, CA 91109-1990.
3. Rev. Ron Zenefski, unpublished thesis, Claremont Graduate School of Theology.
4. Thomas J. Peters and Robert H. Waterman, Jr., *In Search of Excellence* (New York: Warner Books, 1982), 239.
5. Ibid.
6. The Charles E. Fuller Institute of Evangelism and Church Growth, conducts regular training programs for consultants, called "Diagnosis with Impact," in conjunction with Fuller Theological Seminary.
7. Here is a more complete description of the six types of groups:
   (1) Membership groups—Formal commitment to be members of local church. May be divided into active, inactive, resident, nonresident, etc. No size limits.
   (2) Worship groups—Celebrate or worship God. No size limits.
   (3) Fellowship groups—Subcongregational groups that provide a feeling of fellowship for participants. May be same as Worship group in smaller churches. May also be Sunday school classes, choirs, men's groups, church suppers, etc. Ideal size from 30–100.
   (4) Cell groups—Provide a small, family-like relationship for participants. May be Sunday school classes, choirs, or other groups meeting at the church; usually work best when meeting in homes for activities such as prayer and Bible study. Ideal size from 4-12.
   (5) Discipleship groups—Apprenticeship groups that meet the need for skills development in evangelism, music, teaching, Christian living, etc. Ideal size from 2-3.
   (6) Stewardship groups—Operational center groups that administer the church include staff, boards, ministry committees. Can have dynamics like groups 3, 4, 5.
8. John Naisbitt, *Megatrends* (New York: Warner Books, 1984).
9. For an example of the kinds of trends that could be detected, see Melvin F. Schell, "Ripe Fields Can't Wait," *Global Church Growth Bulletin* (Jan.–Feb. 1984).

Part 6

CHURCH GROWTH
AND THE HOLY SPIRIT

All the church growth technology in the world is not sufficient for bringing the lost to Jesus Christ. Drawing a man or woman to himself in love is the work of the Holy Spirit. The Bible says that while Paul plants and Apollos waters, God and God alone gives the increase. Every church growth advocate recognizes this, and no book on church growth is complete without a section explaining the role of the Holy Spirit.

Eddie Gibbs, who recently moved from England to America to teach at Fuller Seminary, raises some necessary warnings to those who would see church growth as a mere application of principles. If the principles are to produce a church which glorifies God, the power of the Holy Spirit must be operative from the very beginning. Elmer Towns looks closely at the spiritual gift of faith and shows how God uses this gift particularly in pastoral leadership. He distinguishes between instrumental faith, insight faith, and interventional faith.

F. J. "Joe" May is the one contributor to this volume who is a classical Pentecostal. No one is better qualified to show how the supernatural anointing of the Holy Spirit plays an essential part in church growth. His chapter will inspire many to seek a deeper relationship with God. The final chapter by John Wimber surfaces one of the newer areas of church growth research and practice—supernatural signs and wonders. Wimber advocates power evangelism and practices it in his church, Vineyard Christian Fellowship of Anaheim, California, which has rapidly grown to over 5,000 members.

19
THE POWER BEHIND THE PRINCIPLES
Eddie Gibbs

Much church growth writing revolves around the *principles* of church growth. Some authors' major concern is to expound these principles from a biblical perspective, while others, with a more practical disposition, focus attention on their significance in specific church growth situations at home or overseas. The fruit of their labors is either the reaffirmation of the validity of the principle or its reformulation in the light of a theological critique or field investigation.

But church growth exponents do not confine themselves to the area of reflective analysis. They are even more concerned with the application of those principles to guide the formulation of new mission strategies. Sometimes their expertise is needed in situations of rapid growth to help leaders function more effectively to facilitate and not frustrate the God-given momentum. At other times their counsel is sought in drawing up plans and seeking appropriate personnel for a pioneering church planting project. In both instances their work is assisted by the operation of a spiritual dynamic to which the principles can be harnessed.

It is a different matter, however, when church growth thinking is applied in a context of church decline and spiritual stagnation. The danger then is that church growth becomes regarded as a rescue program to shore up a crumbling organization and thereby give it a further lease of life. Church growth thus becomes a ploy to avoid facing the deeper need of church renewal. Any church growth consultant or pastor thinking along these lines will sooner or later have to face the inadequacy of applying methodological solutions to cure spiritual ailments. He or she will have been treating symptoms while ignoring the causes. Authentic church growth requires power as well as principle. The principles do not of themselves cause church growth; they simply explain it.

My purpose in this chapter is to draw attention to the fact that the presence and activity of the Holy Spirit is integral to church growth at every phase. The principles are no substitute for the power, and experience of the power does not make the principles superfluous. Let us, therefore, trace the operations of the Spirit in the six essential phases of the church growth cycle.

Phase One: Mobilizing the Witnesses

It is widely recognized that sustained church growth requires a well-mobilized laity prepared to witness to their faith. In order to achieve this goal many churches organize training courses to prepare workers and implement visitation programs to provide them with witnessing opportunities. Such activities, as highly commendable as they are, will only be effective if the Holy Spirit is present to provide the witness with the necessary motivation, the appropriate words, and a sense of timing. A witnessing church is not just one that is talkative. Our Lord orders his followers to remain still and keep quiet until the Holy Spirit has come upon them (Luke 24:49; Acts 1:4, 5). Witness that is authentic and effective results from the overflow of the Spirit through the individual believer and the local church. It results from our "being" before it can be promoted by our "doing" (see Acts 1:8). The Holy Spirit must first witness to our spirits before he can minister through us to the world.

Witness has four aspects. We bear witness to what Christ has done *for* us by his crucifixion and resurrection; to the work of God *in* us bringing about conviction of sin, conversion, regeneration, and adoption as children of God; to the work of God *through* us as he ministers to challenge and restore misdirected or broken lives; and to the work of God *around* us as we report on what we have seen God do through the ministry of others.

When we have something worth sharing then the Holy Spirit can lead us to needy individuals, as he did Philip to the Ethiopian official (see Acts 8:29), and to entire communities and countries, as he did Paul and his companions on their missionary journeys (see Acts 16:6ff.).

Without this essential work of the Spirit, our witnessing will lack both credibility and endurance. On the other hand, when the church is witnessing in the Spirit's power, even the gates of hell will be forced to give way.

Phase Two: Equipping the People of God for Ministry

A growing church is one that is enabling its entire membership to discover and deploy their gifts for ministry. By "ministry" we mean the concerned activity of Christ expressed through individuals in his body to meet human needs both within the Christian community and in the world at large. Without due regard to the role of the Holy Spirit, the church is in danger of regarding ministry as little more than the harnessing of natural talents. The net result may be an impressive display of human creativity and energy, but it only focuses attention on humans and not on God.

While acknowledging the role of the Holy Spirit in our conception and development, for he is at work in the total creative process and not just in the gaps, we must emphasize the need for natural talents to be converted into spiritual gifts. In consecrating our lives to God, we hand back to him all the gifts that we have marred and misused in our sinful state for him to refurbish, re-energize, and redirect. In so doing we find that our subsequent use of those gifts points beyond ourselves to the source as we begin to give of Christ along with ourselves.

We recognize that there is both continuity and discontinuity between our pre- and post-conversion nature. Not only are old talents transformed into spiritual gifts, but new gifts are bestowed that we may achieve all that God desires to accomplish through us. The wide range of gifts we find scattered throughout the New Testament makes us aware of the many facets of Christ's ministry. No individual follower could encompass the totality of that ministry, but each is called and equipped to share a part. The church provides our training ground, support base, and immediate sphere of service, but the world represents an equally vital area of involvement. Our ministry is a continuation of that of Christ, who went into the world to seek and to save the lost.

Phase Three: Creating a Climate of Receptivity

It is an axiom of church growth thinking that highest priority must be given to presenting the gospel to the receptive rather than wasting effort in futile attempts to convince the resistant. To help the evangelist and church planter identify receptive soil there are a number of indicators, most of which point to people in transition or trauma. But unless due regard is given to the work of the Spirit, this church growth principle is liable to be unscrupulously exploited rather than conscientiously applied.

People who find themselves disoriented by unfamiliar surroundings or distressed by a life crisis can be taken advantage of. Christian ministry serves to enrich people—never to manipulate them. We therefore require the wisdom and gentleness of the Spirit to approach people who have acute needs with integrity and sensitivity. Otherwise, we are in danger of becoming peddlers rather than proclaimers of God's Word—that is, people out to make a quick sale rather than to bring about a profound change (see 1 Thess. 2:3-5). The concept of receptivity does not represent an attempt to provide a more palatable, ecclesiastical version of a commercial salesman's marketing strategy. By slick sales talk people may be pressured into buying a convenience-packaged religion, but which on opening is revealed to contain something very different from the gospel of the New Testament.

Factors contributing to receptivity are not exclusively circumstantial. But factors such as war, liberation, sickness, bereavement, unemployment, and other traumatic events have been observed to contribute to increased receptivity to the gospel among nations, communities, and individuals. However, they may or may not represent the superintendency of the Spirit to prepare people to hear the gospel. People either in advantageous or adverse circumstances may be distracted rather than made aware; they may be hardened rather than softened. Life changes serve to unsettle, but the direction of the subsequent movement is uncertain. What is clear is that there needs to be a caring, articulate Christian presence at such times to be available to the Spirit in presenting the riches and claims of Christ.

Are we to become so preoccupied with the responsive that we neglect the resistant? Such might occur if we neglect to follow the leading of the Spirit or to be aware of his role in preparing the resistant to respond. How does he bring about such a dramatic change? Sometimes, as we have noted, he brings a dramatic change in circumstances. At other times the Spirit uses Christians within the resistant group to demonstrate an attractive alternative life-style and show self-giving concern toward those from whom they expect little in return. In addition, the Holy Spirit, who is the Spirit of Christ, burdens our hearts, as he did that of the Apostle Paul for his people, with a deep longing that the hearts of the unresponsive might be softened (see Rom. 9:30–11:12). Such a burden is expressed in agonized intercession for the people as a whole and support for any isolated believers among them.

Phase Four: Effecting Regeneration

Church growth entails much more than recruiting individuals and peoples to support a cause and enlist like-minded people. Underlying any observable ethical, sociological, and vocational change, there is an indispensable spiritual dynamic at work. No individual can qualify for true church membership without a supernatural work of God taking place deep within his or her personality. This is the role of the Holy Spirit: to reveal to us that God intended us to be made in his image, to make us uncomfortably aware of how far off course we have wandered in our sinful state, to startle us into the realization that Christ died for us personally to remove our guilt, to unshackle us from bondage to sin, and to give us a new nature powerful enough to overcome the old. The Holy Spirit thereby shows us the relevance of the gospel and takes up residence within us that we might live by the power of that message. This brings about a change so radical that it can only be described in terms of regeneration, new birth, or new creation.

By giving due recognition to this irreproducible and unpredictable work of the Spirit of God, we will be safeguarded from cheapening church growth by reliance on human gimmicks and manipulation to enlist members, and by going for the soft option of achieving "growth" by persuading the Christian clientele around us to change their church allegiance by offering more spectacular attractions. Our "need for success" stress is lifted as we recognize that our human endeavors, as important as they are, are only a small part of the total operation, and that all that we do must be under the superintendency of the Holy Spirit.

Phase Five: Incorporating into the Body of Christ
One of the most generally recognized contributions of the Church Growth Movement has been its stress on continuing discipleship following the initial decision to follow Christ and on the corporate nature of this life commitment. Again, this is only achieved through the working of the Spirit. We need look no further than the sad history of fragmentation and factionalism of so much of the Protestant movement to recognize our need for constant reliance on the Spirit to hold us together while at the same time expressing our diversity. Once we neglect the Spirit's work we are driven either to a monotonous, monopolistic uniformity or a confining, competitive multiplicity. But when the Spirit is present to orchestrate and conduct, a beautiful symphony can be produced.

In a rapidly urbanizing world—where the city itself symbolizes both the search for identity and the need to express individuality—the church must exist in a prophetic role. Only by the supernatural operation of the Spirit will the church be able to anticipate the heavenly city. To do this with any measure of credibility, the community of believers in a city must think beyond their own fellowships, work together to achieve visibility, and formulate a strategy in which each fellowship plays a vital and distinctive part. The church's retreat from the city into suburbia must be halted. There are signs that the Spirit is directing us to repossess the central zones—both the centers of commercial, political, and media power, and the ghettos made derelict by neglect and exploitation. In such tough places only a ministry empowered by the Spirit is likely to survive and achieve significant gains.

Phase Six: Involving the Church in the Ministry of Christ
This sixth phase completes the church growth cycle. The church is not only a messenger of the reign of Christ—the community

194

of the King—it is also a model. The new believer is as influenced by the example portrayed as by the message proclaimed. The church is in the process of becoming, and in its proclamation not only offers itself but points beyond itself. It is a community created and sustained by the Word and power of God. A church composed of forgiven sinners recruited from one generation to the next is in constant need of renewal. Once again we are led to appreciate the strategic ministry of the Spirit to ensure that new believers entering its fellowship do not find an aging, tired, and tarnished community of believers. The Spirit comes to bring renewed energy, to present fresh challenges so that new converts are not corralled within the church's existing fellowship circle but commissioned for service in the world. As Canon Michael Green reminds us in *I Believe in the Holy Spirit* (Eerdmans, 1975), "The Comforter comes not in order to allow men to be comfortable, but to make them missionaries."

As the Christian community fans out into the world to proclaim the gospel of the kingdom, it must exercise its ministry both in the name and power of Christ to be effective. Only when communication combines both verbal proclamation and powerful demonstration will lives be radically and permanently changed. The Spirit is present to confirm the spoken word with appropriate signs and wonders so that the power of darkness over peoples' minds and bodies might be broken. Such supernatural manifestations are not granted to titillate the curious but to shake the cynical from their spiritual stupor and liberate those in bondage to evil spirits, demonstrating that the power of the living Lord is greater than the most powerful malevolent or capricious spirit. Such "signs following" are presently in the form of physical healing or deliverance from demonic oppression.

Such clashes between the power of God and the power of darkness are referred to as "power encounters." These have tended to occur more often on the frontiers of missionary activity and are associated with "heathen lands afar." But now that much of the Western world has entered a post-Christian phase there is an upsurge of interest in these areas and an increase in recorded occurrences. It must again be emphasized, however, that this is not the Lord putting on a show to draw an audience, but his staging of a showdown to defeat the enemy. Such a spiritual victory may result in the liberation of a territory and a people, producing an immediate, community-wide response to the gospel. Church growth is as much concerned with the spiritual dynamic brought about by the sovereign Lord as it is with the application of principles.

Divested of the power of the Spirit our church growth principles are in danger of becoming cliches. When God's Spirit is in operation, those principles are powerfully and impressively evident.

20
THE GIFT OF FAITH IN CHURCH GROWTH

Elmer L. Towns

A study of the largest churches in America has led to the conviction that the faith of the pastor was one of the main contributing reasons for the church's growth.[1] Jerry Falwell, pastor of the Thomas Road Baptist Church, Lynchburg, Virginia, has identified faith as a source of the church's growth.[2] Peter Wagner states that the spiritual gift of faith was a common denominator found in the pastors of the largest churches. He goes on to explain that the pastors he has observed in large churches have had different gifts. Some pastors were extraordinary preachers, while others were average speakers. He saw differences in the gifts of administration, counseling, and teaching, but he felt all the pastors of large churches had the spiritual gift of faith. Wagner concluded, "The superchurch pastors I know all have this gift (the gift of faith)."[3]

Whole books and dissertations discuss the spiritual gifts in general and tongues, miracles, and healings in specific. A study of the spiritual gift of faith has been neglected too long.[4]

The gift of faith is a spiritual gift that is bestowed upon certain believers to edify the body of Christ and is employed to get extraordinary results. The spiritual gift of faith is more than saving faith, but obviously all who exercise the gift have experienced conversion. Kenneth Kinghorn observes that "while all Christians possess the grace of faith, not all Christians possess the gift of faith."[5] Kurt Koch makes a distinction between the gift of faith and justifying faith: "When faith is mentioned in the list of gifts of the Spirit, this does not mean the justifying faith that everyone must have who believes for eternal life. The faith that comes as a gift of the Spirit is the daring and conquering faith that 'removes mountains.' "[6] Howard Carter believes that "the gift of faith is a wonderful gift that has not been fully understood, we fear, because it is generally confused with ordinary faith, or saving faith."[7] B. E. Underwood notes that the spiritual gift of faith "is not the ordinary faith of the believer."[8] Donald Gee concludes, "The spiritual gift of faith must be distinguished from ordinary faith."[9] Leslie Flynn observes that "the gift of faith, listed by Paul in 1 Corinthians 12:9, is more than saving faith."[10] I conclude, therefore, that the spiritual gift of faith is not synonymous with saving faith (even though it is generally confused with saving faith) but that it is more than saving faith.

The spiritual gift of faith has been generally described as "faith of miracles"[11] by Gee who quotes older theologians; "special faith"[12] in the *Living Bible's* paraphrase of 1 Corinthians 12:9; "wonder working faith"[13] by Underwood; "daring faith"[14] by Koch; and "the gift of prayer"[15] by John MacArthur. All of these titles indicate that the gift of faith is special. As Friesen describes it, "The gift of faith is rather a special God-given ability. . . ."[16]

But even when those who write about the gift of faith recognize that it is special, they do not generally agree on a definition. Perhaps their disagreement arises because (1) little is said of the gift of faith in Scripture, (2) the church has largely ignored the gift of faith and its practice, and (3) Christian writers have not researched the topic thoroughly.

Three Views of the Gift of Faith

There seem to be three different approaches to understanding and interpreting the gift of faith. First, some interpret the gift of faith as an *instrument* to be used in Christian service, as one would use the Bible, prayer, or preaching to accomplish the work of God. The instrumental view appears to be the traditional or historical Christian view. Second, the gift of faith is interpreted as *insight* or *vision*. The person with the gift of faith discerns what God wants accomplished in a situation, then uses every resource available to accomplish his vision. This seems to be the recent interpretation and is held by most evangelical Christians who are now writing on spiritual gifts. Third, the gift of faith is interpreted as the ability to move God by faith so that he divinely *intervenes* in a crisis that faces the Word of God or supernaturally intervenes in Christian service so that he accomplishes what the person with the gift believes will happen. This interventional interpretation is held mostly by Pentecostals, who believe that miracles are occurring in the work of God, and by non-Pentecostals, usually pastors identified with large churches[17] (plus other leaders with dynamically growing works). They may or may not believe the day of miracles has passed, but they believe they have experienced the intervention of God in their Christian service.

Perhaps the three interpretations of the gifts of faith are not three exclusive interpretations but three progressive steps in expressing the gift of faith. If this is true, the three views are different points on a continuum. Those who believe the first step have used faith as an instrument (see Eph. 6:16), but they do not necessarily deny the work of God in the next two steps. They just have not continued to a higher level of usefulness. The same can be said of those who hold the second interpretation of the gift of faith, for they have used faith as a vision to see what God can accomplish. The third position does not interpret the gift of faith differently, but it includes the first two aspects and then adds the interventional factor.

1. The gift of faith as an instrument. The gift of faith is interpreted to be the ability of the Christian to use the instruments of Christianity to carry out the work of God in person or in a church. In Ephesians, chapter 6, Paul describes other instruments that help the Christian fight the enemy: truth (v. 14); righteousness, the knowledge of imputed perfection (v. 14); the gospel (v. 15); the helmet of salvation (v. 17); and the sword, the Word of God (v. 17). He also defends himself with the shield of faith (v. 16), which is an instrument.

Howard Carter believes that "the gift of faith can be defined as faith imparted by the Spirit of God for protection in times of danger, or for divine provision, or it may include the ability to impart blessing."[18] This definition does not include insight or the intervention of God. The gift of faith includes the ministries that God has already promised, such as protection, provision, and blessing. Later Carter describes the gift of faith with more intentionality. "This remarkable gift brings into operation the powers of the world to come; it causes God to work for you."[19]

St. Thomas, the Roman Catholic, suggested a traditional view in his discussion of the gift of faith: "Faith believes in God . . . without involving itself in inquiry or judgment concerning matters of faith. It performs no operation other than that of believing."[20]

The instrumental view is more conformable to a historic Protestant view, that is, that the day of miracles has passed. They say that since miracles are viewed as a demonstration of authority to validate the message from God, there is no longer a need for miracles because the content of revelation is complete (see Jude 3). This view implies that God does not supernaturally intervene in the Christian work, but he works through the means of grace (the instruments, including faith) that he has already supplied. Therefore this view would regard the interventional gift of faith as having similar properties to a miracle, hence not applicable to this age of grace.

The instrumental view takes a passive view of the person with the gift of faith. As such, both the person and his gift are channels or vehicles used by God. God's power is within the Scriptures (see Heb. 4:12; James 1:17, 18; 2 Pet. 1:4) and the Holy Spirit (see Acts 1:8). Power (including the instrumental gift of faith) is not resident within the human, for he is an earthen vessel (see 2 Tim. 2:21), so that power is of God, not man. The Christian accomplishes the work of God through the Word of God by the Holy Spirit who indwells him. Only when the person has the gift of faith is he an instrument to accomplish what God has promised.

Perhaps those who hold the instrumental view see God controlling the destiny of this world (their extreme predestination has led to fatalism); therefore, they reject the interventional view because they believe man cannot change the order of events by his faith. To them faith is only instrumental, so it accomplishes only what God has predetermined. As such, they have not been aggressive (interventional) in changing the natural course of

Christian service, but they surrender their initiative in the Word of God.

Others may view the gift of faith as passive because they relate the gift of faith to other ministries. They feel spiritual gifts are given to persons such as preachers, teachers, evangelists, and others (see Eph. 4:11), and God works through persons who are identified by their gift (i.e., prophets have the gift of prophecy, teachers have the gift of teaching, etc.). But no ministry is identified with the gift of faith, such as a "faither." Therefore, they see God working in the world through secondary sources, such as his laws, the influence of his Word, the Holy Spirit, and the affairs of life. They do not see the gift of faith as an intervention by God in an active or direct role, but they see the gift of faith in an instrumental or indirect (secondary) role.

2. The gift of faith as insight. The view interprets the gift of faith as the Holy Spirit giving the Christian the ability to see what God desires to perform regarding a project. After Christians perceive what can be accomplished, they dedicate themselves to its accomplishment. Perhaps the best known definition is suggested by Peter Wagner: "The gift of faith is the special ability that God gives to some members of the Body of Christ to discern with extraordinary confidence the will and purposes of God for the future of His work."[21]

The strength of this definition is in the Christian's ability to see what God can do in a given situation; hence, it is implied that the Christian must see God's nature and purpose, and these are understood only through his Word. Kenneth Kinghorn supports this insight approach by stating, "The gift of faith is given to some Christians as a special ability to see the adequacy of God and to tap it for particular situations."[22] To this definition, Leslie Flynn adds that the gift of faith is a Spirit-given ability to see something that God wants done and to sustain unwavering confidence that God will do it regardless of seemingly insurmountable obstacles."[23]

The insight view recognizes that God is the source of all Christian work, but the person who exercises faith senses his responsibility to carry out the project through his vision of the work. This view places a high degree of responsibility and accountability on the person. God is active in giving vision, but we are passive in receiving the vision; then we allow God to work through us to accomplish the project. This view implies that the work of God is accomplished in relationship to the ability of the worker; including human knowledge, wisdom, motivational powers, leadership ability, and other factors. Of course, God gave these abilities to people, but God gave them through secondary means, such as training, reading, and role-modeling, and God works through people by secondary means.

The gift of faith may be the supernatural ability of a person to determine what God will do in a church in the next ten years or at any future date. As a result, those who have the gift of faith are growth-oriented, goal-oriented, optimistic, and confident.[24] Some people with natural faith may display these four aspects and build a chain-store empire or a multimillion dollar business. These characteristics can come from the power of positive thinking. The cause is the spiritual gift of faith or vision; the result is a confident attitude that usually produces results in the work of God. Because this gift has become such a strong conviction, some pastors who can communicate the vision to the congregation will work and sacrifice to accomplish the project.

Perhaps a problem with limiting the gift of faith to the insight view is that it makes it synonymous with vision, which might imply that faith is the passive ability to see what God wants done. But faith seems to be active and is used by God to change circumstances. Yet no one could honestly deny that vision is inherent in faith. In saving faith, a person must see his sin, see God, and see the remedy that God has provided in the gospel. In serving faith, a person must incorporate the role of the seer/prophet (see 1 Sam. 9:9), which is seeing the need first, seeing farthest into the future, and seeing the greatest thing that God could accomplish in any situation.[25] Perhaps the gift of faith not only incorporates vision, but it goes to the next aspect where the man of God intervenes in the circumstances of life.

3. The gift of faith as intervention. This view interprets the gift of faith as the ability to move God to divinely intervene in a crisis that is facing a project or to change the expected order of events so that the work of God goes forward. This view holds that the gift of faith is active, the person is responsible, but God is the source of the gift and the source of accomplishment. Traditionally called the gift of miracles,[26] it features divine intervention in a miraculous way.

The leader usually has divine certainty that God will intervene (perhaps because of insight); hence, the leader makes an expression of faith. Gee explains:

> The spiritual gift of faith is a special quality of faith, sometimes called by our older theologians the "faith of miracles." It would seem to come upon certain of God's servants in times of special crisis or opportunity in such mighty power that they are lifted right out of the realm of even natural or ordinary faith in God— and have a divine certainty put within their soul that triumphs over everything. It is a magnificent gift and is probably exercised frequently with far reaching results.[27]

B. E. Underwood's definition is not as long but implies the same elements: "This is extraordinary wonder-working faith for a particular occasion."[28]

Harold Horton clearly indicates that the initiation of moving the mountain begins with man exercising the gift of faith: "The Gift of Faith is a supernatural endowment by the Spirit whereby that which is offered or desired by man, or spoken by God, shall eventually come to pass."[29] The verse often quoted in connection with the interventional view is the one linking speaking and exercising faith. "Whosoever says to this mountain, 'Be removed and be cast into the sea,' and does not doubt in his heart, but believes that those things he says will come to pass, he will have whatever he says" (Mark 11:23, NKJV). Three times Jesus admonished his disciples to say exactly what they wanted to see happen in order to get the desired results. The gift of faith is an active faith that changes the circumstances of a person's ministry.[30]

Earlier the objection was raised that the interventional view made the gift of faith similar to the gift of miracles, tongues, and healings, which are called the power gifts—manifestations of supernatural phenomena in today's world. Horton answers the objection:

> The operation of miracles is more an act, as when the waters were opened by Moses and Elijah; while the operation of the gift of faith is more a process. . . . Faith, the gift, is equally miraculous with all the other gifts, but we might say that its power or manifestation is of greater duration than those of the gifts of healing or miracles.[31]

So interventional faith is an ability given by the Holy Spirit whereby a person overcomes problems (mountains) in a normal ministry, so that the work of God goes forward.

Interventional faith is based on and grows out of using faith as a vision and using faith as an instrument. Although the interventional view of faith is similar to the two previous positions, interventional faith is initiated by those who have the unique gift of faith. The three views of the spiritual gift of faith indicate there are differences in interpreting the biblical data. But in all three, the power comes from God, and the accomplishments come from God.

THREE VIEWS OF THE GIFT OF FAITH					
Name	Initiation	Vision	Power	Accomplishment	Available
1. Instrumental	God	God	God	by God	to all
2. Insight	God	person**	God	by God	to chosen
3. Interventional	person*	person**	God	by God	to chosen

*God is the source of all Christian work, but by exercising the gift of faith, the person of God senses a responsibility for church growth and uses faith to carry it out.

**God gives a vision through his Word for all Christian work, but in the exercise of the gift of faith, the person of God perceives a particular project in time and place.

1. Elmer Towns, *The Ten Largest Sunday Schools* (Grand Rapids: Baker, 1969); Elmer Towns, "The Seventy-five Largest Sunday Schools in America," *Christian Life* (August 1970), 15.
2. Elmer Towns and Jerry Falwell, *Stepping Out on Faith* (Wheaton: Tyndale, 1984); Elmer Towns and Jerry Falwell, *Capturing a Town for Christ* (Old Tappan, New Jersey: Fleming H. Revell, 1973).

3. C. Peter Wagner, *Your Spiritual Gifts Can Help Your Church Grow* (Glendale: Regal Books, 1979), 159.

4. A statistical study of the gift of faith was done using a sociological model of a growing church. See Elmer Towns, "The Gift of Faith in Church Growth" (D.Min. thesis, Fuller Theological Seminary, 1983). The pastors of Liberty Baptist Fellowship, Lynchburg, Va., were surveyed to determine their attitudes to five factors of church growth. They were asked to assess the strength of their faith on a scale of 1 to 10 in relationship to the five areas. The decadal growth rate (DGR) was then determined for all churches in the Liberty Baptist Fellowship. It was concluded that those pastors who had the fastest growing churches also assessed their faith stronger than the pastors with average growth. This measurement of faith did not prove that faith produced church growth, but it revealed a strong correlation between the two. The results of the thesis were printed by Towns and Falwell in *Stepping Out on Faith*.

5. Kenneth C. Kinghorn, *Gifts of the Spirit* (Nashville: Abingdon, 1965), 65.

6. Kurt E. Koch, *Charismatic Gifts* (Montreal: The Association for Christian Evangelicals, 1975), 90-91.

7. Howard Carter, *Spiritual Gifts and Their Operation* (Springfield: Gospel Publishing House, 1968), 37.

8. B. E. Underwood, *The Gifts of the Spirit* (Franklin Springs, Georgia: Advocate Press, 1967), 31.

9. Donald Gee, *Concerning Spiritual Gifts* (Springfield: Gospel Publishing House, 1972), 42.

10. Leslie B. Flynn, *Nineteen Gifts of the Spirit* (Wheaton: Victor Books, 1975), 140.

11. Gee, *Concerning Spiritual Gifts*, 43.

12. *The Living Bible* (Wheaton: Tyndale, 1971), 924.

13. Underwood, *The Gifts of the Spirit*, 30.

14. Koch, *Charismatic Gifts*, 91.

15. John MacArthur, Jr., *The Church, The Body of Christ* (Grand Rapids: Zondervan, 1973), 144.

16. Harold Friesen, "A Model for a Church in Ministry by Employing Spiritual Gifts Resulting in Spiritual and Numerical Growth" (D. Min. diss., Fuller Theological Seminary, 1979), 138.

17. Towns and Falwell, *Stepping Out on Faith*. This volume tells of ten pastors who experienced church growth because of the gift of faith.

18. Carter, *Spiritual Gifts and Their Operation*, 37.

19. Ibid., 42.

20. St. Thomas, *The Gifts of the Holy Spirit*, 243.

21. Wagner, *Your Spiritual Gifts Can Help Your Church Grow* (Glendale: Regal Books, 1979), 158.

22. Kinghorn, *Gifts of the Spirit*, 65.

23. Flynn, *Nineteen Gifts of the Spirit*, 141.

24. Towns, *The Ten Largest Sunday Schools*. The author made this observation in chapter 13 after interviewing the pastors who were the leaders of the largest Sunday schools in America.

25. Elmer Towns and Jerry Falwell, *Church Aflame* (Nashville: Impact Books, 1971), 44-45.

26. Gee, *Concerning Spiritual Gifts*, 43.

27. Ibid.

28. Underwood, *The Gifts of the Spirit*, 31.

29. Harold Horton, *The Gifts of the Spirit*, (Springfield: Gospel Pub., 1975), 31.

30. Elmer Towns, *Say-It-Faith* (Wheaton: Tyndale, 1983). This volume got its title from the command of Jesus that a person should say what problem (mountain) he wants God to remove (see Mark 11:23). It discusses six expressions of faith, of which the gift of faith is the ultimate expression.

31. Horton, *The Gifts of the Spirit*, 131.

21
SUPERNATURAL ANOINTING AND CHURCH GROWTH
F. J. May

A careful study of the growth of the early church, as recorded in the book of Acts, reveals one outstanding fact: The supernatural power of God was at work in miraculous proportions in the ministries of those early Christians. Armed and anointed by the Holy Spirit, they launched a militant assault on the kingdom of Satan. Darkness was dispelled, demons were defeated, diseases were healed, prisoners of sin were delivered, and the church was established. The record states: "And they went out and preached everywhere, while the Lord worked with them, and confirmed the word by the signs that followed" (Mark 16:20, NASB). "God also bearing witness with them, both by signs and wonders and by various miracles and by gifts of the Holy Spirit according to His own will" (Heb. 2:4).

There is no way these early believers could have succeeded with such glorious triumph without the supernatural anointing upon their lives. They had great power to preach, to witness, and to overcome the barriers that stood in their way. They were clothed with power from on high and relied completely on the Holy Spirit. Writing on this point, David Watson has emphasized the importance of our total reliance on the Holy Spirit. He quotes Dr. Carl Bates who says, "If God were to take the Holy Spirit out of our midst today, about 95 percent of what we are doing in our churches would go on and no one would know the difference." Then Watson continues: "The Spirit of God was the key to everything in the New Testament Church. If God had taken the Holy Spirit out of their midst in those days, about 95 percent of what they were doing would have ceased immediately. Everyone would have known the difference."[1] Their success in evangelism and church growth brings to us a strong message. Explosive church growth, New Testament style, can only be accomplished by Christians who are endued with power from on high and are carrying out the Great Commission of the Lord.

Supernatural Anointing and the Great Commission

As we review the last instructions of our Lord to his followers just before his ascension, we are impressed with the fact that the Great Commission was uppermost in his mind. This can be clearly demonstrated by three relevant points from Acts 1:1-8.

First, they were to be endued with power from on high (see Acts 1:4-5). Jesus considered it a matter of top priority for his disciples to receive the power of the Holy Spirit before they should undertake any further ministry. They were commanded to wait in Jerusalem until they had received the "promise of the Father" (compare Luke 24:49). Before they preached any sermon, before they attempted to be witnesses of Christ, before they made any efforts at winning the lost, they were to be "clothed with power from on high." Christ knew what it would take for his people to do his work, and he insisted that they be fully equipped for the challenge before them. Therefore, he said, "You shall be baptized with the Holy Spirit not many days from now" (Acts 1:5).

Next, they were not to get side-tracked on theological issues (see Acts 1:6-7). It would appear that the disciples were concerned with a problem of far greater interest to them than being empowered for service. They wanted Christ to reveal to them the prophetic calendar for the last days. They questioned: "Lord, is it at this time You are restoring the kingdom to Israel?" Jesus sternly rebuked them: "It is not for you to know times or epochs which the Father has fixed by His own authority." To Jesus, the eschatological role of Israel in the end times was not a matter of top priority at the moment. Receiving the power of the Holy Spirit was. He brought them back on track by saying ". . . but you shall receive power when the Holy Spirit has come upon you . . ." (Acts 1:8).

This does not mean that eschatology is not important. On the contrary, it is vital to evangelism and church growth, as Michael Green has so ably argued.[2] He shows us that eschatology gives us evangelistic motives such as "a sense of responsibility" and "a sense of concern." He states emphatically that "there can be no doubt that the expectation of the imminent return of Christ gave a most powerful impetus to evangelism in the earliest days of the church" (compare 1 Thess. 1:5-10). He adds later that ". . . not only in the first and second centuries, but in later periods of the church, missionary zeal has often flowered most notably in circles which held a strongly realistic hope and a likely expectation of the coming kingdom."

What Jesus did mean was, at that particular time, the disciples needed to put first things first. They should be mostly concerned with receiving the equipment for carrying out his command of evangelizing the world. The manifestation of the supernatural anointing upon their ministries would be the greatest sign of the coming of the kingdom. Later, they would preach powerful, effective sermons warning their hearers about the events of the last days.

Next, Jesus restated to them the far-reaching implications of the Great Commission. He said, "You shall be My witnesses both in Jerusalem, and in all Judea and Samaria, and even to the remotest part of the earth" (Acts 1:8). It was necessary for these disciples to understand fully the broad scope of their challenge (compare Matt. 28:19-20). They were to wait in Jerusalem for the outpouring of the Holy Spirit; then, they were to launch an all-out evangelistic thrust which would reach all the nations of the entire world. Thus, we can see the dynamic relationship between the supernatural anointing of God and the Great Commission.

Supernatural Anointing and Preaching

At this point in the development of the Church Growth Movement, not enough has been said about the relationship of preaching and church growth. We have heard much of the pastor who has strong leadership qualities equipping and mobilizing his people for ministry. But what is the best method for activating people? My opinion is that anointed preaching, backed up by supernatural manifestations of God's grace, is the best possible method of quickening the pace of God's work in the world. Church history shows us again and again that in times of great revivals and spiritual renewals, powerful preaching has been a vital part of the movement.

Anointed preaching has certainly been a central part of the Pentecostal movement since the turn of the century. Pentecostal preachers have been certain of their call. They have had unwavering faith in the Word of God and have relied totally on the power of the Holy Spirit to enable them to have effective delivery. As a result, Pentecostals have had the fastest growing churches in the world.[3]

Ray H. Hughes, president of the Church of God School of Theology in Cleveland, Tennessee, and a Pentecostal preacher of worldwide renown, has shown the relationship of Pentecostal preaching to the supernatural anointing of the Holy Spirit. In his book *Pentecostal Preaching,* he has developed this thesis: "The man of God who is called and anointed of the Holy Spirit, and who will faithfully yield to the leading of the Spirit, has the same commission and enablement as was given the disciples of old."[4] In the chapter, "The Uniqueness of Pentecostal Preaching," Hughes describes some of the special characteristics of Pentecostal preaching: It (1) convicts of sin and produces revival, (2) moves men and women to be baptized with the Holy Ghost, (3) produces faith, (4) confronts demonic powers, (5) produces godly fear and respect for the church, and (6) is confirmed by the operation of the spiritual gifts.[5]

Thus, a close look at fast growing Pentecostal churches today would reveal that behind the aggressive evangelistic activity there is divinely inspired and anointed preaching, based on a sound conservative theology, with a strong emphasis on the transforming power of the Word of God.

When we turn to the Scripture, we see the power of anointed preaching and teaching as manifested in the lives of Jesus and the apostles. Our Lord began his ministry by returning from his time of temptation "in the power of the Spirit" (Luke 4:14). His opening sermon in Nazareth was a declaration of the fulfillment of the beautiful servant passage of Isaiah 61. Jesus pronounced: "The Spirit of the Lord is upon Me, because He anointed Me to preach the gospel to the poor" (Luke 4:18). Then, he described what his anointed ministry would accomplish. He would "heal the brokenhearted"; he would "proclaim release to the captives, and recovery of sight to the blind"; he would "set free those who are downtrodden"; and "proclaim the favorable year of the Lord." His anointed preaching and teaching would be accompanied by the miracles of the supernatural power of God.

The same could be said of the preaching of the disciples of Jesus. We yet marvel at the astounding results of Peter's preaching at Pentecost and later—thousands believing and turning to the Lord at one time (see Acts 2:41; 4:4). As he preached at the house of Cornelius, the "Holy Spirit fell upon all those who were listening to the message" (Acts 10:44). What powerful preaching! In no way could there be a more glorious confirmation of the gospel than to have the Holy Spirit fall upon believers as they hear the Word.

The Apostle Paul's testimony to the power of anointed preaching is also noteworthy. When he went to the city of Corinth, he faced one of the greatest challenges in his entire career. It was like trying to start a church next door to hell itself.

Therefore, he determined to overcome his own weaknesses and fear by totally relying on the power of the Holy Spirit. He knew that he would never be successful against the power of darkness by using "superiority of speech or of wisdom." Instead, he depended entirely on the "demonstration of the Spirit and of power" (1 Cor. 2:1, 4). He wanted the faith of his converts to stand, not in the wisdom of men, but in the power of God. This bears repeating. Anointed preaching of the Word of God, confirmed by signs, wonders and miracles, is absolutely necessary in order to have church growth, New Testament style.

Supernatural Anointing and the Body of Christ

We now turn our attention from the individual preacher, who plays such a vital role in church growth, to the various members of the body of Christ who are absolutely indispensable to the work of Christ in the world. Our point is this: God has abundantly provided power and abilities for each Christian through divine grace. The best summary statement concerning these grace gifts is found in 1 Corinthians 12:4-6. Paul says: "Now there are varieties of gifts *[charismaton]*, but the same Spirit. And there are varieties of ministries *[diakonion]*, but the same Lord. And there are varieties of effects *[emergematon,* power], but the same God who works all things in all persons."

This summary statement shows the Holy Trinity in unity providing every gift, every ministry, every power necessary for doing the work that God wants done in the world. In other words, this summary reveals the broad scope of the total charismatic structure of the church that is to be manifested through the members of the body of Christ. Much has been written in great detail concerning all these various gifts, ministries and powers.[6] A discussion of all of these gifts is not appropriate here, but some general statements follow.

The charismatic structure of the church is beautifully described by Hans Kung in his book *The Church.* In one chapter he portrays "the Church as the Creation of the Spirit" and discusses the "Continuing Charismatic Structure" of the body of Christ. He talks about gifts of power, such as healings and miracles, and then places other "charisms" in categories of preaching, service, and leadership. One of his main points of emphasis is that these gifts are not just for a few Christians, but that "each Christian is a charismatic," and each has his own special gift from God (see 1 Cor. 7:7; 12:7).[7]

As already stated, our main point is that God has abundantly provided supernatural power for every kind of ministry needed in the church today. The big question is, How do we come to the place where these abilities can be manifested through us? The answer can be found in Scripture and from the testimony of those who have enjoyed success in miraculous church growth.

In 1 Peter 4:10, the Apostle Peter states: "As each one has received a special gift, employ it in serving one another, as good stewards of the manifold grace of God." The astounding truth in this verse is that God has made his children the stewards of his manifold grace. A steward is one who has been appointed to manage someone else's property. God's "property" is his power and grace. Therefore, it is God's plan for his children to manage, in a sense, his divine grace. He expects us to respond in faith and obedience to his generous gifts and use them to edify the church and evangelize the world. Through prayer, consecration and faith, we are to make ourselves available to be used of God.

Perhaps the most outstanding testimony of miraculous church growth in our time is the story of Paul Yonggi Cho and his church in Seoul, Korea. In his book *Prayer: Key to Revival*, Cho discusses the secret of learning to minister in the power of the Holy Spirit. He says that "prayer opens the door for the Holy Spirit." He illustrates this point by telling of a life-changing experience in prayer. He had been working hard to win the lost and had meager results. In prayer he sought God about this problem. He relates how God spoke to him with a question: "How many quail would Israel have caught if they had gone quail hunting in the wilderness?" Cho's answer was, "Lord, not too many." Then God said, "How did the quail get caught?" Cho realized that God sent a wind which brought the quail. Cho explains what God was teaching him: "The Lord was trying to show me the difference between chasing souls without the Holy Spirit's strategy and working in cooperation with the Holy Spirit." Then Cho says that the Lord said something to him that totally changed his life. He said, "You must get to know and work with the Holy Spirit!"[8]

Indeed, this is the key to revival and evangelism. Through prayer and faith we must come to understand what the Word of God says to us about gifts of the Spirit. Through consecration we must come to know and work with the Holy Spirit. As we do this, we can minister in the power and authority of the supernatural anointing of God. This is a vital key to church growth.

1. David Watson, *One in the Spirit* (UK: Hodder and Stoughton, 1973), 13.
2. Michael Green, *Evangelism in the Early Church* (Grand Rapids: Eerdmans, 1970), 265-269.
3. See Peter Wagner's evaluation of the growth of Latin American Pentecostal churches in *What Are We Missing?* formerly, *Look Out! The Pentecostals Are Coming* (Carol Stream, Illinois: Creation House, 1973).
4. Ray H. Hughes, *Pentecostal Preaching* (Cleveland, Tennessee: Pathway Press, 1981), 159.
5. Ibid., 147-159.
6. For detailed discussions of the various gifts see Peter Wagner, *Your Spiritual Gifts Can Help Your Church Grow* (Glendale: Regal Books, 1979), and Eddie Gibbs, *I Believe in Church Growth* (Grand Rapids: Eerdmans, 1981), 313-356.
7. Hans Kung, *The Church* (New York: Sheed and Ward, 1967), 150-203.
8. Paul Y. Cho, *Prayer: Key to Revival* (Waco: Word Books, 1984), 44.

22
SIGNS AND WONDERS
IN THE GROWTH
OF THE CHURCH

John Wimber

In examining the growth of the church worldwide, one thing is clearly evident. Not only is the church flourishing, it is often growing as a direct result of the effect of "signs and wonders."

These supernatural manifestations are occurring both in and out of the immediate supervision of the Western church and its agencies. Early indications are that the church seems to be growing most rapidly where the Western church has the least immediate influence.

In Latin America, for example, there were 50,000 Protestant Christians in 1900. Research conducted by C. Peter Wagner indicates that at the present rate of growth there will be 100 million Christians in that region by the year 2000. Professor A. M. Rasmusson, of Oral Roberts University, reports that the phenomenon of healing is a major emphasis of church growth in the countries of Latin America. In Guatemala, where 22 percent of the population is Christian, signs and wonders have been in great evidence, particularly during a recent drought in which God miraculously provided water for believers to share with the needy.

In Africa, where there were only four million converts in 1900, conservative predictions estimate that by the turn of the century there will be 351 million Christians on the continent. The fastest growing Lutheran church in the world is in Ethiopia, where 470,000 have joined that denomination since 1960. After extensive research, denominational leaders found that the church is increasing at such a rapid rate because 60 to 80 percent of the new believers became Christians as a result of first-hand experience with signs and wonders.

In 1900 there was no discernible number of Christians in Korea. By 1980 over 20 percent of the population were believers, with six new churches being planted every day. By 1990, 50 percent of the population may be Christian. The Yoido Full Gospel Church of Seoul, the world's largest church, has 500,000 members, and during its rapid growth phase was adding 5,000 to 10,000 members a month. Members meet regularly for prayer at a mountain near Seoul. Hundreds of sick and poor people are drawn to "prayer mountain," and members document at least one miracle a day. Often several signs and wonders are witnessed daily.

After Communism took over China in 1950, Christianity was thought to be all but stamped out. Now the most conservative estimate is that over fifty million Christians are active behind the bamboo curtain. Those involved in researching Christianity in China report that there are three main reasons for the growth of the church in that country. First, Confucianism and then Marxism left the people with a spiritual void which could only be fulfilled through Christ. Second, when the Communist forces overran the country, those who had already been converted maintained a strong, loving witness in the face of severe persecution. Third, there have been spontaneous outbreaks of signs and wonders in every province throughout China.

Power Encounter
One of the primary evidences of signs and wonders being manifested is *power encounter.* C. Peter Wagner defines power encounter as a visible, practical demonstration that Jesus Christ is more powerful than the false god(s) or spirit(s) worshiped or feared by members of a people group. When these divinely appointed encounters occur, the church grows—although not on every occasion. Sometimes there are other mitigating factors which keep the church from growing, such as lack of leadership to foster and nurture the respondents and the negative backlash of power entities in the community who are threatened by God's display of power.

Paul Yonggi Cho, the pastor of Yoido Full Gospel Church in Seoul, believes the Holy Spirit enables them to win lost people. He would further encourage us to believe that much of this evangelistic growth has occurred through power encounter. The issue of power encounter and the need for signs and wonders accompanying the proclamation of the gospel must be examined in the light of every culture. This is especially true where we see little church growth or receptivity to the gospel. Countries that are under the dominating influence of a false religion are relatively easy to identify and analyze. But what about a country with a significant Christian history where the church is not growing? What are the growth-inhibiting supernatural factors there? These issues and factors must be identified and examined.

The Problem of Minimal Growth in the Western Church
In the Western world, particularly in the United States, Canada, and Europe, the church is not growing in the dramatic way that it is elsewhere in the world. In Europe we see sporadic hints of revival, but for the most part, the church is weak and stagnant. The church in the United States and Canada is maintaining a solid population base, even growing minimally in the last decade, but in comparison with the church in the Third World, it is increasing very little. One explanation for this is that because of its rational, empirical worldview the Western church has omitted a main factor of keeping the church alive and vibrant before a watching world: supernatural signs and wonders.

The Problem of Worldview. The worldview to which one ascribes will determine the way in which one theologizes and participates in a signs and wonders ministry. Very few persons are conscious that they even hold to a worldview. They assume that the way they view life is the way in which everybody else sees life. Their assumption is that what they see is reality, while, in fact, their worldview determines what they see and interpret as "reality." A person's worldview is his or her "control box," as Charles Kraft says.

The Western worldview has a blind spot which keeps most Westerners from dealing with or understanding problems related to spirits, ancestors, or anything supernatural. Paul Hiebert calls this "the flaw of the excluded middle."

To become involved in a signs and wonders ministry calls for a paradigm shift in those people whose worldview prohibits God from continuing to act or to be the same in each dispensation.

Western Christians need to rediscover, develop, and practice a theology which includes this middle zone; a theology which includes God in human history, now, in the affairs of nations, peoples and individuals; a theology of divine guidance, provisions, signs and wonders, healings, invisible powers, suffering, misfortune, and even death.

We have, it seems, excluded God and his power from our theology and thus from our churches. Fearing that which we could not control or understand, we have thrown the baby out with the bathwater. We have said, "It simply does not exist." When confronted with manifestations of God's power, we have rejected such things with the excuse that they are too divisive!

The Problem of a Worldview-Inhibited Theology. In order to honestly study the failures of our Western worldview, we must examine our practice in light of the Scriptures. What does the Bible teach about the importance of signs and wonders?

Signs and wonders were (and are) at the heart of the ministry of Jesus. In the Great Commission, the authority of God was imparted to the church. At Pentecost the power of God was imparted. Jesus began his ministry after he was empowered by the Spirit at his baptism.

Jesus saw himself in conflict with Satan. He and the gospel writers viewed sickness as a work of Satan.

The ministry of Jesus in signs and wonders was based on his relationship with the Holy Spirit, who is imaginative and creative. Therefore, one should not try to reduce the ministry of Jesus to a group of simplistic principles.

The disciples, who were the embryonic church, were empowered to work the same ministry that Jesus worked. The result was the supernatural signs and wonders which we see throughout the book of Acts. There is a close relationship between their occurrence and the growth of the early church. The church grew whenever the gospel was preached, and signs and wonders followed. The activities of the New Testament church demonstrated an anticipation of supernatural involvement. The church was led by supernatural means: that is, visions, visitations, and prophecies. When a power encounter took place, signs and wonders were concurrent. Both success and failure are recorded for us in the New Testament. The letters especially share some apparent failures.

Signs and wonders were often performed as a witness to apostleship and the gospel message. They were and are the emblem of God's compassion toward his people.

The Kingdom of God

In order to fully understand the validity of a signs and wonders ministry, we need to study the concept of the kingdom of God. The kingdom of God is the rule of God (the age to come) which has invaded the kingdom (rule) of Satan (this present evil age) and is the arena in which signs and wonders occur. They are the "marks" (signs) of the kingdom. Understanding the kingdom of God is fundamental to understanding the ministry of Jesus; the kingdom of Satan was his real enemy. A war is on! Jesus was sent by God to shatter the strongholds of Satan. His one purpose was Satan's defeat. Jesus accomplished this through his death, resurrection, and ascension. This demonstrated who was the victor, but Satan is not yet cast out and will not be until Christ returns to establish his kingdom forever. The church is God's army in the continual fight which goes on with Satan as the church lives "between the times."

Acts 2:22 defines what we should look for as signs *(semeion)* and wonders *(teras)*. They are the works which were performed by Jesus while on earth. The word *signs* is found seventy-seven times in Scripture. *Wonders* occurs sixteen times and only in connection with *signs*.

The Gospels record numerous healings (signs) of Jesus, many released from demons, three dead persons raised, eight miracles. These are signs of God's kingly rule.

Jesus' words and works are the beginning of the new age, the age to come. The miracles (signs) are the foreshadowing and a promise of the coming universal redemption. The casting out of demons signals God's invasion into the realm of Satan and Satan's final destruction (see Matt. 12:29; Mark 3:27; Luke 11:21, 22; John 12:31; Rev. 20:1ff.). The raising of the dead announces that death will be forever done away with (see 1 Cor. 15:26; Rev. 21:4). The miraculous provisions of food are telling us about the end of all human need (Rev. 7:16ff.). The stilling of the storm points forward to the complete victory over the powers of chaos which threaten the earth.

A Continuing Ministry among the Church Fathers

Not only is a close examination of the biblical record necessary, but a look at the historical testimony is also vital. Signs and wonders did not cease with the close of the first century or with the completion of the canon. They have continued to occur in each of the three major historical periods (Patristic, Medieval, Reformation-Modern).

When the ones in authority endorsed the gifts, they occurred openly and widely within the church. When those in authority no longer endorsed the gifts, there appears to have been a decline in their usage and their occurrence. The gifts usually became manifest among the pietistic God-seekers and more frequently among the lesser educated, although not always so. When anything happened outside the norm that tended to threaten the structure or status quo, the institution (power base) would try to put a stop to it.

Almost every major personality of church history had some exposure to and acceptance of signs and wonders. Augustine, for example, listed several miracles in his voluminous work, *The City of God.* In Book 22 he confesses that there are simply too many to adequately record. "Actually," he wrote, "if I kept merely to miracles of healing and omitted all others . . . I should have to fill several volumes and, even then, I could do no more than tell those cases that have been officially recorded and attested for public reading in our churches." Augustine concludes by saying that "it is a simple fact that there is no lack of miracles even in our day. And the God who works the miracles we read in the Scriptures uses any means and manner He chooses."

Martin Luther, in a letter to a tax collector and a councilor, advised that the best way to cure a particular affliction in a man was to "lay your hands upon him and say, 'Peace be with you, dear brother, from God our Father and from our Lord Jesus Christ.'" He encouraged them to continue with the Lord's Prayer and "the Creed." "Then, when you depart," he wrote, "lay your hands upon the man again and say, 'These signs shall follow them that believe; they shall lay hands on the sick, and they shall recover.' . . . This is what we do," he concludes, "and what we have been accustomed to do, for a cabinet maker here was similarly afflicted with madness and we cured him by prayer in Christ's name."

After recording a great number of various healings and exorcisms in his journal, John Wesley wrote to Thomas Church in June 1746: "Yet I do not know that God hath anyway precluded Himself from thus exerting His sovereign power from working miracles in any kind or degree in any age to the end of the world. I do not recollect any Scripture wherein we are taught that miracles were to be confined within the limits either of the apostolic or the Cyprianic age, or of any period of time, longer or shorter, even till the restitution of all things."

The Resources for a Spirit-Empowered Church

Obviously, church history brims with the accounts of signs and wonders, written by great men instrumental in the spread of God's message. Indeed, these reports align directly with those accounts and instructions given in Scripture. If we in the Western world desire to see the church grow in our own sphere, we must seek to experience what we see recorded in Scripture and in the history of the church. How, then, can we begin?

We must reevaluate our theology and experience concerning spiritual gifts. These gifts are the expression of God's power at work in the world (church) today. A believer does not *possess* gifts, a believer *receives* gifts from God to be used at special times for special occasions. Gifts are the attestation of the empowering of the Holy Spirit and are vital in a signs and wonders ministry. Spiritual empowering equips one for service. The gifts are the tools which enable one to fulfill the ministry required. The gifts of the Spirit are received by impartation. The gifts (except the private use of tongues) are given to us and through us to use for others, and are developed in a climate of risk-taking and willingness to fail.

The gifts *(charismata)* or "gracelets" (a term coined by Russell Spittler of Fuller Theological Seminary) of the Holy Spirit are the trans-rational manifestations of God. They are given by God for the purpose of ministry taking place for the good of the body of Christ (see 1 Cor. 12:7).

There is a sense in which both the person and God's Spirit are involved in the giving/receiving of gracelets. There is rationale in the sense that the person must be aware of what he is observing. They are trans-rational in the sense that God, at his own discretion, anoints the person for an effect which he wishes produced.

There is a difference between the possession of gracelets, and gracelets being used by God through us at a special time and occasion. Many teachers of spiritual gifts have suggested that each person has a gift and it is his/her possession; that they are dispensed to us and become our property. This does not appear to be the case. In 1 Corinthians 12:4-7 we find that there are varieties *(diairesis)* or assignments of gracelets.

Their source: The same Spirit gives the gracelets.

Their use: The root word here gives us our word *deacon/servant*. Jesus is both the one ultimately served by the use of the gracelet and the one who directs to whom the service will be given.

Their effect: The root word is *energy,* and is used here not in the active but completive sense. God sees that the effects of the gracelet being used are accomplished.

Their manifestation *(phanerosis):* The English word *manifestation* comes from two Latin words which mean *the festive hand* or the *dancing hand* (Mel Roebeck). So the manifestations of the Spirit in verse 7 are the dancing hand of God, which can be seen by all who observe. The word *given* in verse 7 is present tense, implying continuous action, and could be translated "to each one (God) is giving and keeps on giving. . . ." The word is also passive. This means that each one receives the giving from an outside source; that is, the Spirit. This is not something which can be "worked up" by oneself.

As God sees fit, his dancing hand anoints (gives a gracelet to) a believer. It is a festive occasion for all to witness. The gracelets are given by the Spirit. As they are used, service is effected by the power of God.

The Biblical Mandate: Power Evangelism

Perhaps the activity best suited to the use of spiritual gifts is the area of evangelism. This was Paul's testimony to the Corinthians concerning his initial efforts in their lives: "My message and my preaching were not in persuasive words of wisdom, but in demonstration of the Spirit and of power" (1 Cor. 2:4, NASB). In Athens, he had used persuasive words with meager results. At his next apostolic stop, Corinth, many believed. It appears that in Corinth Paul combined proclamation with demonstration, as Christ had done throughout his ministry. What we are dealing with here is both content (proclamation) as well as context (the situation impregnated with God's mighty presence). The Word and works of God, coupled in an expression of God's divine will and mercy, culminate in the conversion of individuals as well as groups.

I call this type of ministry that Paul had in Corinth power evangelism: a presentation of the gospel that is rational but also transcends the rational. The explanation of the gospel comes with a demonstration of God's power through signs and wonders. It is a spontaneous, Spirit-inspired, empowered presentation of the gospel. It is usually preceded and undergirded by supernatural demonstrations of God's presence.

More than any other issue, it is the influence of materialism and antisupernaturalism that inhibits Westerners from experiencing evangelistic power as illustrated in the New Testament. Throughout Scripture there is continuous interaction between natural and supernatural beings and activities (angelic visitations, dreams, visions, prophecies, etc.). These interactions were one of the means God used to communicate his desires and direction to his people. In our contemporary society people screen out the possibility of supernatural interaction with the natural. We refuse, for the most part, to even study or allow for the reality of supernatural activity in our day.

One of the indicators of the Messiahship of Jesus was the demonstration of God's power in his ministry. In Luke 7:20, the disciples of John the Baptist asked Jesus, " 'Are You the One who is coming, or do we look for someone else?' " Jesus did not reply by giving a set of logical proofs. He viewed his ministry from a different perspective. He saw it from a power demonstration point of view. He told the disciples to tell John that he could be assured by what he had seen and heard (that is, by the curing of the sick and expulsion of evil spirits). The early church was effective because it understood evangelism from this same perspective—power demonstrations!

In power evangelism, the Holy Spirit has the power, not us. Through him we will be encouraged to say and do things we wouldn't ordinarily do. Under the anointing of the Holy Spirit, Jesus manifested all of the gifts of the Holy Spirit. Jesus' prayers for the sick, his evangelistic messages, even his recruiting techniques ("Come, follow me . . .") are notable for their simplicity. Obviously he was operating in an unction greater than personal words. It is this unction that is to characterize power evangelism and its practitioners.

While program evangelism is, to a limited degree, effectual, power evangelism has always been, and still is, the best means of church growth. In order to see God's church multiply as it is doing in the rest of the world, the Western church must become involved in power evangelism. We must allow the Holy Spirit to empower us and lead us to those who are in need of him. When we encounter the lost, we must have power—the ability to see into men's hearts and know their sin and their need, the ability to heal those who are ill, the ability to free those who have been bound by Satan.

Part 7

WHO'S WHO IN
CHURCH GROWTH

Hundreds of church leaders are now practicing church growth principles in America and around the world. The editors have compiled this list of representative church growth leaders who have made significant professional-level contributions to the Church Growth Movement. No such list could possibly be exhaustive, and undoubtedly some names which should have been included are absent. We regret this, but feel that it is worth such a risk to make these individuals known to the general Christian public. Contributing editors to this volume have longer biographical sketches than the others.

Delmar L. Anderson was born in Swedeburg, Nebraska, in 1929. He is a graduate of Knox College, Galesburg, Illinois, and North Park Theological Seminary, Chicago, Illinois. In addition, he has done postgraduate studies in counseling at the University of Chicago, completed Diagnosis with Impact Consultation Training at Charles E. Fuller Institute of Evangelism and Church Growth, and in 1983 received his Doctor of Ministry degree from Fuller Theological Seminary. All of his D.Min. studies were in the area of church growth and evangelism. His D.Min. dissertation, entitled *Accelerating Church Growth through a Ministry of Consultation in a Denominational Context,* outlines the creation, development, and results of his ministry as Director of Church Growth in the Evangelical Covenant Church. He is one of the first denominational level Directors of Church Growth on the American scene.

Anderson is an ordained pastor in the Evangelical Covenant

Church, having served churches in Illinois, Virginia, Washington, and Minnesota. For three years before becoming Director of Church Growth for the denomination he served as superintendent of the North Pacific Conference of Covenant Churches, and supervised the planting of several new churches. The North Pacific Conference comprises Oregon, Washington, Idaho, and Montana. His longest pastorate was ten years at Newport Covenant Church, Bellevue, Washington. The church relocated, went to multiple services, and effectively used a subcongregation parish system. Delmar Anderson's ministries cover a wide range of involvement: he was a youth pastor in a suburban church, a home missionary in Lee County, Virginia, a pastor in a city church, and a supervisor of churches.

On the denominational level Delmar Anderson is a past member of the Board of Christian Education, past chairperson of the Board of World Mission, and has served as dean for two Christian Education Laboratory Training Schools. He spearheaded Churches Alive Experiences weekend training events while serving as superintendent. He is a certified film workshop leader for the Robert H. Schuller Institute for Successful Church Leadership, Field Ministries Division, and also represents *Churches Alive: Growing by Discipling.*

Anderson is an excellent teacher and speaker. He is an adjunct professor at North Park Theological Seminary, where he taught the first discipling course offered. The course was entitled "Discipling, Theology, and Practice." He has wide experience in conducting diagnostic analysis evaluations in the churches of the denomination. He is a certified consultant with Performax Systems International, Inc., and is author of *Church Growth Monographs* distributed by the denomination to pastors and church chairmen. Monograph titles are: "Communication Gaps Checkup," "Church Growth and Revival," "Equipping Christians for Ministry," "Destination Sickness," "Growing Plans for Static Churches," and "Why Join a Church?" Anderson has guided several churches through modular training programs. His modular training specialties are: *Purpose and Needs Oriented Planning* and *Body Evangelism.* Several of Anderson's articles have been published in the denominational magazine *Covenant Companion,* the most significant one entitled, "Is Your Church Drifting?" He and his wife, Darlene, have three grown children, two of whom are married. Delmar and Darlene are happy grandparents, currently residing in Chicago, Illinois.

Delmar Anderson contributed chapter 17 to this volume: "Church Growth Consultation in the Denominational Context."

E. S. "Andy" Anderson, growth promotion specialist for the Southern Baptist Sunday School Board, Nashville, Tennessee, was a Florida pastor for nineteen years. Not content with a Sunday school that was failing to reach new people, he developed the ACTION Program of Sunday School Enrollment. What happened at the Riverside Baptist Church in Fort Myers, Florida, is history—from 1,094 to 2,600 enrollment, and from 400 to 1,150 in average attendance.

Anderson has developed a practical system to initiate and sustain growth in the Sunday school. It is called "The Growth Spiral." Goals are set, evaluations are made, workers are trained, space is provided, and visitation is encouraged. Through the new approach, churches are growing and people are being saved and baptized.

Anderson was a pastor for twenty-nine years, serving churches in Georgia and Florida. He is the author of several books, including *The Growth Spiral Workbook, Fasting Changed My Life, Where ACTION Is,* and *Effective Methods of Church Growth.* He travels over three hundred days each year conducting regional growth conferences in the United States, Canada, and the Caribbean.

Anderson attended the Atlanta Baptist Institute, and received degrees from Luther Rice Seminary, Jacksonville, Florida.

W. Charles "Chip" Arn is the foremost designer of church growth training curricula and resources used by individual churches and regional districts across the Protestant spectrum. He is vice-president of Research and Development for the Institute for American Church Growth in Pasadena, California, and has been the primary designer of over twenty major church growth products available through either the Institute or individual denominations.

Chip Arn (son of Win Arn) has led numerous pastors' training conferences across the country and provides regular consultation to churches and regional executives in effective application of growth principles. Arn has done much of the research and design for the highly effective "Two Year Growth Process" (offered through the Institute), in which several hundred churches are now involved.

Arn's most significant contribution to date is probably his work in *The Master's Plan for Making Disciples,* which is the first strategy of evangelism building on and incorporating the principles of church growth into a practical method for equipping laypersons and congregations to effectively reach their unchurched friends and relatives. *The Master's Plan* includes a variety of teacher and student material, video training, overhead transparencies, and additional resources to help local church leaders train their laity in this process. *The Master's Plan* is one of the most talked about and increasingly used new tools for evangelism throughout the church today.

Chip Arn, who holds the Ed.D. degree from the University of Southern California, contributed two chapters to this volume: chapter 4, "Evangelism or Disciple Making?" and chapter 9, "Lay Ministry: A Closer Look."

Win Arn, president and founder of the influential Institute for American Church Growth, is widely respected as a pioneer and major spokesperson for the American Church Growth Movement. His contributions in the field of church growth are creative and wide-ranging. He has conducted more church growth seminars and training sessions for pastors, individual churches, consortia of churches, and denominations than any other person. Arn continues to be actively involved in leading churches in the discovery and application of church growth insights.

He has produced or coproduced almost every film now in use in the area of church growth. Some of these titles include: "But . . . I'm Just a Layman!" "The Gift of Love," "Discover Your Gifts," "The Great Commission Sunday School," "The Possibility Sunday School," "For the Love of Pete," "See You Sunday?" ". . . And They Said It Couldn't Be Done!" "Reach Out and Grow," "How to Grow a Church," and "The Ministers." Films

Arn has produced that are particularly oriented toward establishing new churches are: "Planned Parenthood for Churches," "A Church Is Born," "A Matter of Urgency." Arn has helped many denominations tailor these films to their particular needs and include their own executives into the script. It is estimated that his films have been seen by over two million people.

Win Arn has written a variety of church growth books, articles, and curriculum material. Books he has authored, coauthored, or edited include: *How to Grow a Church, Ten Steps for Church Growth, Back to Basics, Growth: A New Vision for the Sunday School, The Master's Plan, The Pastor's Church Growth Handbook, Volumes I and II.* In addition, he has been editor of the magazine *Church Growth: America* and is presently publisher of *The Win Arn Growth Report.* Several of the research studies done by Arn have been reported in *Time* magazine, *Newsweek* magazine, and the Associated Press. He has written articles and regular columns for numerous denominational magazines and national Christian periodicals.

To help the concepts of church growth become a reality throughout America, Arn has produced a variety of diagnostic and training materials. The teacher training kit, "A New Vision for the Sunday School," has brought new life and growth to educational ministries of churches in over fifty different denominations. "Let the Church Grow" is a twelve-week curriculum study. "Spiritual Gifts for Building the Body" enables laity in a church to identify and use their spiritual gifts. "The Caring System" provides a church with an effective way to respond to potential new members in a systematic and individual way. *The Master's Plan,* produced along with Charles Arn, is a process of training laity in evangelism based on the natural networks of relationship among unchurched friends and family, and is a strategy that is mobilizing hundreds of congregations for effective outreach. "The Growth Opportunity Survey" and other diagnostic materials have been developed under Arn's leadership. They enable a church to look creatively and effectively at its strengths and weaknesses and build a growth plan.

Win Arn has been instrumental in the research and development of computer software which builds on the principles of church growth for the local church. Through this church growth software, churches are now finding it possible to enter an entirely new dimension of ministry possibilities.

The Institute for American Church Growth, under Arn's direction, has developed a uniquely effective "Two Year Growth Process" for individual churches and regional judicatories. This growth process includes consultation, seminars, computer monitoring, materials, and video training—all of which come together to help churches break through roadblocks and grow to their full potential in disciple making. He also serves as a consultant to several major denominations as well as regional judicatories and individual churches.

Win Arn, who received his D.Rel.Ed. degree from Eastern Baptist Theological Seminary, is associate editor of this volume and has contributed two chapters: chapter 6, "Understanding and Implementing Growth for Your Church," and chapter 8, "How to Use Ratios to Effect Church Growth."

Charles Chaney is president of Southwest Baptist University in Bolivar, Missouri, a 106-year-old liberal arts and professional college affiliated with the Southern Baptist Convention. He has served in that position since 1983. Previous to that he was Dean of the Courts Redford School of Theology at the same institution.

Before entering academia, Charles Chaney had a distinguished career as a pastor and denominational executive. As a pastor, he served three churches in Texas, three in Kentucky, and one in Illinois. While in First Baptist Church of Palatine, Illinois, he became committed to sharing Christ in the great metropolitan centers of the world. The Palatine church became the mother church to several daughter congregations while he was pastor. In 1972, Chaney became director of the Church Extension Division of the Illinois Baptist State Association (Southern Baptist). His primary responsibility was planting new churches, and he supervised the planting of more than two hundred congregations. His book *Church Planting at the End of the Twentieth Century* (Tyndale, 1982) grew out of that experience. It took form in the annual church growth lectures which Chaney delivered at Fuller Theological Seminary in 1980.

Chaney's experience with numerous plateaued and declining churches in Illinois motivated him to join with Ron Lewis to write *Design for Church Growth* (Broadman, 1977), one of the recognized church growth texts. He holds the B.D. and Th.M. from Southern Baptist Theological Seminary, and the Ph.D. from the University of Chicago.

Ronald K. Crandall is the McCreless Professor of Evangelism at Asbury Theological Seminary in Wilmore, Kentucky. Born and raised in Michigan, he graduated from Michigan State University with honors in 1964. Under a Rockefeller grant he attended Fuller Theological Seminary focusing on missions and evangelism. While studying under Dr. Donald McGavran he became a missionary intern to Viet Nam where he studied church growth. He received the D.Th.P. degree from Fuller in Pastoral Theology in 1969.

As a United Methodist minister Crandall has served growing churches in California and Arizona. In 1977 he was appointed to the United Methodist General Board of Discipleship in Nashville, Tennessee, where he served for six years as director of evangelism for the local church. Crandall has preached, taught, and published widely, including articles, denominational resources, and books. Developing a special interest in the smaller membership churches, he has recently coauthored with L. Ray Sells a book entitled *There's New Life in the Small Congregation* (Nashville: Discipleship Resources, 1983). He is secretary/treasurer of the Academy for Evangelism in Theological Education and a member of working groups on evangelism for the Oxford Institute of Wesleyan Theological Studies and the Lausanne Committee's Consultation on the Work of the Holy Spirit and Evangelization.

Chester J. Droog is the western field secretary for the Synod of the West, Reformed Church in America, with his office in Cerritos, California. He has responsibility for church planning and development in thirteen western and southwestern states. During the past ten years the baptized membership of the synod has grown from 81,448 to 95,799. Fifty new congregations have been started during this same ten year period. Droog conducts numerous church growth workshops and is a popular church growth speaker. His doctoral study, completed in 1976, was entitled *Priorities, Principles, and Programs for the Growing Church,* wherein he outlined a variety of helpful suggestions for seeing church growth become a reality in Reformed Churches. He has written a *Church Planning and Development Manual*, presently being used in his denomination; a history of the Reformed Church in America on the West Coast from 1920 to 1985; and numerous church growth articles for his denominational magazine, *The Church Herald*. For the past five years he has edited a semiannual church growth newsletter sent to churches in the synod.

Chester Droog is a graduate of Hope College and Western Theological Seminary in Holland, Michigan, and California Graduate School in Glendale, California. Prior to assuming his present position in 1973 he served the Hope Reformed Church in Spencer, Iowa, the Fifth Reformed Church in Grand Rapids, Michigan, and the Bethel Reformed Church in Bellflower, California.

Frederick J. Finks has been vice president of Ashland Theological Seminary in Ashland, Ohio, since 1982. He is responsible for the daily operations and organization of Ashland Seminary, and teaches in the field of church growth. Prior to coming to Ashland, Finks was senior pastor of the Winding Waters Brethren Church in Elkhart, Indiana. During the ten years of his pastorate at Winding Waters, he led the congregation to a 300 percent decadal growth rate. Perhaps even more important for the future of the church was the development of a ministry concept which helps people discover their spiritual gifts and then incorporates them into ministry positions within the church.

In 1981 Finks was elected moderator of the General Conference of the Brethren Church. In this capacity, he also served as chairman of the Spiritual State of the Churches Committee which entailed travel throughout the nation to ascertain the health of the denomination. He has written articles on church growth subjects for the *Brethren Evangelist* and the *Ashland Theological Journal*.

Fred Finks holds the B.A. in psychology from Ashland College, the M.Div. from Ashland Seminary, and the D.Min. in church growth from Fuller Theological Seminary.

Carl F. George is the director of the Charles E. Fuller Institute for Evangelism and Church Growth in Pasadena, California. The Fuller Institute is an outgrowth of the ministry of Charles E. Fuller, who through the "Old-Fashioned Revival Hour" became the most listened to voice on American radio several decades ago. The Fuller Institute is affiliated with Fuller Theological Seminary as one of several action-oriented institutes radiating from the academic center.

The Fuller Institute was founded in 1975 through the vision of C. Peter Wagner, then director of the Fuller Evangelistic Association. John Wimber became the first director of the Institute, turning it over to Carl George in 1978. Under George's leadership, the Fuller Institute has become the foremost center of church growth consultation and the training of consultants. A nationwide network of over seventy church growth consultants has been trained through the acclaimed "Diagnosis with Impact" program.

Carl George is the senior editor of the "Church Growth Modular Training System," a set of tools used by professional consultants to guide the process of church growth in local congregations as well as in judicatories and denominations. It is a flexible system which does not cause the consultant to be locked into some predetermined pattern or program.

Further, the Fuller Institute is a resource center for a wide variety of materials which are being used in hundreds of churches across America with good growth results. Particularly noteworthy is a line of materials on spiritual gifts keyed in to C. Peter Wagner's best-seller, *Your Spiritual Gifts Can Help Your Church Grow*.

Carl George holds an M.A. in interpretative speech and post graduate studies in social psychology and church growth. After serving as youth minister in a Baptist church in Miami, he went to Gainesville, Florida, where he founded the University Baptist Church and pastored it for thirteen years. During that time he was instrumental in sponsoring several new church starts, one of which was a church among new middle-class blacks. George serves as an adjunct faculty member of the Fuller Seminary School of World Mission where he helps teach in the church growth courses of the Doctor of Ministry program. He is also executive vice-president of the Fuller Evangelistic Association.

Carl George contributed chapter 16 to this volume: "Church Growth Consultation."

Eddie Gibbs has been at the forefront of church growth thinking in the United Kingdom for the past seven years. Since his ordination into the Church of England ministry twenty-one years ago, he has been concerned about the persistent decline of the mainline denominations in Western Europe, and especially about their failure to relate to the working classes, or nonbook culture, as he prefers to call them. This emphasis is understandable in the light of his own working class background.

A second growing area of reflection for Gibbs has been the need for the renewal of the local church and the developing of dynamic and flexible structures in response to the chronic problem of nominal Christianity and the increasing missionary challenge of British post-Christian society.

After serving a curacy in the south London parish of Wandsworth, in 1966 he went to Chile under the auspices of the South American Missionary Society, where he was involved in pastoring two Spanish-speaking Anglican churches. In addition, he taught at two Pentecostal evening institutes, and worked on the radical reshaping of the organizational structures of an Anglican diocese which at that time covered three republics. His South American experience provided the seedbed for much of his subsequent thinking as he observed the rapid growth of the Pentecostal churches in nonbook cultures and struggled to discover appropriate strategies for the new Anglican urban evangelistic and church planting projects.

The South American Missionary Society called him to work on the home front as Home and Education Secretary, where from 1970 to 1977 he was much in demand at conferences and in local churches interpreting his Latin American experience in terms appropriate to the United Kingdom situation.

While at pains to emphasize that there were few transferable models, there were a number of key principles to be identified and applied. Present at one of his conferences was Canon Colin Buchanan, principal of the Anglican theological college of St. Johns', Nottingham, who encouraged Gibbs to write up his presentation as one of the series of Grove Booklets which he edited.

The booklet was entitled, *Urban Church Growth—Clues from Latin America and Britain,* which has proved to be one of the best-sellers in the Grove series.

At about this time his growing reputation in the church growth field gained national recognition. Tom Houston, then executive director of Bible Society (now president of World Vision), invited Gibbs to develop a church growth ministry within the overall objectives of the organization.

A tentative start was made in 1971 with a basic course for ministers and lay leaders. From the outset Eddie Gibbs insisted on training core groups of leaders rather than isolated individuals to enhance the chances of concrete action being taken as an outcome of the teaching given. The snowballing demand for these courses was such that a second staff member (Roy Pointer) was appointed within a year to share the teaching load and further develop the concepts and strategies embodied in this ministry. At the present time over 15,000 leaders have been trained from 4,000 churches. One remarkable aspect of this project has been the breadth of interests across the denominations, spanning a broad theological spectrum. A sample of 175 people who had attended the basic course showed that 50 percent came from churches that were either declining or static, and that since the course one-half of that number were reporting numerical growth.

At the start of his career with Bible Society he was encouraged to enroll in the church growth concentration of the D.Min. program at Fuller Seminary. He was also approached by Edward England, the religious editor of Hodder and Stoughton, to contribute a volume on church growth in the prestigious "I Believe" series, which Hodder published jointly with Eerdmans. *I Believe in Church Growth* was accepted as his Fuller dissertation and on publication received high praise by reviewers both outside as well as within the evangelical constituency. He was honored by an invitation to become the first president of the British Church Growth Association and to join the adjunct faculty of Fuller Seminary School of World Mission.

In the summer of 1982 he handed over the leadership of the Bible Society's church growth ministry to Roy Pointer to become the National Training Director of Mission England. This is a three-year evangelistic program incorporating church growth principles, in which Billy Graham had a major input from May to July 1984 when he held crusades in six major British cities. On completion of the training phase of Mission England in 1984 he moved to the United States along with his wife, Renee, and their four children. He now serves as Assistant Professor of Church Growth at the Fuller Seminary School of World Mission.

Eddie Gibbs contributed chapter 19 to this volume: "The Power behind the Principles."

Larry Gilbert is president of Church Growth Institute, Lynchburg, Virginia. Called into the ministry later in life, Gilbert founded Steps in Living Ministries, Inc., in 1978, which later became Church Growth Institute. Leaving behind fourteen years of business, he graduated from the Institute of Biblical Studies of Liberty Baptist College. He has also attended classes at Liberty Baptist Seminary and the Maryland Institute, College of Art in Baltimore.

Gilbert's major contribution to the Church Growth Movement is his program on spiritual gifts titled *How to Build a Championship Team for Effective Church Growth*. He presents positive teaching on the "task-oriented" gifts, showing their relationship to the life of the believer, the local church, and the Church Growth Movement. The Church Growth Institute continually expands its resources of evangelistic stewardship, discipleship, and lay involvement programs.

John A. Gration is professor of missions in the Wheaton Graduate School, Wheaton, Illinois. Previous to that he served as a missionary to Africa under the Africa Inland Mission, working closely with the churches in Zaire and Kenya in evangelistic outreach and development. He continues working with the African churches in their encounter with their cultural context.

Gration attended Moody Bible Institute, Gordon College, and the Wheaton Graduate School. He received his Ph.D. from New York University with a dissertation entitled *The Relationship of the Africa Inland Mission and Its National Church in Kenya between 1895 and 1971.* He has written articles for *Evangelical Missions Quarterly, Missiology,* and the *International Bulletin of Missionary Research.*

Joe A. Harding is senior pastor of the Central United Methodist Church in Richland, Washington, where he has served for over fifteen years. The church, also known as Central United Protestant Church, has received nationwide recognition for the rapid growth of the worship attendance and the congregational membership during recent years. Worship attendance is now over 1,200.

One of Joe Harding's contributions to church growth is his book *Have I Told You Lately?* (Church Growth Press, 1982), which is the first attempt at relating preaching to church growth. His church is featured in two films: "Finding the Way Forward" (United Methodist Church) and "But . . . I'm Just a Layman" (Christian Communications). Harding regularly conducts seminars at his church, and he has addressed church growth conferences in over thirty-five states for numerous denominations.

Harding holds theological degrees from Candler School of Theology and Boston University School of Theology, and his D.Min. from San Francisco Theological Seminary.

George G. Hunter III is dean and professor of church growth of the new E. Stanley Jones School of World Mission and Evangelism of Asbury Theological Seminary. Hunter and his five colleagues provide mission and evangelism instruction for M.A.R., M.Div., Th.M., D.Min., and D.Miss. students.

Previously Hunter served as Secretary of Evangelism for the United Methodist Church (1977-83), as Assistant Professor of Communication and Evangelism at the Perkins School of Theology, S.M.U. (1972-77), as a staff director with the former Methodist Board of Evangelism, and as pastor of churches in Florida and Great Britain.

As a writer, George Hunter is best known for *The Contagious Congregation*, an Abingdon Press "classic" now approaching its seventh printing. Hunter has also written *Church Growth: Strategies That Work* (with Donald McGavran, Abingdon, 1980), *Finding the Way Forward, And Every Tongue Confess* (Discipleship Resources).

Hunter is currently developing manuscripts on the church growth strategies of John Wesley and on the management of congregational growth. He is in wide demand as a platform speaker, mission preacher, large scale trainer, and church growth consultant with churches, judicatories, and denominations. Such work has been expressed across the U.S.A. and Canada and more than a dozen foreign countries.

Hunter is a member of the Lausanne Committee for World Evangelization, and has served on the World Methodist Council's Evangelism Committee and the board of the Institute for American Church Growth. He frequently speaks at Billy Graham Schools of Evangelism.

Hunter received his education from Florida Southern College (B.A.), Emory University (B.D.), Princeton Theological Seminary (Th.M.), and Northwestern University (Ph.D.). He has taken additional studies at Fuller's School of World Mission, American Management Association, and NTL Institute.

One of Hunter's prevailing interests focuses on the western church's "mega-problem"—how to communicate the gospel to "secular people," who lack a Christian vocabulary, assumptions, memory, and frame of reference. As a contributor and interpreter of church growth theory, Hunter is a "traditional McGavranite"—believing that Donald McGavran's established historic insights are better founded and more needed today than are some of the "newer wrinkles in the literature." He believes that the valid forward progress of the discipline will be achieved as church growth becomes more intentionally an applied behavioral science, drawing hypotheses from the communication and management disciplines to test in many contagious congregations— which are the laboratories of the Lord of the Harvest.

Hunter, 46, is married to the former Ella Faye Price, a professor of psychiatric nursing. They have three children: Gill, Monica, and Donald.

George Hunter contributed chapter 5 to this volume: "The Bridges of Contagious Evangelism: Social Networks."

Kent R. Hunter is director of the Church Growth Center, Corunna, Indiana. He founded the Center in 1977 for the purpose of "the transformational change of the Christian church toward the effective implementation of the great commission (Matt. 28:19-20)." The Center's ministry is concentrated in three areas: workshops and seminars, resources, and parish consultations. The Center has served churches of several denominations on the North American Continent.

Hunter holds the Master of Divinity degree from Concordia Theological Seminary, St. Louis, Missouri, the Doctor of Sacred Theology degree from the Lutheran School of Theology at Chicago, and a Doctor of Ministry degree in church growth from Fuller Theological Seminary. He has also studied at Luther Seminary, Adelaide, South Australia. An ordained minister of the Lutheran Church—Missouri Synod, Hunter has served several churches and effectively applied church growth principles in diverse ministries such as a racially changing urban community in Detroit, Michigan, and a rural church in northeast Indiana. He has taught church growth at several colleges and seminaries as a guest lecturer. He also serves as a presenter for the Yokefellow Institute in Richmond, Indiana.

He is the author of numerous articles and several books, including *Launching Growth in the Local Congregation, Foundations for Church Growth, Your Church Has Doors: How to Open the Front and Close the Back, Gifted for Growth: An Implementation Guide for Mobilizing the Laity, Six Faces of the Christian Church: How to Light a Fire in a Lukewarm Church,* and *Your Church Has Personality.* Hunter sees his major contribution to the Church Growth Movement in the area of theology. He sees church growth as an ecclesiologist and has developed theological articulations for areas such as gospel-motivated mission thrust and quality church growth. His "historical growth axion" states that "the church has grown in quantity and quality when it has been clear on its own identity and purpose." He has done much work in the area of helping congregations develop a philosophy of ministry that declares the personality of the local body of Christ.

With his colleagues at the Church Growth Center, Hunter has been instrumental in developing the "Two-Year Church Growth Process," an in-depth experience aimed at changing attitudes from maintenance to mission and developing "church growth eyes" on the congregational level. The process is designed for clusters of churches of the same judicatory or in a particular geographical area. The process has been effective in several areas of the United States and Canada among various types of churches. It combines regional workshops which teach church growth principles with follow-up materials used in the local parish where the principles are put into practice. Computer tracking and consultant monitoring help the churches through the process. A variation of the "Two-Year Process" has been developed for churches wanting to participate individually.

The Church Growth Center is emerging as a significant consulting ministry for Christian churches. With some guidance from parish consultant Lyle Schaller, Hunter and his associates have developed a consultation ministry which combines the best of Schaller's years of experience with the insights of church growth principles on the one hand, and the latest input from computer technology on the other. The Center's computer analyst and programmer is developing a system of rapid access to an expanding data base that will help staff consultants to efficiently deal with those aspects of parish life which can be measured and analyzed.

The Church Growth Center has trained a staff of consultants and presenters who are located all across the United States, and its resources are used in several countries around the world. Several of the resources are available in Spanish. The Center continues to develop Bible studies and implementation guides for comprehensive church growth at the local level.

Kent Hunter contributed two chapters to this volume: chapter 7, "Membership Integrity: The Body of Christ with a Backbone" and chapter 11, "The Quality Side of Church Growth."

Raymond W. Hurn is a general superintendent of the Church of the Nazarene. Previous to taking this position, Hurn served the Church of the Nazarene as director of Home Missions/ Church Extension. Under his leadership a thirty-year decline in church planting in the Church of the Nazarene was reversed in the U.S.A. and Canada. In the period 1980-1985, 592 new works were officially launched.

Hurn is a graduate of Bethany Nazarene College and was later honored with a Doctor of Divinity degree from his alma mater. He has taken graduate studies in church growth at Fuller Theological Seminary. His published books include *Mission Possible, Black Evangelism: Which Way from Here?*, *Finding Your Ministry*,

Spiritual Gifts Workshop, and *Mission Action Sourcebook.* For fifteen years he published a bimonthly tabloid, *Mission Alert,* which circulated widely within and without his denomination.

Raymond Hurn is a member of the board of the Institute of American Church Growth, a founding member of the North American Society for Church Growth, and was program chairperson for Houston '85, a National Convocation on Evangelizing Ethnic America.

Medford H. Jones has been an innovator in mission since his conversion in 1935. He is a first generation Christian of frontier stock having grown up in the mountains of eastern Oregon and the Black Hills of South Dakota.

He earned a B.Th. degree at Northwest Christian College coupled with class work at the University of Oregon. During this period he ministered to rural churches, preached revivals in the three west coast states and superintended a downtown rescue mission for one year.

Graduate study was done from 1942-1949 at Butler University School of Religion, where he earned the M.S. degree in Church Management and M.Div. in church history. Specialized research was carried out in evangelism and ministry. In this period he effectively led a city church from an average attendance of fifty to over three hundred and enlarged the property. Twenty-five young people were recruited for ministry, and they now serve around the world.

From 1949-1965, Medford Jones led the Jones-Keister Evangelistic Team in evangelistic crusades for churches in thirty-five states. The plan of evangelism was comprehensive and intensive, mobilizing the resources of the church for maximal evangelistic thrust. Churches served experienced an average 16 percent gain in membership with a higher assimilation record than they had had with Sunday-by-Sunday additions. His largest single church crusade reaped 241 new members and his largest multiple church crusade in Portland, Oregon, gave 1,251 new members to local churches. Each church served developed a group of experienced evangelists who continued in service.

After doing program consultation and church fund-raising along with evangelism, Medford Jones developed his "Church

Growth Consultation" program for churches in 1960. This program diagnosed the church in the context of the community and its own internal circumstances. This was a unique program in its time and showed the way to growth for churches in over ten states.

Milligan College honored Medford Jones with a doctorate in recognition of his pioneering and innovation in evangelism and church growth in 1963.

At Emmanuel School of Religion in 1965, Jones opened what is believed to be the first Department of American Church Growth in a seminary. Here he convened the first Church Growth Colloquium in 1968 which drew participants and top executives from a wide theological spectrum involving twenty-one denominations. During this period he was in close contact with Dr. Donald McGavran, developing ties that continue today.

Pacific Christian College called Medford Jones to its presidency in 1969. The College increased in size and moved from Long Beach to Fullerton, California. The college became characterized by its emphasis upon the priesthood of believers ministry with stress upon mission involvement regardless of occupation. Every student was challenged and equipped to contribute to the growth of a local church congregation either as a volunteer or as an ordained minister.

In 1981 Jones asked to be transferred from the presidency of Pacific Christian College to professor of church growth in the College's Graduate School of Church Dynamics. After a year of study leave, Jones assumed the deanship of the Graduate School of Church Dynamics. The centerpiece of this growing school is a thirty-six-semester unit M.A. designed for the Bible college graduate in Ministries. The emphasis is upon church growth and effective field ministry.

As a diagnostic church consultant, Medford Jones ministers to churches and seminar groups nationally. He is generating new ideas and challenges out of his long experience and study. Recent computerized research done with several thousand churches has enriched this ministry.

Medford Jones contributed chapter 13 to this volume: "Dynamic Churches Come in All Sizes."

Brian Kingsmore, a native of Belfast, Northern Ireland, is the director of evangelism and church growth for the Columbia Graduate School of Bible and Missions in Columbia, South Carolina. His former positions include pastor of three churches, evangelist of the Presbyterian Church in Ireland, chaplain to New University of Ulster (five years), church planter and conference speaker. He was educated at Edinburgh University, Scottish Congregational College, Queens University (Belfast), and Union Theological Seminary (Belfast). He holds the D.Min. in church growth from Fuller Theological Seminary.

Kingsmore was a member of the board of the British Church Growth Association; the board of Evangelism Explosion (Great Britain); vice chairman of Eurofest '75; chairman of Youth Reach 1978 to 1983; delegate to Lausanne, Switzerland, and Pattaya, Thailand; and seminar speaker at the World Itinerant Evangelists Conference, Amsterdam '83.

Lloyd E. Kwast is a professor in the School of Intercultural Studies at Biola University and is professor and chairman of the department of world missions at Talbot Theological Seminary, La Mirada, California. He has also taught church growth and missions-related courses at Fuller School of World Mission and School of Theology, Pasadena, California; the North American Baptist Seminary, Sioux Falls, South Dakota; and the Institute of International Studies at the William Carey University, Pasadena, California. From 1963 to 1971 he served with his family as missionaries in the Cameroon, West Africa.

Kwast holds graduate degrees in theology, Christian education, church growth, and missiology, and has authored two books on church growth in Cameroon, *The Discipling of West Cameroon* (Eerdmans, 1972) and *The Origins and 19th Century Development of Protestant Christianity in Cameroon* (University Microfilm, 1980). He is a contributing author to books edited by Donald McGavran: *Crucial Issues in Missions Tomorrow* (Moody Press, 1972); Alan Tippett, *God, Man and Church Growth* (Eerdmans, 1973); and Ralph Winter, *Perspectives on the World Christian Movement* (William Carey, 1981).

Kwast has conducted church growth seminars and workshops

245

in fifteen countries of Africa, Asia, Latin America, the Caribbean and Micronesian Islands. He holds the B.D. from American Baptist Seminary of the West and the M.A. (Missions) and Doctor of Missiology from the Fuller Seminary School of World Mission.

Robert C. Larson is the executive secretary of the Department of Church Growth and Evangelism of the Evangelical Covenant Church. He is an ordained minister of that denomination. He is a graduate of North Park Theological Seminary (B.D.) and holds the degrees of M.U.P. and Ph.D. in Urban Planning from the University of Washington in Seattle. He is a member of the American Institute of Certified Planners.

Larson has been involved in the Church Growth Movement with papers presented to numerous meetings including the Theological Conference of the International Federation of Free Evangelical Churches in Oslo in 1980. His special interest is in locational factors for local churches, and he incorporates church growth principles in his consultive role in this regard. He teaches as an adjunct member of the faculty of North Park Theological Seminary in the field of church growth.

E. Leroy Lawson has been senior pastor of the Central Christian Church, Mesa, Arizona, since 1979. The church had 800 members when he assumed his pastorate and it now has doubled to 1,600. The congregation is currently relocating to a 33-acre campus. Previously to going to Mesa, Lawson planted and pastored other churches, as well as serving a two-year term as vice president of Milligan College in Tennessee.

Leroy Lawson has authored a dozen books, the best known of which include *Introducing Church Growth* and *Church Growth: Everybody's Business* (both with Tetsunao Yamamori), *The Lord of the Parables,* and *The New Testament Church Then and Now.* He holds the B.A. (Northwest Christian), A.B. (Cascade), M.A.T. (Reed), and Ph.D. (Vanderbilt). He is chairperson of the board of the Christian Missionary Fellowship and was president of his church's North American Christian Convention. He lectures frequently in America and abroad on church growth and related themes.

Roger W. Leenerts is an executive with the Lutheran Church— Missouri Synod, serving as associate executive secretary for North

America missions on the Board for Mission Services. He has been a key instrument in introducing church growth principles and practices into the LCMS through sponsoring church growth seminars and workshops for key denominational personnel. Under this new emphasis, church planting became the primary mission emphasis for the synod. In the mid seventies only twenty new congregations were being started per year. Currently the number is over 100, and the goal for 1990 is 500 new congregations per year.

Leenerts, a graduate of Concordia College and Concordia Theological Seminary, has taken graduate work in church growth at Fuller Theological Seminary. He has coauthored a Bible study and seminar materials on spiritual gifts.

Ron S. Lewis is the founding president and senior consultant for Church Growth Designs. Since 1979 Church Growth Designs has served clients across the Southern Baptist Convention, evaluating church and community trends and offering strategy suggestions to accomplish the evangelistic task of the local church. Before moving into his present position, Lewis pastored several churches and served as the director of church development of the Illinois Baptist Convention. He also spent some time working with the Baptist Sunday School Board.

Ron Lewis is the coauthor (with Charles Chaney) of *Design for Church Growth* (Broadman, 1977) one of the most popular introductions to the field. He speaks on a regular basis at evangelism conferences, church growth conferences, and other programs as a specialist in church growth. He works with a number of churches as a consultant. Lewis is a graduate of Oklahoma Baptist University and Southwestern Baptist Theological Seminary. He has done graduate work at southern Baptist Seminary and in the church growth field at Fuller Theological Seminary.

David Chia-en Liao has been associate professor of missions at Biola University, La Mirada, California, since 1980. He teaches church growth and other missions-related subjects for both graduate and undergraduate students. Born in mainland China of Christian parents, he grew up in a strong indigenous Brethren movement. He joined Overseas Crusades in Taiwan in 1955 and has since devoted himself to serving the church in Taiwan and elsewhere in the fulfillment of the Great Commission. He received his advanced training in church growth from the School of World Mission at Fuller with the M.A. and D.Miss. degrees.

In Taiwan, David Liao was one of the charter members of the Taiwan Church Growth Society, and for seven years he was the editor of *Co-Workers Monthly,* a pastor-oriented magazine dedicated to promoting evangelism and church growth. His recent assignments prior to teaching at Biola included an eighteen-month term in Thailand as a full-time consultant to the nationwide interdenominational Thailand Church Growth Committee, and another eighteen-month term as Program Consultant preparing for the "Consultation on World Evangelization" held at Pattaya, Thailand, in June 1980. Liao is the author of *The Unresponsive: Resistant or Neglected?* (Moody Press, 1972), and the editor of *World Christianity: Eastern Asia* (Mission Advanced Research Center, 1979). Also, as one of the first writers to introduce the church growth school of thought to the Chinese Christian public, he is editor and translator of two Chinese books containing various articles on church growth by McGavran, Wagner, and others.

Larry McCracken has been general director of the Conservative Baptist Association of Oregon since 1982. He serves as a pastor to pastors, cares for general administrative responsibilities, and functions as an instructor and consultant in church growth and church planting. He also serves as a Sunday school consultant for a major publishing company, and has traveled to several foreign countries training leaders in Christian education.

McCracken's training in church growth has come through studies at Fuller Seminary, the Institute of American Church Growth, and Lyle Schaller's seminars. Under his leadership a number of new churches have been established and many existing churches have experienced vigorous growth. McCracken holds the B.A. from Westmont College and the M.R.E. from Western Conservative Baptist Seminary in Portland, Oregon.

Donald A. McGavran is the founder of the Church Growth Movement. See chapter 1, "A Tribute to the Founder."

Gary L. McIntosh is vice president of the Institute for American Church Growth where he oversees the "Two-Year Growth Process" involving over five hundred churches in the United States and Canada. He also directs the Church Growth Associate program which each year trains twenty-five to thirty denominational executives to be associate consultants with the Institute. In a typical month, McIntosh will analyze ten to twelve churches, helping pastors and leaders identify and eliminate growth-restricting barriers and structure plans for new growth and outreach. Recently he analyzed two entire denominations in the United States.

McIntosh's articles have appeared in *Church Growth: America, The Win Arn Growth Report, Leadership,* and several denominational publications. He is a contributor to the *Pastor's Church Growth Handbook II* (Church Growth Press, 1982) and has developed and taught seminars on effective church advertising and staffing the church for growth. Recently he wrote a major 200+ page manual for use by local church growth task forces as they work through the application of growth principles in their particular situations.

McIntosh holds the B.A. and M.Div. degrees as well as the Doctor of Ministry in church growth from Fuller Theological Seminary.

Tim E. Matheny is the executive director of the Center for Church Growth in Houston, Texas—a non-profit corporation dedicated to helping Churches of Christ grow. Each year he makes over forty trips to help churches grow and spends over 200 hours speaking at workshops and seminars. He has preached in twenty-three states and six foreign countries. From 1977-1981 he served as minister of evangelism for the Madison Church of Christ (4,000 members) in Madison, Tennessee.

In 1974 Matheny was awarded the B.A. degree in speech and Bible at Harding University and in 1977 he received the M.Th degree in church growth from Harding Graduate School of Religion. He is currently a doctoral candidate in church growth at Fuller Theological Seminary in Pasadena, California. In 1981 he authored *Reaching the Arabs: A Felt Need Approach.*

John Ed Mathison is the senior minister of the Frazer Memorial United Methodist Church, Montgomery, Alabama, the fastest growing United Methodist Church in America. Frazer has seen a net gain of 2,000 members in the last five years, with an average worship attendance for the Sunday services of 3,000. Over 2,600 people are involved in specific areas of ministry. The church has set a goal of no more than 10 percent of the resident membership as inactive (anyone who misses three consecutive Sundays is considered inactive), and the church is presently staying within that goal. Frazer utilizes many part-time staff persons and secures most of its staff members from the local congregation.

Mathison holds the B.A. degree from Huntingdon College, B.D. from Candler School of Theology, Th.M. from Princeton Seminary, and D.Min. from Candler School of Theology. In 1963 he traveled with the Venture for Victory Basketball Team through several countries in the Orient. The basketball team competed against Olympic teams and college teams in Oriental countries, and at half-time presented a Christian witness. The team spoke to more than 20,000 people every day. He was selected as "Man of the Year" in Montgomery for 1978 and received the Distinguished Service Award from the Jaycees in 1979.

Elmer W. Matthias is associate professor of practical theology at Concordia Seminary, St. Louis, Missouri, an institution of the Lutheran Church–Missouri Synod. He joined the faculty of his alma mater after thirty-two years as a parish pastor. Matthias began his ministry in 1946 as the founding pastor of Peace Lutheran Church, Galena Park, Texas. After ten years of work in this suburb of Houston, he became senior pastor of Zion Lutheran Church, Anaheim, California, in 1956. This became a growing congregation in a rapidly expanding area. While serving the parish he enrolled in the Doctor of Ministry program in church growth at Fuller Theological Seminary, receiving his degree in 1977. At Concordia Seminary he became the first trained church growth seminary instructor in Lutheran circles, teaching church growth, evangelism, and parish administration.

In addition to these responsibilities, Matthias has conducted church growth workshops for parish pastors in over fifteen districts of his denomination throughout the United States. He also serves on the staff of the Church Growth Center, Corunna, Indiana. His article "This Lutheran Sees Value in Church Growth" appeared in the March 1984 issue of *The Concordia Journal*, perhaps the first positive article on church growth to appear in any Lutheran theological journal. He holds membership in the Academy for Evangelism and Theological Education, The North American Society for Church Growth, The Society for Continuing Education and Ministry, Interim Network, and American Society of Missiology.

Flavius Joseph May, known to his friends as Joe, was born in 1927 in Neshoba County, Mississippi, the fifth child of the Reverend and Mrs. G. N. May. Growing up in the home of a country preacher/farmer, May learned some very important lessons which were of great value in his later life. He learned the value of a good day's work, an appreciation for music, and love and respect for his parents. He learned early to respect God and the church. Since his father was a pioneer evangelist in the Church of God (Cleveland, Tennessee), Joe learned firsthand what was involved in planting new churches. Also, he learned the importance of caring for the soil, about planting crops, cultivation, and harvest. All these kinds of experiences formed a valuable foundation for his later life in the ministry.

In 1945 he graduated from high school at Yazoo City, Mississippi. The next year he married his classmate and high school sweetheart, Lavelle Carpenter. At this very young age, Joe and Lavelle May began their ministry in the Church of God. For the first nine years, 1945-1954, May served as an evangelist and new field pastor, working in Mississippi, Alabama, and Missouri. He planted two new churches—one in Fort Payne, Alabama, and one in Cape Girardeau, Missouri. In 1954, he was elected to serve as pastor of a self-supporting church. His remaining experience as a pastor is as follows: 1954-1959, Hattiesburg, Mississippi; 1959-1965, West Frankfort, Illinois; 1965-1967, Minot, North Dakota; and 1967-1975, Louisville, Kentucky.

During these years in the pastorate, May devoted some of his time to college and seminary. He attended the University of Southern Mississippi and William Carey College, both in Hattiesburg. He graduated from Southern Illinois University, receiving the B.A. degree with a major in English and a minor in philosophy. He received seminary training while at Louisville, Kentucky, graduating from Southern Baptist Theological Seminary with the Master of Divinity degree. He is now working on the Doctor of Ministry program in church growth at Fuller Theological Seminary.

During these years in the pastorate May rendered service to his denomination beyond his ministry in the local church. He was elected to serve on the State Council in several states—Missouri, Mississippi, Illinois, North and South Dakota, and Kentucky. He served for eight years as a member of the Board of Directors of Lee College, Cleveland, Tennessee. He is now serving on the national Executive Council of the Church of God.

For many years Joe May's ministry has been marked by a teaching-preaching style of pulpit delivery. This means that he has devoted his preaching almost completely to the expository method. As a result of this kind of preaching, he has been highly honored by his church. He has served as Bible teacher in sixty state camp meetings. Beyond this, he has been a special speaker in renewal, evangelism, and church growth conferences throughout the United States and also in Canada, Mexico, Puerto Rico, South Africa, Germany, and England.

In 1975, when the Church of God School of Theology was begun, May was selected by the Executive Committee of the Church of God to move to Cleveland, Tennessee, and serve as a teacher in the new seminary. He has been teaching there ever since. He serves as associate professor in pastoral ministries and English Bible. He teaches several courses in practical theology, ministry of the Word, expository preaching, pastoral ministries, church growth, and evangelism and renewal. He teaches several Bible courses: John, Mark, 1 Corinthians, Amos-Hosea, and others.

As May fulfills his ministry at the School of Theology, he also stays in contact with the local church. He preaches each Wednesday evening at the prestigious North Cleveland Church of God and fills weekend appointments to local churches where he preaches and teaches seminars on renewal, evangelism and church growth.

F. J. May contributed chapter 21 to this volume: "Supernatural Anointing and Church Growth."

Ben Merold is senior minister of Eastside Christian Church in Fullerton, California. Since 1969 this church has grown from 180 to over 2,200 in attendance. During this time, the church has started three new churches and helped strengthen weak churches by sending them staff members or members. He has been considered a friend to the small church. He has held over five hundred local church evangelistic meetings. Most of these have been one week in length and are usually held in small towns or rural communities. He also holds many Sunday school and church growth seminars for district leadership groups.

Ben Merold was president of the 1978 North American Christian Convention and is a member of the Executive Committee of that convention at this present time. He attended Johnson Bible College, Knoxville, Tennessee, and Lincoln Christian College, Lincoln, Illinois. He has an honorary doctorate from Pacific Christian College, Fullerton, California. His six-part video series entitled "Principles of Church Growth" has been very popular in the U.S. and Australia.

Delos Miles is professor of evangelism at Southeastern Baptist Theological Seminary in Wake Forest, North Carolina. He previously served as pastor and then as Southern Baptist state evangelism executive in Virginia and North Carolina. Miles has written a textbook for an introductory church growth course entitled *Church Growth—A Mighty River* (Broadman, 1981). The book provides a historical overview of the Church Growth Movement and enters into constructive dialogue with Donald A. McGavran, C. Peter Wagner, and others. Presently, Miles is writing a study guide for an introductory course on church growth for use by the Seminary External Education Division of the six Southern Baptist seminaries.

Delos Miles holds degrees from Furman University and Southeastern Baptist Theological Seminary. His S.T.D. is from San Francisco Theological Seminary. He is an active member of the Academy for Evangelism in Theological Education and a founding member of the North American Society for Church Growth. Other published works include *Master Principles of Evangelism,*

How Jesus Won Persons, Introduction to Evangelism, and *Overcoming Barriers to Witnessing.*

Juan Carlos Miranda is the founding director of the Hispanic Church Growth Department of the Charles E. Fuller Institute of Evangelism and Church Growth in Pasadena, California. He is also supervisor of the missionary work of the Missionary Board of the Brethren Church in Mexico and southern California. In that capacity, with the help of his wife, Maria, he has planted eight churches in the last seven years.

Miranda has translated and adapted the Fuller Institute church growth resources into Spanish and has written the first church growth book originally in Spanish, *Manual de Iglecrecimiento* (Editorial Vida, 1985). He presents seminars and workshops on church growth to an average of 2,000 church leaders per year. In high demand for counsel on Hispanic Christian organizations, Miranda has been elected regional vice president of CONELA (Latin American Evangelical Confederation) for the U.S.A. and Canada. He also served as a member of the planning committee of Houston '85, the National Convocation on Evangelizing Ethnic America.

Juan Carlos Miranda, a native of Argentina, holds the D.Min. degree in church growth from Fuller Seminary.

James H. Montgomery, missionary with Overseas Crusades for twenty-seven years and now president of Dawn Ministries, has served as editor of *Global Church Growth* since 1976. He is the originator of the D.A.W.N. (Discipling A Whole Nation) movement, now gaining momentum worldwide. Dawn Ministries is committed to communicating the vision of saturation church planting on a worldwide basis. Montgomery serves as a consultant to leaders desiring national programs of this nature. The pilot project in the Philippines resulted in doubling the rate of growth of the participating churches. A second project in Guatemala aims at seeing the nation become 50 percent evangelical by 1990.

Montgomery is the author of *New Testament Fire in the Philippines, When God Was Black, The Discipling of a Nation* (with Donald A. McGavran), and *La Hora de Dios para Guatemala.* He holds the B.A. and M.A. from Wheaton College and has done graduate work in church growth in the Fuller Seminary School of World Mission.

Charles Mylander is general superintendent of the Friends Churches in California and Arizona (California Yearly Meeting of Friends Church). He holds a D.Min. degree in church growth from Fuller Theological Seminary. His contributions to the Church Growth Movement are both conceptual and practical. On the conceptual side, he developed the "composite membership" method of measuring growth and contributed to the understanding of "sociological strangulation." On the practical side he has written on stimulating church morale, good staff relationships, and effective incorporation and assimilation of recent visitors to a church.

Mylander has led numerous church growth conferences and pastors' seminars. He has written *Secrets for Growing Churches* (Harper & Row, 1979). Along with staff members of Rose Drive Friends Church, he has written the *Operation Andrew, Philip, and Barnabas* visitation manual. He has also written various articles related to church growth in *Christianity Today, Eternity,* and *Church Growth: America* magazines. He serves as an adjunct professor of the Graduate School of Theology of Azusa Pacific University where he teaches church growth and related subjects.

Robert D. Noble is founder and director of Noble Ventures in Faith, an organization designed to teach liturgical churches the concepts and skills of evangelism and church growth. Noble is also an experienced church planter and works for the Diocese of San Diego as a consultant in church planting. For twenty-five years he was rector of Episcopal churches in California and Idaho. From 1976 through 1981 he worked part time for the National Episcopal Church and the Province of the Pacific of the Episcopal Church as a consultant in evangelism and church growth with responsibility for the region from the Rocky Mountains to Taiwan.

In conducting these ministries, he has developed many innovative workshops for liturgical congregations. He has published *Discovery Weekend: Commitment Through Community* (1979), *The Episcopal Church: It's Greek to Us* (1981), and *Spiritual Gifts: Your Portion of Christ's Bounty* (1985). Noble is completing his Doctor of Ministry thesis at the Pacific School of Religion. He graduated from the Church Divinity School of the Pacific, Berkeley, California with a M.Div. in 1958 and from the University of California, Berkeley, with an A.B. in Social Psychology in 1953.

Vernon E. Olson is director of church extension for the Rocky Mountain District of the Evangelical Free Churches of America. He is a visiting professor at Colorado Christian College in Denver teaching in the areas of church growth, church planting, and the small-membership church. He specializes in workshops for small-membership and newly planted churches, and has helped manage a number of church growth and church planting seminars. Olson has served as pastor of churches in both urban and rural areas, and has been the first full-time pastor of three newly planted suburban churches.

Vernon Olson is the author of many journal articles and one book, *Goals for the Teacher.* He holds degrees from Trinity Evangelical Divinity School in Deerfield, Illinois, from Trinity Seminary in Chicago, and from Denver Seminary. His D.Min. from Denver Seminary was done in the area of church growth strategies for the small-membership church.

Paul R. Orjala is the professor of missiology at Nazarene Theological Seminary, Kansas City, Missouri. He and his wife pioneered the work of the Church of the Nazarene in Haiti for fourteen years, beginning in 1950, resulting in a movement of 47,000 full and probationary members in 1984. In 1961 he met Donald McGavran and the next year started teaching church growth in the annual Nazarene missionary orientation seminars. Elected to the faculty of Nazarene Theological Seminary in 1964, he and his colleagues have developed a comprehensive missiology program, including courses in general church growth, cross-cultural church growth, church planting, and American church growth. He has impacted his denomination as a consultant researcher, planner, and trainer in church growth.

Orjala received his education at Pasadena College, Nazarene Theological Seminary, and the Kennedy School of Missions of Hartford Seminary Foundation, from which he received the Ph.D. in 1970. Among six books and numerous articles, his book

Get Ready to Grow (Beacon Hill, 1978) has reached the widest public (almost 60,000 copies) as a training text for local churches.

Robert Orr is vice president of the Institute for American Church Growth in charge of seminars and professional training. He was formerly the director of the Canadian branch of the Institute and prior to that served as pastor for a number of years in Winnipeg. Orr has traveled extensively in the U.S.A., Canada, and overseas communicating state-of-the-art insights in church growth since 1975. He is a keen leader and practitioner in the field of church growth, putting him in high demand as a church consultant, guest speaker, and seminar leader.

After graduating from Winnipeg Theological Seminary, Orr worked in revitalizing a downtown church in a changing neighborhood then in a suburban parish which, prior to his arrival, had undergone two splits in ten years. Within eighteen months the church had been revitalized and had added a full-time associate and secretary. In addition, he has been responsible for planting three churches.

Bob Orr has developed a series of three growth task force study manuals on "Assimilating New Members," "Spiritual Gifts and the Growing Church," and "Master Planning for Church Growth." Presently he is working closely with a number of churches in a special two-year emphasis in systematic application of long-term church growth principles.

Archie B. Parrish is the founding president of Serve International, an Atlanta-based organization which integrates church growth principles with a relational system of evangelism aimed to achieve body evangelism in local churches. It does this through a cumulative curriculum for local churches dealing with renewal, personal evangelism training, follow-up, and mobilization. For ten years previous to this, Parrish served as chief executive officer of Evangelism Explosion out of Fort Lauderdale, Florida.

Archie Parrish became an ordained Presbyterian minister in 1961 and served several churches before going to Coral Ridge Presbyterian Church in Fort Lauderdale in 1969. He holds the M.Div. from Gordon-Conwell Seminary and the D.Min. in church growth from Fuller Theological Seminary.

James E. Persson is director of church growth for the Evangelical Covenant Church with his office in Littleton, Colorado. He functions as a church growth consultant to local churches and conferences of churches. Currently he is working with others on designing and implementing a creative strategy for church planting in Houston, Texas.

Before assuming his current position, Persson served as executive secretary of evangelism for his denomination and as director of new church development in the Pacific Southwest Conference of the Evangelical Covenant Church. At that time he planted seven new churches and designed a regional strategy for church growth.

James Persson is an adjunct professor of church growth at North Park Theological Seminary and has had significant impact in designing a seminar curriculum in American church growth. He holds a B.D. from North Park and a D.Min. in church growth from Fuller Theological Seminary. He has completed the "Diagnosis with Impact" program of the Charles E. Fuller Institute and is an associate consultant with the Institute.

J. Mark Platt has been the associate director of Vision 2000 Churches (Conservative Baptist Association of Northern California) since 1982. In the first three years in that position, he began three churches personally and directed the birth of an additional sixteen churches. He has a goal of 200 churches by A.D. 2000. Platt also serves as a church growth consultant to 100 established churches and has served as an adjunct faculty member at Dallas Theological Seminary, Western Conservative Baptist Seminary, and International School of Theology. He has been an associate pastor, senior pastor, and a church planting pastor.

Platt holds degrees from California State University, Fresno (B.A.); Bethel Theological Seminary (M.Div.), and Fuller Theological Seminary (D.Min. in church growth). He is a charter member of the North American Society of Church Growth. Platt has published in *Church Growth America* and is working on a new book titled: *Church Obstetrics: How a Church Is Born.* Dr. Platt's office is located in Saratoga, California.

R. Daniel Reeves has been a church growth consultant with the

Charles E. Fuller Institute for Evangelism and Church Growth for eight years. He is the author, with Ron Jensen, of a popular introductory church growth book entitled *Always Advancing: Modern Church Growth Strategies* (Here's Life Publishers, 1984). He has also published articles in *Global Church Growth* and *Church Growth America,* and he continues to conduct research on the cutting edge of church growth science.

Reeves has over fifteen years of experience as an evangelist, mission executive, pastor, and teacher. He has served in England and France as well as the United States. Part of his career was spent as a Campus Crusade for Christ worker. He now balances his time between teaching, consulting, writing, and research. Reeves holds the Doctor of Missiology degree in church growth from the Fuller Seminary School of World Mission.

Barbara Rivera is the founder/director of ACORNE Associates (Associated Consultants for Outreach, Renewal, Nurture and Evangelism), a consulting firm through which she gives lectures, workshops, and seminars on church growth, church management, stewardship, evangelism, and other related subjects. She has also served as a seminar leader for the Institute of American Church Growth, conducting basic ten-hour seminars in Mexico accompanied by her husband, the Rt. Rev. Victor M. Rivera, Episcopal Bishop of San Joaquín.

Rivera was a charter member of the Diocesan Church Growth Commission, and was active in presenting church growth programs to the churches in the diocese. She is a consultant to the Episcopal Three-Year Plan for Church Growth, as well as a certified trainer for the L.E.A.D. program headed by John Savage. Rivera is the church growth page coordinator for the *San Joaquin Star,* and has written the chapter "Evangelism in the Family" for *Being God's Family* (Episcopal Church, Department of Lay Ministries).

Barbara Rivera holds degrees from the University of San Francisco and the Mennonite Brethren Seminary in Fresno, California.

Lyle E. Schaller has been parish consultant since 1971 with the Yokefellow Institute, a retreat center in Richmond, Indiana, founded by D. Elton Trueblood. During the past quarter century he has consulted with more than four thousand congregations from three dozen denominations in forty-nine states, four provinces in Canada, and in Guyana. He also has conducted approximately eight hundred workshops on church growth, parish planning, leadership, and related subjects.

For the past fourteen years Schaller's work has been concentrated in three areas: (1) consulting with individual congregations and clusters of churches, (2) conducting workshops for both laity and clergy, and (3) doing research and writing. The typical year will find him spending approximately 175 days in parish consultations and in conducting workshops in the United States and Canada.

Schaller is the author of twenty-five books, including *Growing Plans* (Abingdon, 1983), *Assimilating New Members* (Abingdon, 1978), *Effective Church Planning* (Abingdon, 1979), and *Activating the Passive Church* (Abingdon, 1981). He also has contributed chapters to two dozen other books and is the general editor of the twenty-two volume *Creative Leadership Series* published by Abingdon. He is the editor of the monthly newsletter *The Parish Paper*, which focuses on local church concerns including church growth, and has published over five hundred articles in fifty different periodicals. Schaller holds four academic degrees from the University of Wisconsin and the B.D. from Garrett Biblical Institute in Evanston, Illinois.

Melvin F. Schell, Jr., is a multifaceted church growth specialist. He is president of Church Growth Ministries of Atlanta, Georgia. Church Growth Ministries, in turn, is affiliated with the Charles E. Fuller Institute of Evangelism and Church Growth in Pasadena, California.

Schell was thirty-five years old when he came into the ministry in 1973. Prior to that he spent thirteen years working with International Business Machines in a variety of positions. His last position involved the use and marketing of the IBM small computer line.

He began his ministry at the First Alliance Church of Atlanta, Georgia. That led to his becoming executive director of the Atlanta office of Evangelism Explosion. It was through this that

Mel Schell came in touch with the Church Growth Movement, studying in the first church growth course taught off campus through the Doctor of Ministry program of Fuller Theological Seminary. This course was taught by Peter Wagner and John Wimber at the Coral Ridge Presbyterian Church in Fort Lauderdale, Florida.

This eventually led to a change in focus for the Evangelism Explosion ministry in Atlanta, and in 1976 it was reorganized as Church Growth Ministries. It also led to a much closer relationship with both the Fuller Institute of Evangelism and Church Growth and the Fuller Theological Seminary. Church Growth Ministries, in addition to its affiliation with the Institute, also sponsors the Seminary's Doctor of Ministry extension program held in Atlanta, Georgia.

Schell's background in evangelism and his training in computer services has enabled him to develop what he calls "Total Church Growth," a systemic approach to the understanding of church organization and ministry. Briefly, it sees the task of the church in three major growth areas: (1) external growth, (2) internal growth, and (3) organizational growth. External growth focuses on all aspects of conversion and transfer growth, while internal growth deals with Christian nurture and renewal in the church. Organizational growth concentrates on the infrastructure and administration of the church.

In an attempt to guide Total Church Growth, Mel Schell has developed the "Congregational Growth profile," a computerized profile analysis of the local church. He has also developed a complete set of computer programs that can be used by churches of all sizes to help implement and guide Total Church Growth. These programs are marketed internationally by Omega Information Systems, Inc., of Atlanta, Georgia. Omega is also headed up by Schell and was formed in 1979 to meet the growing need for high quality software to support the ministry efforts of churches.

His understanding of computer systems led to recognition of Schell as an international authority on the use and application of computers in the church world. He has been involved with such organizations as the United States Air Force, the A. B. Dick Company, and the American Christian Management Association.

Through all of this, however, Schell has continued to promote evangelism through Total Church Growth. From 1974 through 1983 he either taught or led training programs for more than ten thousand American church leaders.

This has resulted in two very significant developments. One of them is the *Comprehensive Plan for Total Church Growth,* a six-volume set of training manuals for use by church growth consultants. This set includes video tape instruction and is available from the Charles E. Fuller Institute of Evangelism and Church Growth.

Through an experience with church leaders in Johnstown, Pennsylvania, which suffers from one of the nation's highest unemployment rates, Schell began a major project in targeting church growth to major areas of unemployment. He formed a national group called the "United States Ripe Fields Commission."

In addition to his involvement with the Fuller group, Church Growth Ministries, Omega Information Systems, and the Ripe Fields Commission, Mel also makes time for his wife, Dollie, and sons, Mark and Jeremy. Dollie and Mark work for Church Growth Ministries and Omega Information Systems, respectively.

Schell did his undergraduate work in Bible and psychology at a Baptist school—Tennessee Temple College. He did his masters level work in church history at Columbia Theological Seminary, a Presbyterian school. His doctoral level work has been done through the interdenominational Fuller Theological Seminary. He was ordained both by the Christian and Missionary Alliance and the Briar Lake Baptist Church, where he and his wife are members.

Schell contributed chapter 18 to this volume: "Using Computers to Support Total Church Growth."

Joe Schubert is president of the Center for Church Growth in Houston, Texas, an organization designed to help Churches of Christ grow through the use of seminars, workshops, and consulting services for church leaders. From 1973 to 1983, he served as pulpit minister of Bammel Road Church of Christ in Houston. In that length of time, the congregation grew from 200 to 1,200 members and was reportedly the first church ever to contribute $1,000,000 in a single Sunday collection.

A native of Oklahoma, Schubert graduated from high school in Muskogee, Oklahoma. He attended Abilene Christian University (Abilene, Texas) where he received his B.A. and M.A. degrees in Bible. In 1967, he was awarded the Ed.D. degree from the University of Southern California (Los Angeles).

L. Ray Sells is the executive secretary and director of the Center for Congregational Life of the General Board of Discipleship of the United Methodist Church. He came to the Board in September 1978 as a director in the Section on Evangelism. The Center for Congregational Life is a project committed to the growth and development of the local congregation as a vital center of faith and discipleship.

Sells is a graduate of Ball State University, Muncie, Indiana, and the Methodist Theological School in Delaware, Ohio. He received a Doctor of Ministry from McCormick Seminary in 1975. His graduate project at McCormick led to the development of a church growth program for the local congregation, published as *The Caring System*. It has been a widely used kit for assimilation and nurture of new members. He is also the coauthor of three books: *There's New Life in the Small Congregation; 101 Ways to Reach, Welcome, and Include New Members;* and *The Small Membership Church: Growing, Caring and Serving.*

In addition to leading seminars and workshops, Ray Sells serves as a church growth consultant to annual conferences and local congregations.

Charles B. "Chuck" Singletary began building his vision for church growth in 1956 after his graduation from West Point. With his new bride, Pat, he began a disciple-making ministry as a lay leader with the Navigators on several army bases. This helped prepare him for harder times when he flew over one thousand hours of combat helicopter time in Vietnam. After seventeen years of military service, Singletary's vision carried him to a different type of ministry. He served as regional director and as U.S. coordinator for Community Ministries with the Navigators. Later he served as the Director of Discipleship at

Briarwood Presbyterian Church in Birmingham, Alabama, a church noted for its discipleship and shepherding emphasis. While serving there, he graduated from Fuller's School of World Mission where he majored in church growth studies.

In the midst of all this ministry, Singletary became acutely aware of the need of many churches for assistance in developing, mobilizing, and multiplying laborers who could become agents of growth for the cause of Jesus Christ. In response to this need, in July 1980, he founded and became the first president of a church growth oriented ministry called Church Resource Ministries (CRM).

CRM attempts to be what its name implies—a resource of talent and knowledge that can help churches grow. Because churches, like individuals, are unique, CRM offers no set program for the challenge of developing laborers for Christ. Instead it offers a broad spectrum of resources to the local church. It may take the form of CRM staff working with carefully chosen laymen either in a small group ministry or on a one-on-one basis. It may mean personally working with pastors to help them actively model and implement discipleship building as an important aspect of their overall ministry. It may mean helping start new church-growth oriented churches. It may mean using a variety of diagnostic tools and analyses to help a church identify its strengths and areas needing improvement. It may mean presenting specialized programs, such as small-group leaders seminars, workshops, and conferences in areas that are designed to fit the needs of the specific church.

Pastor Chuck Swindoll, senior pastor of First Evangelical Free Church of Fullerton, California, says of CRM: "There are four reasons I believe in, support, and endorse CRM. One, the structure and strategy are thoroughly biblical. Two, those involved in the leadership have integrity. Three, from start to finish, there is a strong commitment to the local church. Four, the process is obtainable—it works!"

He goes on to say, "CRM fits in so beautifully with a sensitive spirit in a desire to work alongside the pastoral staff adapting to the philosophy of each individual ministry. The CRM team is available to get next to those who wish to be involved in discipleship. By investing hands-on time and energy with key people in a congregation, CRM encourages the involvement of people in the lives of one another. The enemies of close fellowship—isolationism, unaccountability, 'Sunday only religion,' and spiritual indifference—are broken down. And best of all, the body becomes the healthy organism it was intended to be. I sincerely recommend Church Resource Ministries. I am grateful that such an organization is no longer a distant dream—it is a present reality."

CRM is rapidly expanding throughout the U.S. It has staff teams in Los Angeles, San Diego, Baton Rouge, Akron, Phoenix, Memphis, Birmingham, Atlanta, and Athens (Georgia). The organization plans to open additional resource centers throughout the U.S. and plans are under way to place a team in Europe in 1986. CRM's practical, conceptualized application of church growth principles to the church which is serious about being mobilized toward the task of world evangelization should contribute immeasurably toward helping fulfill the Great Commission.

Singletary contributed chapter 10 to this volume: "Organic Growth: A Critical Dimension for the Church."

Ebbie C. Smith is professor of Christian ethics and missions at Southwestern Baptist Theological Seminary in Fort Worth, Texas, and served fifteen years as a Southern Baptist missionary in Indonesia with major responsibilities in theological education and church planting. He founded an extension Bible school for lay pastors during his last five years on the field. Presently Smith has major responsibilities for teaching missionary strategy, including anthropology, church planting, church development, and cross-cultural communications.

Ebbie Smith's degrees include a B.A. from Harden-Simmons University (1954); M.Div. and Ph.D. from Southwestern Baptist Theological Seminary (1957, 1961); M.A. missiology from School of World Mission Institute of Church Growth, Fuller Theological Seminary (1970); and further study toward M.A. in sociology and Ph.D. in urban studies at University of Texas, Arlington. His publications include *God's Miracles: Indonesian Church Growth*

(William Carey Library, 1970); *A Manual for Church Growth Surveys* (William Carey Library, 1976); and *Balanced Church Growth* (Broadman Press, 1984).

A. Timothy Starr is executive secretary of the Home Mission Board of the Fellowship of Evangelical Baptist Churches in Canada. As a result of his direction, counsel, and encouragement, over one hundred Canadian churches have been planted. Prior to assuming his present position, Starr pastored four churches, all of which experienced significant numerical growth. He is the author of *Church Planting—Always in Season* (Fellowship of Evangelical Baptist Churches of Canada, 1978), which has been an inspiration to thousands.

One of the vehicles Starr uses to foster church growth in his own denomination and other churches is a popular "Church Growth Seminar." This five-hour presentation includes a diagnosis of reasons why many churches do not grow. Starr holds degrees from Coe College, the University of Iowa, and Toronto Bible College. His D.Min. degree is from Luther Rice Seminary.

Bill M. Sullivan is director of the Division of Church Growth for the Church of the Nazarene. He was elected to this position after introducing church growth concepts to the Nazarene churches in North Carolina where he was district superintendent. He initiated a program of rapid church planting in North Carolina and, in consultation with the Charles E. Fuller Institute, facilitated continuous training in church growth principles. When church growth principles were introduced to the denomination, he was elected the first chairman of the District Superintendent's Committee on Church Growth.

As the denominational leader of church growth, Sullivan directs the departments of Evangelism, Church Extension, Pastoral Ministry, and Chaplaincy. He is responsible for growth in the areas of new Christians, new churches, new ministers, and net membership growth rate. He founded the Association of Nazarene Sociologists of Religion to research and promote church growth. He has written several articles on church growth and coedited the book *The Smaller Church in a Super Church Era* (Beacon Hill Press, 1983).

Sullivan holds degrees from Bethany Nazarene College and the Nazarene Theological Seminary. His D.Min. degree in church growth is from Fuller Theological Seminary.

Elmer L. Towns, born in 1932, in Savannah, Georgia, made his first significant contribution to church growth with the research and publication of *The Ten Largest Sunday Schools and What Made Them Grow* (Baker, 1969, ten editions). The findings had a significant influence for several reasons. First, Towns developed a sociological modeling research tool that inducted principles of ministry and church growth from growing churches. Second, these churches in turn became models that motivated many churches to grow (during a period when media reflected a downward trend in church growth). Third, Towns used his position as Sunday school editor of *Christian Life* magazine to popularize the results of his study, especially in the annual listing of the 100 largest Sunday schools.

Towns followed with five other books modeling growing churches: *Church Aflame* (Nashville: Impact Books, 1971); *Capturing a Town for Christ* (Old Tappan, N.J.: Fleming Revell, 1973); *America's Fastest Growing Churches* (Impact Books, 1972); *The World's Largest Sunday School* (Thomas Nelson, 1974); and *Great Soul-Winning Churches* (The Sword of the Lord, 1973). Towns compiled the list of the 100 largest Sunday schools for ten years, 1967-1976 *(Christian Life),* and the list of the fastest growing Sunday schools for ten years, 1973-1982 *(Christian Life* and *Moody Monthly). The Complete Book of Church Growth* (Wheaton, Ill.: Tyndale, 1981) concluded that there were seven church types that were catalysts for growth.

Towns has never left his Sunday school roots. He was first brought to Sunday school as a five-year-old boy to the Eastern Heights Presbyterian Church, Savannah, Georgia, and there he earned fourteen years of Sunday school pins for perfect attendance. His first pastorate was the Westminster Presbyterian Church, Savannah, Georgia, 1952-1953. Even though he was doing research on the phenomenal growth of Thomas Road Baptist Church, 1971-1973, he also served as Sunday school superintendent to implement the laws of growth he had discovered in his research of the largest Sunday schools.

Although Towns is presently known in the field of church growth, his original professional contribution was in religious education. He was associate professor of Christian Education, Midwest Bible College, St. Louis, Missouri, 1958-1961; professor of Christian Education, Winnipeg Bible College, 1961-1965 (he was also president of the college), and associate professor of Christian Education, Trinity Evangelical Divinity School, Deerfield, Illinois, 1965-1971. During this time he wrote *Successful Lesson Preparation* (Baker, 1969); *Successful Church Libraries* (Baker, 1968); *Successful Ministry to Single Adults* (Regal, 1967); *The History of Religious Educators* (Baker, 1975); *Team Teaching with Success* (Standard, 1971); *Teaching Teens* (Baker, 1967).

Towns was a member of the advisory board for the Evangelical Teacher Training Association for whom he wrote two teacher manuals and the textbook *Evangelize thru Christian Education*, 1970. He also wrote for the Accent Teacher Training Series, *How to Grow an Effective Sunday School* (Accent, 1979, translated into three languages).

Finally, in the field of Sunday school, Towns wrote *The Successful Sunday School and Teacher's Guide Book* (Creation House, 1975). This quarter-of-a-million word encyclopedia is characterized as the most complete volume of helps for Sunday school teachers.

Towns went to Fuller Theological Seminary to earn the D.Min. degree in church growth in 1982. In his dissertation he examined the spiritual gift of faith as it is related to church growth. He surveyed the Liberty Baptist Fellowship for church planting and determined that Jerry Falwell's primary strength in church growth was the gift of faith, and this has been communicated to his students. Towns had each pastor measure the intensity of his faith on a scale of one to ten and then showed a correlation between those with the fastest church growth and those with the highest assessment of faith. This sociological assessment of the role of faith in church growth is published in *Stepping Out on Faith* (Tyndale, 1984).

Towns was converted to Christ July 15, 1950, at a small Presbyterian mission in Bonnabella, Georgia. He attended Columbia Bible College, South Carolina, 1950-1953, where he met his wife, Ruth Forbes. He graduated from Northwestern College,

Minneapolis, in 1954. The next four years were spent at Dallas Theological Seminary where he became a Baptist under the preaching of Dr. W. A. Criswell, pastor of First Baptist Church. There he received a love for large, growing churches. While in Dallas he attended Southern Methodist University and earned his M.A. in education in 1958. He also received a Th.M. from Dallas Seminary the same year.

Towns taught at the small Midwest Bible College, St. Louis, Missouri, from 1958 to 1961, where Christian education was his main field, but he also taught theology, Bible, evangelism, and philosophy. But most importantly he was secretary to the national committee that brought the National Sunday School Convention to St. Louis in 1960. Because of his research on Thomas Road Baptist Church, Lynchburg, Virginia, Towns was asked to be cofounder of Liberty Baptist College, Lynchburg, Virginia. This gave him an opportunity to train pastors to produce church growth. The college exploded in growth from nothing to 900 students in three years. Because of multiplied administrative responsibilities, Towns left to research and write full time, moving to Savannah, Georgia, in 1973.

The following year Towns was asked to help merge seven small Bible colleges in South Carolina, Georgia, and Florida, and he worked with Baptist University of America for the next three and one-half years (1974-1977). The college moved from Miami to Tampa to greater Atlanta, Georgia.

Towns returned to work with Falwell in 1978 as editor-in-chief of the magazine, books, and newspapers and as dean of Liberty Baptist Seminary, where he presently serves.

During his ministry, Towns has given lectures at over fifty colleges and seminaries in this country and abroad. He and his wife have three children, two daughters and a son, Sam Towns, professor of Christian education, Arlington Baptist College.

During the summer of 1984, total sales of his books reached one million copies; three were listed in *The Christian Bookseller's* list of best sellers.

As an associate editor of this book, Towns wrote chapter 3, "Evangelism: The Why and How"; chapter 14, "The Great Commission and Church Planting"; and chapter 20, "The Gift of Faith in Church Growth."

John N. Vaughan is author of *The World's Twenty Largest Churches* (Baker, 1984), *The Large Church: A Twentieth Century Expression of the First Century Church* (Baker), and is coauthor of *The Complete Book of Church Growth* (Tyndale, 1981) with Elmer Towns and David Seifert. He and Elmer Towns published together the only comprehensive listing of the one hundred largest congregations in the U.S.

Referring to Vaughan's book, *The World's Twenty Largest Churches*, Peter Wagner says, "This book is the first one ever to identify and describe large, growing churches on an international scale."

Vaughan has personally visited most of the world's largest churches and has served actively as a church growth consultant to churches in several states. Included in his research is an analysis of the growth patterns of the 118 Southern Baptist churches in Memphis, Tennessee, during the period of 1930-1985. The study traces how the transition of communities within the city have influenced the growth patterns of the congregations of his denomination in this city of 800,000, where one-third of the churches are in decline, one-third have plateaued, and one-third are growing. The growing churches, however, tend to be in developing suburban areas.

He is grateful for the influence and friendship of two church growth leaders who have been his mentors: Elmer L. Towns in American church growth, and C. Peter Wagner in world church growth.

Born in 1941, Vaughan's early years were spent in Baptist and Presbyterian churches. Most of his early education was received from Catholic schools. At the age of sixteen he made his public profession of faith in Christ in the growing 1,600-member Berclair Baptist Church of Memphis, under the leadership of Dr. E. B. Bowen. In 1962, five years later, he married Joanne Wooten, and they now have a son, John, and a daughter, Johnna, both born in Iowa City, Iowa.

A doctoral graduate in church growth from Fuller Theological Seminary, Vaughan's dissertation is *Satellite Groups: Valid Church Growth Strategy.* This study analyzes the presuppositions, definitions, illustrations through Christian history, and the use of small groups in the large churches of the world. Special attention is given to the use of small groups meeting outside the main campuses of the Jotabeche Methodist Pentecostal Church of Santiago, Chile; Yoido Full Gospel Church of Seoul, Korea; and Young Nak Presbyterian Church of Seoul, Korea. All three churches are among the world's ten largest. Vaughan has also earned an M.Div. from Southwestern Baptist Theological Seminary and a B.A. in sociology and history from Memphis State University.

A popular speaker, Vaughan has developed church growth seminars designed to challenge churches and groups of churches with the vision for miraculous growth. Centered on principles used by growing churches around the world and in the U.S., topics include: evangelism strategies, ministry methods, music, staff organization, pastoral leadership, organizational structure, use of small groups, setting growth goals, and overcoming barriers to growth.

Currently Vaughan serves as assistant professor of church growth, Southwest Baptist University, Bolivar, Missouri. He previously pastored Baptist churches in Memphis; Iowa City; Birmingham, Alabama; Texas; and Mississippi.

John Vaughan is listed in *Who's Who in Religion; Who's Who in the South and Southwest;* and *Men of Achievement* (Cambridge, England).

He wrote chapter 12 of this book: "Trends among the World's Twenty Largest Churches."

C. Peter Wagner is the Donald A. McGavran Professor of Church Growth at the Fuller Theological Seminary School of World Mission in Pasadena, California. The School of World Mission became a part of Fuller Seminary in 1965 when Donald McGavran, father of the Church Growth Movement, moved his nonacademic Institute of Church Growth to Pasadena from Northwest Christian College in Eugene, Oregon.

Since that time, Fuller Seminary has been the institutional base for the Church Growth Movement, first in its global expression and later in its North American expression. The faculty of missiology, which McGavran founded, now numbers twelve full-time professors and serves over 500 students annually from sixty to seventy different countries. Studies in church growth are required for graduation in all the degree programs, from M.A. and Th.M. to D.Miss. and Ph.D.

McGavran founded the School of World Mission with the intention of serving students ministering in the Third World. The scope broadened, however, when Peter Wagner joined the faculty in 1971. Previously Wagner had served as a missionary in Bolivia for sixteen years. He did evangelistic work, church planting, Bible school and seminary teaching, and also directed the mission, which is now the Andean field of SIM International. During his furlough of 1967-1968, Wagner enrolled as a student in Fuller (where he had received his M.Div. in 1955) and studied under Donald McGavran. McGavran invited him to become a member of the faculty in 1968, but previous commitments made it impossible at that time. Wagner flew to Pasadena frequently to teach as an adjunct professor, then moved to the U.S. with his family in 1971.

Under Peter Wagner's leadership, the field of American church growth developed along two lines, the theoretical and the practical. The theoretical began with an experimental course taught for American pastors in the fall of 1972. Wagner invited McGavran to team teach with him, and the course was a success. Among its students was Win Arn, who almost immediately stepped out in faith and established the Institute for American Church Growth, also located in Pasadena. Both Wagner and McGavran were members of the founding board of directors. Arn has given brilliant leadership to the Institute for American Church Growth and ranks as the premier communicator of the Church Growth Movement in North America.

In 1975 the Fuller School of Theology began a new Doctor of Ministry program, and Peter Wagner was asked to teach a church growth course. A second course was soon added. Now students can take up to 80 percent of their D.Min. work in church growth. A helpful feature is that all classes are two weeks in length, and only three two-week sessions are needed for the program. Auditors as well as credit students are admitted. Helping Wagner with the teaching are John Wimber, Carl George, and Eddie Gibbs. As of this writing, over 1,200 pastors and denominational executives have received church growth training in the Fuller Doctor of Ministry program.

Wagner's practical contribution to the Church Growth Movement was related to his position as executive director of the Fuller Evangelistic Association which he assumed simultaneously with his professorship at the seminary. Recognizing the need for professional church growth consultation, in 1975 he invited John Wimber to become the founding director of what is now the Charles E. Fuller Institute of Evangelism and Church Growth. Wimber got the Institute off to an excellent start, then left to become the founding pastor of Vineyard Christian Fellowship of Anaheim and Vineyard Ministries International. Carl George was called to replace Wimber, and the Fuller Institute has since become a leader both in providing church growth consultation for churches and denominations, as well as training consultants in its acclaimed "Diagnosis with Impact" program.

Besides his two degrees from Fuller, Wagner holds the Th.M. from Princeton Seminary and the Ph.D. from the University of Southern California. He did his undergraduate work at Rutgers University.

Peter Wagner is a prolific author with twenty-seven published titles in missions and church growth. His best selling book is *Your Church Can Grow* (Regal 1976, rev. ed., 1980), with over 100,000 copies in print. *Your Spiritual Gifts Can Help Your Church Grow* (Regal, 1979) is approaching the 100,000 mark. A newer book, which Wagner regards as his most helpful book for pastors, is *Leading Your Church to Growth* (Regal, 1984). *Church Growth and the Whole Gospel* (Harper and Row, 1981) is a scholarly discussion of criticisms of the Church Growth Movement from the viewpoint of social ethics, in which Wagner did his doctoral work. *Spiritual Power for Church Growth* (Strang, 1986) tells the story of explosive church growth among Pentecostals in Latin America.

Wagner was instrumental in the organization of the North American Society for Church Growth, and became its founding president in 1984. In the same year he was honored by Fuller Seminary with the Donald A. McGavran Chair of Church Growth.

Wagner lives in Altadena, California, with his wife, Doris, who is also his secretary. They have three daughters and two grand-sons.

Wagner edited this book and contributed the first two chapters.

Stephen A. Wagner is senior pastor at Prince of Peace Lutheran Church in Carrollton, Texas. In addition he serves as chairman of the Church Growth Task Force of the Texas District, Lutheran Church–Missouri Synod.

Wagner has served as a presenter at church growth conferences for both clergy and laity, representing the Institute for American Church Growth, the Church Growth Center in Corunna, Indiana, and the continuing education department of Concordia Seminary in St. Louis, Missouri. He is the author of *Heart to Heart: Sharing Christ with a Friend* (Corunna, Indiana: Church Growth Center). He is also a contributing author to the *Church Planting Manual* (North American Missions Department of the Lutheran Church–Missouri Synod, 1985), and he has written articles for denominational publications.

Wagner is a graduate of Concordia Seminary, St. Louis, 1973. Currently he is a candidate for the Doctor of Ministry degree in church growth from Fuller Theological Seminary in Pasadena, California.

In 1981 the Institute for American Church Growth in Pasadena, California, named him the "Outstanding Church Growth Leader in America."

Waldo J. Werning is director of the Stewardship Growth Center of Fort Wayne, Indiana, and an adjunct professor at Concordia Theological Seminary, Fort Wayne. He teaches a seminar course and conducts seminars which focus on "supply side stewardship," integrating church growth principles with a stewardship program. He is a regular seminar speaker for the National Association of Evangelicals, and is a consultant on stewardship with his denomination, Lutheran Church–Missouri Synod.

Werning is the author of fifteen books, the best known of which are *Vision and Strategy for Church Growth* (Baker), *The Radical Nature of Christianity* (William Carey), and *Christian Stewards Confronted and Committed* (Concordia). He has served on the Lutheran Church–Missouri Synod Board of Missions and on the Board of Directors of Lutheran Bible Translators. Werning has conducted seminars in Brazil, Taiwan, Hong Kong, Nigeria, England, Norway, Haiti, and New Guinea.

John Wimber is pastor of the Vineyard Christian Fellowship of Anaheim, California. Currently one of the outstanding figures in the field of church growth, he has a fascinating background. Very much involved in the early days of rock 'n' roll, he was responsible for the birth and popularity of such groups as the Righteous Brothers. Converted in the mid sixties, he walked away from a lucrative and rising career in order to follow Jesus.

In the first few years of Wimber's Christian life, he showed several thousand people how to follow Jesus. Eventually entering the pastorate full time, he began to develop and implement concepts which brought his church to growth and maturity. He left the pastorate in 1975 and became Director of Church Growth at Fuller Evangelistic Association in Pasadena, California. This enabled him to teach the church growth concepts that he had implemented to pastors throughout the world.

In 1978 God called Wimber to leave what is now called the Charles E. Fuller Institute for Evangelism and Church Growth and pastor a small fellowship in Yorba Linda, California. That tiny group, now the Vineyard Christian Fellowship, has grown to well over five thousand active participants. He has also been instrumental in planting a whole network of Vineyard Christian Fellowships throughout the United States.

In January of 1982, he taught a course at Fuller Theological Seminary, where he is an adjunct professor, called "Signs, Wonders, and Church Growth." Wimber taught this course for four years and it became one of the most popular courses at Fuller.

In 1983 Wimber began another ministry which is called Vineyard Ministries International, the vehicle which sends his ministry teams to England and South Africa as well as many areas in the continental United States. In June 1984 and February 1985, Wimber held a popularized version of his Fuller course at the Vineyard Anaheim with a composite attendance of four thousand.

In addition, he has been a regular television teacher on the Trinity Broadcasting Network, Santa Ana, California. During the last year and a half he has taught four thirteen-week courses including "Healing for Today" and "Spiritual Gifts," plus a daily five-minute presentation called "Doin' the Stuff."

John Wimber has written articles for or been interviewed by *Christian Life, Commonlife, Pastoral Renewal, Charisma, Leadership, New York Times, Los Angeles Times,* and CBS. His first book for national distribution is *Power Evangelism* (Harper and Row, 1986).

He contributed chapter 22 to this book: "Signs and Wonders in the Growth of the Church."

Flavil R. Yeakley, Jr., is the director of the Center for Church Growth Studies at Abilene Christian University in Abilene, Texas. This center conducts church growth research and provides various growth-related services to the Church of Christ. He served as a minister and church planter in the Church of Christ for over twenty-five years.

Yeakley received the B.A. and MA. degrees in psychology and communication from the University of Houston in 1970 and 1972 and the Ph.D. degree in communication from the University of Illinois in 1975. Since 1970 he has conducted extensive survey research on patterns of growth in the Church of Christ. He is the author of *Persuasion in Religious Conversion, Why Churches Grow, Church Leadership and Organization,* and many church growth articles. He is a charter member of the North American Society for Church Growth.

W. Thomas Younger was born in 1928 in Gary, Indiana. He came to Christ at age sixteen through the influence of the Glen Park Baptist Church.

Younger's education was gained at Baptist Bible Seminary in Johnson City, New York, and Fort Wayne Bible College in Indiana. He holds a bachelor's degree from Fort Wayne and an honorary doctor's degree from Cedarville College in Ohio.

His professional career began in 1950 with brief stints in Jermyn, Pennsylvania, and at the Baptist Bible Union, Purdue University. In 1951 Younger joined seven families in Arcamum, Ohio, to plant a new church in Darke County. In that farm community of nine hundred, the Immanuel Baptist Church prospered through five years of his ministry, engaging in two building projects. Growth was primarily the result of conversions. Immanuel still prospers, now under the leadership of David Huffman.

Younger was called in 1956 to Fort Wayne, Indiana, to pastor the Immanuel Baptist Church with a membership of approximately three hundred. Fresh from the experience of planting a church, his dream for the city of Fort Wayne, then with a population of 170,000, was to plant churches by means of sending out families from the home church. During his seventeen years of ministry, Immanuel realized the dream of seeing more than one hundred families leave to become church planters in and around Fort Wayne. Twelve new congregations were born.

In 1973 Tom Younger went on to Salem, Oregon, to become president of Western Baptist Bible College. It was there in Salem—in the chapels, classrooms, dormitories, and in his home—that he challenged students to become interested in evangelism and church planting.

In 1982 Younger and his wife, Davi, moved to Walnut Creek, California, where he became pastor of First Baptist Church. They are proud parents of five adult children.

Younger's professional career has been from within the General Association of Regular Baptist Churches, a fellowship he has served well as pastor, educator, writer, missions and church planting consultant, and as a leader of its central body, the council of eighteen. He has traveled extensively in the United States and other countries, sharing his expertise both in church planting and friendship evangelism in leadership seminars.

He wrote chapter 15 of this book: "The Local Church as a Church Planting Base."

C. Wayne Zunkel has been pastor of the Panorama City and Glendale, California, Churches of the Brethren since 1976. He has been active in church growth efforts within his denomination and interdenominationally both in the U.S. and overseas. He authored a paper on "Diminishing Membership" for his denomination's annual conference. He coauthored a denominational study guide entitled *Invitation to Adventure*. A graduate of Manchester College, Indiana, and Bethany Theological Seminary, Oak Park, Illinois, he served as pastor in Harrisburg, Pennsylvania, in an inner city setting, and a college related congregation in Elizabethtown, Pennsylvania. He received the Doctor of Ministry degree in church growth from Fuller Theological Seminary in 1983.

Zunkel is the author of *Growing the Small Church: A Guide for Church Leaders* (David C. Cook, 1982), and *Growing the Small Church: A Guide for Church Members* (David C. Cook, 1983). He has conducted workshops for clusters of churches or individual congregations across the U.S., interdenominationally, and for his own denomination. In 1985 he wrote *To Follow in Jesus' Steps: A Manual for Participation in the Church of the Brethren* (Elgin, Ill.: The Brethren Press, 1985), being translated into various languages for use globally by new congregations.

Part 8

A GLOSSARY OF CHURCH GROWTH TERMS

ACCULTURATION. The dynamic process by which a society in contact with other societies changes its culture, adapts to the new situation, accepts some innovations, and modifies its system.

ADHERENTS. A term to refer to the unbaptized members of a declared Christian community in which many individuals are baptized believers—deeply interested in Christianity.

AFRICASIA. A term representing Africa, Asia and Latin America or the Third World. Later changed to LATFRICASIA. See EURICA.

ANNUAL GROWTH RATE (AGR). A statistic showing the rate of a church's membership growth using data from two consecutive years. The equation is: This year's membership minus last year's membership divided by last year's membership $\times$ 100 = _____. Final answer is read as percent of annual growth.

ANTHROPOLOGY. One of the human sciences, describing how people innovate, how they govern themselves, what restraints they set up for society, how they think, etc.

A-1, A-2, A-3. See CULTURE AND ASSIMILATION FACTORS.

ARCHBISHOPS' DEFINITION OF EVANGELISM. A definition which recognizes the goal of evangelism as persuasion (3-P) or making disciples. Developed in 1918 by the Anglican Archbishops' Committee, it states: "To evangelize is so to present Christ Jesus in the power of the Holy Spirit, that men and women shall come to put their trust in God through Him, to accept Him as their Saviour, and serve Him as their king in the fellowship of His church." See PERSUASION EVANGELISM.

ARRESTED CHURCH GROWTH. Caused by: (1) excessive feeling of "family" spirit within the church and feelings of irritation toward "outsiders," (2) undue attention toward "Christian perfection," and (3) "bad air" generated by self-centered bickering in the congregation.

ARRESTED SPIRITUAL DEVELOPMENT. A disease of church growth that occurs when the people of a church are not growing in their relatiionships with God or with one another in an adequate manner.

ASSIMILATION FACTORS. See CULTURE AND ASSIMILA-TION FACTORS.

AUTOPSY. The study of a church that has died, for the purpose of discovering clues that may save the lives of other churches.

AVERAGE ANNUAL GROWTH RATE (AAGR). A statistic showing the rate of the membership growth of a church for periods more than one year apart. The equation is: Latest membership divided by earlier membership = y^x number of years between them $1/x$ = preliminary answer $\times$ 100 = secondary answer minus 100 = _____ . Final answer is read in percent average annual growth.

AWAKENING. A movement of the Holy Spirit in Christ's Church bringing about a revival of New Testament Christianity.

AXIOMS FOR CHURCH GROWTH. Four preconditions for growth in a church: (1) The pastor must want the church to grow and be willing to pay the price. (2) The people must want the church to grow and be willing to pay the price. (3) The church must agree that the goal of evangelism is to make disciples. (4) The church must not have a "terminal illness."

BIBLICAL BARRIERS. These must not be removed, and they include: (1) the offense of the cross; (2) to repent of one's sins and turn from them; and (3) to confess Christ before others and be baptized.

BIOLOGICAL CHURCH GROWTH. Church growth derived from those born into Christian families.

BODY EVANGELISM. A perspective which emphasizes the goal of evangelism as making disciples who are incorporated into the body of Christ, the result of which is church growth.

BODY LIFE. The clustering of Christians together in a shared intimacy to achieve growth by all members of the body working together and building up one another.

BRIDGES OF GOD. Intimate and natural relationships through which the gospel can spread. See WEB MOVEMENTS.

BRIDGING GROWTH. The increase of a church's membership through the process by which new churches are planted in cultures different from the culture of the base church; represented in two degrees: first degree (designated as E-2 evangelism)—in cultures somewhat different from the base church; second degree (designated as E-3 evangelism)—in cultures greatly different from the base church. Cross-cultural church planting.

CATS. Abbreviation for catalysts, those persons equipped to make something happen and get new projects started. See OPS, ORGS.

CELEBRATION. That segment of the church's structure which represents its collective, corporate identity as it expresses itself in the primary function of worship and praise to God; the sum total of worshipers represents the whole church family.

CELL. Sometimes called a kinship circle; a small group of 8–12 believers; an important part of the church's structure which has the primary functions of spiritual accountability and intimacy and secondary functions of Bible study, prayer, and healing.

CHRISTIANIZATION BY ABSTRACTION. The common mode of evangelism, a one-by-one method of spreading the gospel, extracting converts from their social setting. Usually produces little growth.

CHURCH. An assembly of professed believers under the discipline of the Word of God, organized to carry out the

Great Commission, administer the ordinances, and minister with spiritual gifts.

CHURCH EXTENSION. Planting new churches.

CHURCH GROWTH. The science that investigates the nature, function, and health of Christian churches as they relate specifically to the effective implementation of God's Commission to "make disciples of all the nations" (Matt. 28:19). Church growth is simultaneously a theological conviction and an applied science, striving to combine the eternal principles of God's Word with the best insights of contemporary social and behavioral sciences, employing as its initial frame of reference the foundational work done by Donald McGavran and his colleagues.

CHURCH GROWTH CONSCIENCE. The conviction that God's will is for the body of Christ to grow.

CHURCH GROWTH EYES. A characteristic of Christians who have achieved an ability to see the possibilities for growth and to apply appropriate strategies to gain maximum results for Christ and his Church.

CHURCH GROWTH MOVEMENT. A group of pastors, denominational executives, missionaries, professors, and other Christian leaders who allow their ministry to be governed by the principles of church growth developed by Donald McGavran and fellow participants in the Church Growth Movement.

CHURCH GROWTH PRINCIPLES. Worldwide truths which, when properly applied, along with other principles, contribute significantly to the growth of the church.

CHURCH GROWTH RATES. Rates of growth determined by the School of World Mission at Fuller Theological Seminary, Pasadena, California, which are used for decadal composite membership measurements in the U.S. and Canada:

25% per decade (2.3%AAGR*)—biological growth only: minimal

50% per decade (4.1%AAGR)—fair

100% per decade (7.2%AAGR)—good

200% per decade (11.6%AAGR)—excellent

300% per decade (14.9%AAGR)—outstanding

500% per decade (19.6% AAGR)—incredible
*AAGR = Average Annual Growth Rate

CHURCH GROWTH, TYPES OF. (1) Internal—growth of Christians in grace, relationship to God, and to one another. (2) Expansion—growth of the local congregation by the evangelization of non-Christians within its ministry area. (3) Extension—growth of the church by the establishment of daughter churches within the same general homogeneous group. (4) Bridging—growth of the church by establishing churches in different cultural areas.

CHURCH PLANTING. The type of growth that occurs when, instead of bringing people into the same church, they are gathered into another structure, called a daughter church. See EXTENSION GROWTH.

CLASSES. Ruling bodies over the masses, distinguished by differences in income, language, housing, health, religion, authority, and power. See MASSES.

CLASSES OF WORKERS OR LEADERS. See LEADERSHIP CLASSES.

COMMUNICANT MEMBERS. The hard core of the church, those members who principally finance and support the church's existence.

COMPOSITE MEMBERSHIP. A statistic which represents a comprehensive view of church health and growth. The equation is: Church membership at end of year + average Sunday school attendance over 52 Sundays + average Sunday worship attendance over 52 Sundays ÷ 3 = _____ . Final answer is read directly as the composite membership figure.

CONGLOMERATE CONGREGATION. A local church which draws men and women of many different ethnic, linguistic, and educational backgrounds into one new local family of God.

CONGREGATION. Sometimes called a fellowship group or fellowship circle; a group of 35-80 believers; an important part of the church's structure which has the primary social function of fellowship and the secondary functions of Bible study and Christian growth.

CONGREGATIONAL STRUCTURE. See MODALITY.

CONTEXTUAL FACTORS. National or local forces operating external to the church and influencing it; sociological factors beyond the control of the church. See INSTITUTIONAL FACTORS.

CONVERSION. Participation by non-Christians in a genuine decision for Christ, a sincere turning from the old gods and evil spirits, and a determined purpose to live as Christ would have people live. (1) Individual Conversion—the evangelization of one person at a time in individual counseling time. (2) Multi-Individual—many people participate in the act, each individual makes up his mind, debates with others and decides to either accept or reject Christianity. (3) Mutually Interdependent—all those making the decision are intimately known to each other and take the step in view of what the other is going to do.

CONVERSION CHURCH GROWTH. Those outside the church come to rest their faith intelligently in Jesus Christ and are baptized and added to the church.

CROSS-CULTURAL EVANGELISM. Extending evangelistic efforts beyond cultural, racial, social, or linguistic boundaries. See BRIDGING GROWTH.

CRUSADE EVANGELISM. That method of reaching people with the gospel in the context of a public meeting place in which an evangelist delivers a message and people are asked to respond, with follow-up being the responsibility of the local churches.

C-1, C-2, C-3. See CULTURE AND ASSIMILATION FACTORS.

CULTURAL CHAUVINISM. An attitude contrary to the homogeneous unit principle in which people believe that if other people who are different would become like them, the others would be better off. A form of racism, ethnocentrism.

CULTURAL MANDATE. Jesus' command to have concern for one's neighbor; the mission and ministry of the church as it is expressed in social concerns. Christian social responsibility.

CULTURAL OVERHANG. A condition which occurs when Christians of one culture try to reach out with the gospel to people of another culture, but do so assuming that what is good for their own culture is good for the other one; the

286

extent to which the cross-cultural missionary is unable to totally shed his or her original culture.

CULTURE. The learned set of values and behavior patterns which are mutually understood and accepted by a significantly large social group.

CULTURE AND ASSIMILATION FACTORS. Two sets of symbols measuring rates and degrees of assimilation of minority groups living in nations which have an open society allowing cultural mobility. The relative rate of assimilation is indicated by A-1, A-2, and A-3, A-1 being the slowest assimilators and A-3 the most rapid. The relative degree of assimilation is indicated by C-1, C-2, and C-3, C-1 being least assimilation (nuclear ethnics) and C-3 being virtually complete assimilation into the second (usually dominant) culture.

DEATH. The opposite of biological growth; the decline in church membership which occurs when members die.

DECADAL GROWTH RATE (DGR). The net increase in church membership over an entire decade expressed in percentage. A statistic indicating the rate of membership growth per ten years (decade). There are two equations: (1) When membership figures are available for the beginning and end of a ten year period—The later membership minus the earlier membership divided by the earlier membership × 100 = _____ —the answer is read in percent of decadal growth. (2) When membership figures are available for a period other than ten years—The later membership divided by the earlier membership = y^x number of years between the two figures $1/x = y^x$ 10 = × 100 minus 100 = _____—the final answer is read in percent of decadal growth.

DEMOGRAPHIC STUDY. A study of population statistics relating to births, deaths, geographical location, income distribution, education, population changes, etc.

DISCERNING THE BODY. Seeing a local church or a denomination as it really is and obtaining and analyzing information about it and its members.

DISCIPLE. A Christian who follows Jesus Christ as Savior and Lord, is growing in the grace and knowledge of him, and who is a responsible member of his body.

DISCIPLING. Bringing people to a personal relationship with Jesus Christ. A more refined classification follows:

D-1 The turning of a non-Christian society for the first time to Christ.

D-2 The turning of any individual from nonfaith to faith in Christ and his or her incorporation in a church.

D-3 The teaching of an existing Christian as much of the truths of the Bible as possible, helping him or her grow in grace. See PERFECTING.

DISCIPLING FAMILIES. Groups of approximately six to twenty that meet for discipleship training and friendship activities several times a week.

DISCIPLING—PERFECTING. The two stages of Christianization. *Discipling* means bringing a person or group to commitment to Christ, while *perfecting* means to nurture them in their faith and bring about ethical change.

EGALITARIANISM. Method of mission administration which stresses equality in distributing resources—hindering church growth in responsive areas, beneficial to nonresponsive areas. See HARVEST PRINCIPLE.

EICOS PATTERN. See OIKOS EVANGELISM.

ENGEL SCALE. A linear scale of movement in which the non-Christian travels through different stages toward becoming a Christian and a mature disciple.

ETHCLASS. The term that describes a homogeneous unit of society determined by the dynamics of ethnicity on the one hand and social class on the other.

ETHNE. The Greek word for peoples; the word used in the Great Commission, "Go therefore and make disciples of *panta ta ethne.*"

ETHNIKITIS. A terminal disease in church growth which is common to churches located in changing communities where other kinds of people are moving in and church members begin moving out.

ETHNOCENTRICITY. Tendency to see everything in one's own cultural frame of reference, with the overtone that other cultures are inferior.

EURICA. A term representing both Europe and America; the Western world. See LATFRICASIA.

EVANGELISM, TYPES OF. Reaching the unbeliever with the gospel, employing every available means to bring people to Christ.

E-0 Bringing people to a commitment to Christ (new birth) who are already church members.

E-1 Near-neighbor evangelism of non-Christians whose language and customs are those of the Christian who is witnessing.

E-2 Evangelism across a relatively small ethnic, cultural, or linguistic barrier.

E-3 Evangelism across a relatively large ethnic, cultural, or linguistic barrier.

EVANGELISM. Proclaiming the Good News (gospel) of salvation by grace through faith toward the goal of making disciples of Jesus Christ, resulting in their incorporation into the church. See ARCHBISHOP'S DEFINITION OF EVANGELISM.

EVANGELISTIC MANDATE. Jesus' command to reach others in witness of the gospel; the mission and ministry of the church as it is expressed in spiritual concerns.

EVANGELISTIC MYOPIA. A common symptom of the disease of *koinonitis*, a fellowship that is limited to an inward, self-concern rather than a concern to make disciples of all peoples.

EXPANSION CHURCH GROWTH. Each congregation expands as it converts non-Christians and takes more of them into the same congregation. Growth by transfer is included also.

EXTENSION CHURCH GROWTH. Each congregation plants daughter churches among its own kind of people in its neighborhood or region. See CHURCH PLANTING.

FACTORS OF GROWTH. See CONTEXTUAL FACTORS and INSTITUTIONAL FACTORS.

FAITH PROJECTION. A projected growth goal based on present growth patterns, plus a trust in the Lord for an increase in the harvest. Usually a five-year projection.

FAMILY ANALYSIS. Reveals the intricate network of blood

289

and marriage relationships which tie communities together and have so much to do with the inner life of any congregation.

FELLOWSHIP CIRCLE. See CONGREGATION.

FELLOWSHIP INFLAMMATION. A symptom of the disease of *koinonitis* which represents an overemphasis on Christian fellowship. See KOINONITIS.

FELLOWSHIP SATURATION. A symptom of *koinonitis* that results from a church's unwillingness to divide the congregation and cell structures when they reach beyond their respective tolerances of 80 and 12. See KOINONITIS.

FELT NEED. Describes the conscious wants and desires of a person; considered to be an opportunity for Christian response which stimulates within the person a receptivity to the gospel.

FIELD TOTALS. The number of Christians in all congregations of a given denomination in a given field—may be a whole nation, a state, a province, a district, or a part of a district.

FLUCTUATING RECEPTIVITY. The responsiveness of individuals and groups waxes and wanes due to the Spirit's peculiar activity in the hearts of people.

FOG. Inaccurate guesswork; uneducated opinions that are abundant regarding the growth and decline of the church.

FOLDING. The process by which new Christians are assimilated into the local church.

FOLLOW-UP GAP. The difference between the number of persons who make decisions for Christ in a given evangelistic effort and those who go on to become disciples.

FOURTH WORLD. Peoples who have not yet become Christian.

GIFT MIX. The mixture of the spiritual gifts of an individual Christian or a group of Christians.

GOAL SETTING. The process of exercising faith in the area of trusting God for a given number of new members in the church over a given period of time. See FAITH PROJECTION.

GHOST TOWN DISEASE. Formerly "old age." A terminal

illness of church growth which occurs when the town or community in which a church is located disintegrates with many people moving out and few moving in. Usually a rural disease.

GRAPHS OF GROWTH. Ten-year graphs of the rise and fall of church membership to serve diagnostic purposes. The most common are a ten-year line graph of composite membership and a ten-year bar graph of annual growth rates.

HARVEST PRINCIPLE. The strategy of concentrating the maximum number of workers among receptive segments of population while not bypassing the resistant. See RESIS-TANCE-RECEPTIVITY AXIS.

HARVEST THEOLOGY. The presentation of the gospel which results in the actual decision of nonbelievers to follow Jesus Christ as Savior and Lord. See SEARCH THEOLOGY.

HEART LANGUAGE. Mode of communication employed by our intimates, our mother tongue to which we assess great personal value.

HIDDEN PEOPLE. A people group that does not as yet have a viable church capable of finishing the evangelistic task by E-1 evangelism. An unreached people. See PEOPLE GROUP.

HOMESTEADERS. A term designating new families who move and begin to attend worship at an established church, but who do not have firsthand recollection of the pioneering days of the church. See PIONEERS.

HOMOGENEOUS UNIT. A section of society in which all the members have some characteristic in common. See also PEOPLE GROUP.

HOMOGENEOUS UNIT PRINCIPLE. People like to become Christians without having to cross racial, linguistic, or class barriers to do so.

HOMOGENEOUS UNIT CHURCH. A cluster of congregations of one denomination that is growing within a given homogeneous unit.

HOUTS QUESTIONNAIRE. A list of 125 questions that help Christians begin to discover what spiritual gifts God has given them. Also known as the Wagner Modified Houts Questionnaire.

HYPER-COOPERATIVISM. A disease of church growth that occurs when cooperation between churches becomes an end in itself and, therefore, directs the churches away from the priority goal of evangelism.

HYPOTHESIS OF THE 10 PERCENT. The hypothesis that up to about 10 percent of the people of the average Christian church have the gift of evangelist. See PROBLEM OF THE 9.5.

INDEFINITELY REPRODUCIBLE PATTERN. Planting new churches in such a way that the future growth and development of the churches does not depend on the resources of the mission or the church planter, but rather that they generate their own resources for continual evangelism and multiplication of churches.

INFRASTRUCTURE. The dynamic structures of congregation and cell that undergird and provide permanency to the celebration or membership circle. See CELEBRATION, CELL.

INSTITUTIONAL FACTORS. National or local forces of church growth internal to the denomination or the local church that can be controlled to some extent by church leadership. See CONTEXTUAL FACTORS.

INTERNAL CHURCH GROWTH. Christians growing in their faith and in living out their Christian commitment. See QUALITATIVE GROWTH.

INVERTED DISCIPLESHIP. The tendency within missions to invest an increasing amount of time and resources toward developing maturity in those already converted, at the expense of the unconverted.

KINSHIP CIRCLE. See CELL.

KOINONITIS. A disease of church growth which occurs when too much fellowship causes the church to look inward upon itself, losing sight of non-Christians who need to be won.

LATFRICASIA. Referring to Latin America, Africa, and Asia. The Third World. See EURICA.

LEADERSHIP CLASSES.

Class 1—Leaders whose energies primarily turn inward toward the service of existing Christians and existing church structures.

Class 2—Leaders whose energies primarily turn outward toward non-Christians in an effort to bring them into the body of Christ.

Class 3—Leaders who are unpaid or partially paid and who shepherd new small churches.

Class 4—Leaders who are full-time, paid professional staff of ongoing churches.

Class 5—Denominational or interdenominational leaders.

LEFT END PEOPLES. People groups which find themselves toward the resistant (left end) side of the resistance-receptivity axis. See RESISTANCE-RECEPTIVITY AXIS, RIGHT END PEOPLES.

LIFE-STYLE EVANGELISM. Role modeling by Christians so that non-Christians will identify with the life of Christ in the believer as well as the gospel message, and will better hear the message. This approach to evangelism is rooted in theology and sociology.

MASS MOVEMENT. An archaic term, no longer used. The phenomenon is now called a people movement. See PEOPLE MOVEMENT.

MASSES. The majority or bulk of society that lives in submission to the classes; the proletariat. See CLASSES.

MELTING POT THEORY. A point of view that people of differing cultural backgrounds will automatically develop a commonness and oneness because they are in geographic proximity.

MISSIOLOGY. The study of cross-cultural communication of the Christian faith.

MISSION. The task for which God sends his people into the world. Mission includes the evangelistic mandate and the cultural mandate. See EVANGELISTIC MANDATE, CULTURAL MANDATE.

MISSION STRUCTURES. See SODALITY.

MODALITY. The vertical structure of churches into which people are born and raised; the local church, district, denomination. The congregational structure. See SODALITY.

MOSAIC. The variety of cultural, ethnic, economic, educational, and linguistic groupings of people found in a city, country, state, or nation.

MULTI-CONGREGATIONAL MODEL. An option for a church which serves a pluralistic community; a church structure in which each homogeneous unit forms its own church and worships in its own language and style, yet the churches are all under the umbrella structure of one larger church; frequently the various churches share the same facilities.

MULTI-INDIVIDUAL DECISION. A decision for conversion to Christianity which is made in a culture with a community rather than an individualistic decision-making process. After discussing the pros and cons, the entire group decides to follow Jesus.

MULTIRACIAL OR MULTIETHNIC CHURCH. A church composed of many different peoples from different cultures. See CONGLOMERATE CONGREGATION.

NEAR NEIGHBOR EVANGELISM. Denotes evangelistic efforts to those who have the same language and culture. See EVANGELISM, TYPES OF, E-1.

NOMINALITY. A term used to describe those for whom Christian faith and life are in name only. They participate in the church by a sense of habit or social tradition, with little or no commitment to Christ and the body of Christ.

NONGROWTH EXCUSES. Rationalizations of failure to grow, often used as justification for nongrowth.

OIKOS EVANGELISM. The conversion of whole households and the spread of the gospel along natural lines of relationship. See WEB MOVEMENTS.

OLD AGE. See GHOST TOWN DISEASE.

ONE-BY-ONE CONVERSION. Also called Christianization by abstraction—a mode of conversion that pries individuals out of their social matrix and leads them to become Christians against the tide of society.

OPS. Abbreviation for operators, those persons equipped to manage an organization once established and organized. See CATS, ORGS.

ORGANIC GROWTH. The development of the infrastructure of the church. The boards, committees, activities, training programs, and small groups. See CONGREGATION, CELL.

ORGS. Abbreviation for organizers, or those persons equipped to set in place the organizational structure needed to undergird a new organization. See CATS, OPS.

PANTA TA ETHNE. See ETHNE.

PARALLELISM. This is the methodology whose adherents, consciously or unconsciously, believe all the many activities carried on by missions are of equal value and should therefore receive parallel thrust and priority. See EGALITARIANISM.

PATHOLOGY OF CHURCH GROWTH. The study of the growth-inhibiting diseases of churches, the characteristics and symptoms of those diseases, and the prescriptions to deal with them to achieve the goals of health and growth.

PEOPLE APPROACH. Strategizing the evangelistic and missionary task by first identifying the unreached people groups in a given geographic area and tailoring the approach to each group according to its culture and felt needs. See PEOPLE GROUP.

PEOPLE BLINDNESS. A disease of church growth that occurs when a church does not see significant cultural differences that exist between groups—differences which tend to hinder the natural transmission of the gospel message. See PEOPLE VISION.

PEOPLE FLOW. A term designating the movement of people into the church, how they enter, what type of people they are, and in what quantity.

PEOPLE GROUP. A significantly large grouping of individuals who perceive themselves to have a common affinity for one another. See HOMOGENEOUS UNIT.

PEOPLE MOVEMENT. Results from the joint decision of a number of individuals all from the same people group that enables them to become Christians without social dislocation, while remaining in full contact with their non-Christian relatives, thus enabling other segments of that people group, across the years, to come to similar decisions and form Christian churches made up primarily of members of that people group.

PEOPLE MOVEMENTS, TYPES OF.
(1) Lystran movement—a part of the people becomes Christian and the balance becomes hostile to the Christian religion.
(2) Lyddic movement—the entire community becomes Christian.
(3) Laodicean movement—a movement slows down and stagnates.
(4) Ephesian movement—people who desire to become Christians but simply do not know how are provided with the necessary knowledge.
(5) Web movement—the gospel spreads through natural friendship and kinship ties.

PEOPLE VISION. In contrast to *people blindness,* the ability to discern and respect the numerous significant differences among social groups. See PEOPLE BLINDNESS.

PERFECTING. The process of nurture and development (following discipling) that is required to take believers from the initial acceptance of Jesus Christ to mature faith and obedience; sanctification. See DISCIPLING, DISCIPLING-PERFECTING.

PERSUASION EVANGELISM. A definition of evangelism for which the goal is perceived as making disciples; stresses the importance of not separating evangelism and follow-up. The goal is incorporating people into the body of Christ. Designated 3-P evangelism.

PHILOSOPHY OF MINISTRY. A statement of purpose, priorities, emphases, and style which identifies how one church is unique and different from others; a reflection of the church's identity and image.

PIONEERS. The founding members or the old-timers who,

by virtue of fighting the early battles in the formation of a church, become a tightly knit fellowship and tend to exclude homesteaders. See HOMESTEADERS.

PLANNED PARENTHOOD. A congregation decides to become a mother church and plants a daughter church. Intentional church planting.

PLATEAUING. A growing church ceases to grow and remains about the same year after year.

POWER EVANGELISM. Spreading the gospel with accompanying supernatural signs and wonders.

PRAGMATISM. The principle that demands results from biblically sound strategies; when no results are recorded, the strategy is changed to another one that is equally sound theologically.

PRESENCE EVANGELISM. A definition of evangelism for which the goal is perceived as getting next to people and helping them; doing good in the world; designated 1-P evangelism.

PRIORITIES. Items that have more importance and, therefore, require attention prior to other items; the priority of evangelism is primary for church growth. See THREE PRIORITIES.

PROBLEM OF THE 9.5. Whereas it is hypothesized that up to 10 percent of the members of the average congregation have the gift of evangelist, only 0.5 percent of the members in the average congregation are actively using their gift for regular, structured evangelism ministry, leaving 9.5 percent who have the gift but who need to discover, develop, and use it. See HYPOTHESIS OF THE 10 PERCENT.

PROCLAMATION EVANGELISM. A definition of evangelism for which the goal is perceived as presenting the gospel; the death and resurrection of Christ is communicated; people hear and can respond; designated 2-P evangelism.

PROSPECT. A term used technically in local church evangelistic programs that refers to people who appear to be receptive or responsive to the gospel and the church.

PYRAMID PRINCIPLE. If a church wishes to serve more people, it must first expand its base of organization, ministry, and leadership.

QUALITATIVE GROWTH. The collective improvement in Christian commitment and ministry among the members of a given local church. See INTERNAL GROWTH.

QUANTITATIVE GROWTH. An increase in membership and worship attendance in a given local church.

RECEPTIVE PEOPLE. Those who are positive toward the gospel message as a result of social dislocation, personal crisis, or internal working of the Holy Spirit. They are open to hearing and obeying the gospel of Jesus Christ. See RESISTANCE-RECEPTIVITY AXIS.

REDEMPTION AND LIFT. A phenomenon that occurs when a person or group becomes Christian and thereby is lifted out of his (its)|former environment and separated from it in social and economic respects. This causes a gap between the new Christian(s) and unsaved friends.

REMNANT THEOLOGY. Glorification of littleness in which to be small is to be holy. Slow growth is adjudged good growth.

RESISTANCE-RECEPTIVITY AXIS. A measurement scale by which people are designated according to their openness to the gospel. See RIGHT END PEOPLES, LEFT END PEOPLES, HARVEST PRINCIPLE.

REVERSION. The decline of church membership attributed to those who renounce the Christian faith or become delinquent members of the church. See ROLL PURGING.

RIGHT END PEOPLES. Those people who are receptive to the gospel, who fall on the right end of the resistance-receptivity axis. See RESISTANCE-RECEPTIVITY AXIS, LEFT END PEOPLES.

RIPE FIELDS. Groups of people who will accept the gospel when it is communicated to them. See HARVEST PRINCIPLE, RECEPTIVE PEOPLE.

ROLL PADDING. The practice of adding inactive names to the membership rolls or receiving into membership those who have no intention of following Christ; a useless and dishonest practice.

ROLL PURGING. A process by which the church honestly reflects its actual membership by removing the names of those who no longer belong on the rolls due to inactivity, transfer to another church, or moving away.

SANCTIFICATION GAP. A symptom of *koinonitis* which occurs when a church, turned inward on itself, demonstrates a high degree of visual piety, which in turn causes a new Christian to feel very uncomfortable and often unwanted among the people of that church. See KOINONITIS.

SATELLITE PRINCIPLE. The strategy of planting churches in which the daughter churches are semi-autonomous, relating organically to the mother church and each other.

SEARCH THEOLOGY. A theological justification of the practice of continuing to use a given evangelistic methodology even though it does not result in making disciples.

SHEEP STEALING. A term used to describe the phenomenon of a person in one church being encouraged to join another. Often considered sheep "finding" rather than stealing, based on the premise that active members who are a part of their church cannot be persuaded to leave it unless their needs are not being met.

SOCIAL ACTION. Christian involvement in changing the structures of society in order to help the poor and oppressed. See SOCIAL SERVICE, CULTURAL MANDATE.

SOCIAL SERVICE. Christian social involvement designed to meet the immediate and long-term needs of the poor and oppressed. Also called relief and development. See SOCIAL ACTION, CULTURAL MANDATE.

SOCIOLOGICAL STRANGULATION. A disease of church growth that is the result of overcrowded conditions due to lack of adequate physical facilities. Occurs only in growing churches.

SOCIOLOGICAL TISSUE REJECTION. The sociological phenomenon in which some people would prefer the death of their own social group rather than see it infiltrated with people of a different homogeneous unit; a characteristic not always changed by becoming a Christian.

SODALITY. A task-oriented organization that draws people from various modalities; not, in itself, a church; sometimes called a para-church; requiring a second decision to join, a decision beyond a person's decision to be a Christian. See MODALITY.

SOIL TESTING. An evangelistic strategy that seeks out those people who are open to receiving the gospel at the present time. See HARVEST PRINCIPLE, RECEPTIVE PEOPLE.

SPONTANEOUS GROWTH. Sudden growth in church membership apparently unrelated to conscious planning.

ST. JOHN'S SYNDROME. A disease of church growth which reflects the lukewarm faith and life of nominal Christians; often a phenomenon found in a second generation church.

STAINED-GLASS BARRIER. The barrier between the Christian and the non-Christian; the barrier between the church and the world.

STATIC CHURCHES. Churches in which growth has ceased and a decline in enrollment is imminent.

STEW POT. America's ethnic reality in which many cultural groups are enriched by others without losing their own identity and integrity.

STRATEGY. A mutually agreed upon plan of action to achieve the goals that have been determined by a particular group.

SUPERCHURCH. A church that has demonstrated a strong desire and ability to grow, that has many agencies for growth (synergistic approach to evangelism), that is located on a large church campus, and that has a varied staff of professionals. Superchurches usually number members in the thousands.

SYMPATHIZERS. Distinct from adherents who simply possess an interest in the church, sympathizers attend the evangelical teaching, but do not join the church. They are favorable to Protestants and aid evangelicals when they are persecuted.

THREE PRIORITIES. (1) Commitment to Jesus Christ, (2) commitment to the body of Christ, (3) commitment to the work of Christ in the world.

TRANSFER CHURCH GROWTH. The increase of certain congregations at the expense of others; members go from one church to another.

TWO HUNDRED BARRIER. The most formidable numerical barrier to church growth. This represents a range of 150-250 reasonably active adults.

TYPES OF CHURCHES. These churches are characterized in *The Complete Book of Church Growth.*

(1) *Fundamentalist*—Characterized by organized evangelistic outreach (soul-winning) with individual religious response, pastor-led churches, revivalistic preaching, education that indoctrinates, dependence on literal church principles for administration, emphasis on numbers as evidence of biblical credibility, and ethics that magnify personal purity and separation of the church from carnal influences.

(2) *Fuller Factor*—Characterized by the importance of numerical growth, focus on receptive groups, recognition of the place of people movements, employment of science as a valid tool to determine valid church growth principles, and a belief that right methods properly used will guarantee response.

(3) *Body Life*—Characterized as unified bodies, controlled by love as a life-style, servant leadership, and ministering laity. Church growth is initiated by personal concern (never organized or manipulative).

(4) *Charismatic Renewal*—Characterized by emphasis upon the supernatural power of the Holy Spirit (signs and wonders), sharply altered style of living as a result of spiritual gifts, extreme enthusiasm, priority of healing in the meetings, worship of God through signs, and emphasis upon the organism rather than the organization, resulting in church growth.

(5) *Evangelical Bible*—Characterized by strong Bible teaching and emphasis on the edification of believers. The pastor equips the saints to do the task of evangelization; spiritual leaders are disciplined; an intense caring spirit is manifested; and there is a plurality of godly leaders.

301

(6) *Southern Baptist*—Characterized as emphasizing church growth through the Sunday school and well-structured organization of the total church. The controlling purpose of the church is evangelistic, with a detailed training for staff and teachers, and an effective visitation program for outreach and growth.

(7) *Mainline Denominational*—Characterized by an emphasis on liturgical (traditional) worship, nurture of members, social service outreach, and attention to internal programs. They are accepted by the community and are usually not evangelistically nor church growth oriented.

UNREACHED PEOPLE GROUP. A people group among which there is no indigenous community of believing Christians with adequate numbers and resources to evangelize this people group.

VITAL SIGNS OF A HEALTHY CHURCH. The normal signs of life that are found in healthy and growing churches. Seven vital signs are commonly recognized: (1) the pastor; (2) the people of the church; (3) church size; (4) structure and functions; (5) homogeneous unit; (6) methods; and (7) priorities.

WEB MOVEMENTS. Movement through natural ties of friends and family to compel many to come to Christ. See OIKOS EVANGELISM.

WINNABLE PEOPLE. Those who are considered receptive to the gospel; those who will respond. See HARVEST PRINCIPLE; RESISTANCE-RECEPTIVITY AXIS.

Part 9

A CHURCH GROWTH
READING LIST

Arn, Charles, Donald McGavran, and Win Arn. *Growth: A New Vision for the Sunday School.* Pasadena: Church Growth Press, 1980. 150 p. The first book to make explicit application of church growth principles to the growth of the Sunday school.

Arn, Win, ed. *The Pastor's Church Growth Handbook.* Pasadena: Church Growth Press, 1979. 220 p. A very interesting compilation of articles that have appeared in *Church Growth: America* magazine over the last few years.

————. *The Pastor's Church Growth Handbook, Vol. II.* Pasadena: Church Growth Press, 1982. 191 p. More of the above. An excellent and practical source.

Arn, Win and Charles Arn. *The Master's Plan for Making Disciples.* Pasadena: Church Growth Press, 1982. 176 p. One of the key concepts of church growth theory is to identify people movements that travel along lines of natural webs of relationships. The Arns call this *oikos* evangelism and develop the principle in detail in this excellent book.

Bartel, Floyd G. *A New Look at Church Growth.* Mennonite Publishing House, 1979. 140 p. A contextualized application of church growth principles for Mennonites avoiding to the extent possible over-identification with the Fuller brand of church growth and yet including the principles.

Beasley-Murray, Paul and Alan Wilkinson. *Turning the Tide: An Assessment of Baptist Church Growth in England.* British Bible Society, 1981 (may be ordered from the American Bible Society in New York). 90 p. This is a landmark volume because it contains the first published scientific study of the applicability of Wagner's "seven vital signs" to an empirical situation. Five were affirmed; two questioned.

Benjamin, Paul. *The Growing Congregation.* Lincoln Christian College, 1972. 95 p. (Out of print.) A brief summary of church growth principles by one of the pioneers of American church growth, now director of the National Church Growth Research Center in Washington, D.C.

Chaney, Charles L. and Ron S. Lewis. *Design for Church Growth*. Broadman, 1977. 200 p. Oriented to Southern Baptist philosophy of ministry, this is an excellent general orientation to the whole church growth school of thought.

Cho, Paul Yonggi. *More Than Numbers*. Word Books, 1984. 153 p. Paul Yonggi Cho opens his heart on the personal resources of the pastor, how to motivate and train laity, cell groups in the church, the effective use of media, how revival relates to growth, the kingdom of God, its supernatural power, and much more.

Davenport, D. Dewayne. *The Bible Says Grow: Church Growth Guidelines for Church of Christ*. Church Growth/Evangelism Seminar, Box 314, Williamstown, WV 26187, 1978. Donald McGavran writes the introduction to this fine summary of church growth principles contextualized for the Restoration Movement churches.

Falwell, Jerry and Elmer L. Towns. *Stepping Out on Faith*. Tyndale House, 1984. 219 p. Ten case studies on church planting and growth regarding graduates of Liberty Baptist College. This book is a statistical analysis of the role of faith in church planting and church growth.

Gibbs, Eddie. *Body Building Exercises for the Local Church*. London: Falcon, 1979. 80 p. A creative application and adaptation of Wagner's church pathology to churches in England. This book models how church growth principles can be contextualized.

————. *I Believe in Church Growth*. Eerdmans, 1982. This is the most complete introductory textbook on church growth available. Gibbs, who has a D.Min. in church growth from Fuller, writes from a British perspective, but his insights are universal.

Hamilton, Michael. *God's Plan for the Church—Growth*. Gospel Publishing, 1981. 125 p. This is the first church growth book written from the Pentecostal perspective.

Hunter, George G., III. *The Contagious Congregation*. Abingdon, 1979. 150 p. Hunter has provided fresh insights into local congregational growth. The book has become an Abingdon best-seller.

Hunter, Kent R. *Foundations for Church Growth*. Leader, 1983. 204 p. One of the best introductions to church growth principles. This is written from a Lutheran perspective, but the ideas are practical for all.

————. *Your Church Has Doors: How to Open the Front and Close the Back*. Church Growth Center, 1983. 103 p. Church growth expert Kent Hunter expounds on eight "keys" to open doors to growth in your church: faith, aftercare, incorporation, integrity, assimilation, accountability, pruning, and amputation.

Jenson, Ron and Jim Stevens. *Dynamics of Church Growth*. Baker, 1981. 200 p. This adds to church growth literature by bringing to bear the Campus Crusade insights, laying a strong biblical base, incorporating management principles, and offering practical suggestions for action at the end of each chapter.

Kelley, Dean M. *Why Conservative Churches Are Growing.* rev. ed. Macon, GA: Mercer University Press, 1986. 180 p. This was probably the most discussed religious book in the seventies. It deals with the function that churches have in society and shows how liberal churches usually turn out to be socially weak institutions. It is a must for students of church growth.

Kramer, Bert. *Growing Together.* Everyday Publications Inc., 421 Nugget Avenue, Unit 2, Scarborough, ON Canada M1S 4L8, 1982. 64 p. A concise introduction to church growth by and for Plymouth Brethren.

Kraus, C. Norman, ed. *Missions, Evangelism and Church Growth.* Herald Press, 1980. 168 p. A symposium of several essays written from the Mennonite/Anabaptist point of view, this book is occasionally at odds with church growth thinking, but generally it is supportive.

Lawson, E. LeRoy and Tetsuano Yamamori. *Church Growth: Everybody's Business.* Standard, 1975. 152 p. (Out of print.) A solid, but now rather dated, introduction to church growth principles by two students of McGavran.

McGavran, Donald A. *Understanding Church Growth.* rev. ed. Eerdmans, 1980. 450 p. The classic textbook by the father of the Church Growth Movement, this is the essential starting point for any serious student of the field. Originally published in 1970, the revision has many allusions to American churches.

McGavran, Donald and Win Arn. *How to Grow a Church.* Regal, 1973. 180 p. In a question and answer format, McGavran sets forth his thoughts on American church growth. This is the best-selling church growth book to date with over 125,000 copies in print.

————. *Ten Steps for Church Growth.* Harper & Row, 1977. A substantial sequel to *How to Grow a Church* with many new insights from the authors.

————. *Back to Basics in Church Growth.* Tyndale, 1981. 130 p. A biblical perspective on church growth, so related to the spiritual dimension that it could be read as a devotional exercise.

McGavran, Donald and George G. Hunter III. *Church Growth: Strategies That Work.* Abingdon, 1980. 120 p. One of the best primers on the Church Growth Movement, this book also provides practical tips on motivating people for growth, training laity, helping small churches grow, and planting new churches.

McGavran, Donald and C. Peter Wagner. *Your Church and Church Growth: A Self-Study Course.* rev. ed. Pasadena: Charles E. Fuller Institute of Evangelism and Church Growth, 1982. Six audio cassettes and workbook. The condensation of MC500 or MC520, the fundamental church growth course with Wagner's comments on McGavran's *Understanding Church Growth.* A 25-hour self-study experience.

Miles, Delos. *Church Growth: A Mighty River.* Broadman, 1981. 165 p. (Out of print.) This is the best single book to provide a broad up-to-date summary of the entire field of church growth. While it does not go deeply, it does touch virtually all the bases.

Mylander, Charles. *Secrets for Growing Churches.* Harper & Row, 1979. 140 p. This book draws many practical applications for American churches from general church growth principles. Written by a pastor who is seeing it happen in his church.

Orjala, Paul R. *Get Ready to Grow.* Beacon Hill, 1978. 120 p. Written as a denomination-wide study book by a professor in the Nazarene Theological Seminary, this book sold over 50,000 copies in the first three months and has circulated throughout the Church of the Nazarene.

Reeves, R. Daniel and Ron Jenson. *Always Advancing.* Here's Life Publishers, 1984. 196 p. An up-to-date book introducing church growth principles with new information on church typology and philosophy of ministry.

Schaller, Lyle E. Schaller is undoubtedly the most knowledgeable and skilled church consultant in America today. A United Methodist by affiliation, he works both for the Yokefellow Institute and independently. He comes to the church from the field of city planning. Schaller writes a book a year with Abingdon as well as editing the influential *Creative Church Leadership* series which adds four books per year. His books are all highly relevant to the student of church growth. Eight of his latest books are listed here:

———. *Hey, That's Our Church!* Abingdon, 1975. 192 p.

———. *Survival Tactics in the Parish.* Abingdon, 1977. 205 p.

———. *Assimilating New Members.* Abingdon, 1978. 130 p.

———. *Effective Church Planning.* Abingdon, 1979. 170 p.

———. *The Multiple Staff and the Larger Church.* Abingdon, 1980. 140 p.

———. *Activating the Passive Church.* Abingdon, 1981. 160 p.

———. *Growing Plans.* Abingdon, 1983. 176 p.

———. *Looking in the Mirror.* Abingdon, 1984. 206 p.

———. *The Middle-Sized Church.* Abingdon, 1985. 157 p.

Schuller, Robert H. *Your Church Has Real Possibilities.* Regal Books, 1975. 200 p. In this book Schuller articulates sound church growth and goal-setting principles and inspires the reader with possibility thinking.

Shannon, Foster. *The Growth Crisis in the American Church: A Presbyterian Case Study.* William Carey Library, 1977. 140 p. Originally a D.Min. dissertation at San Francisco Theological Seminary, this book analyzes reasons for the decline in United Presbyterian membership.

Shumate, Charles R. *On the Grow!* Warner Press, 1984. Case studies of thirteen growing Churches of God (Anderson, Ind.) with a summary chapter on common factors of church growth.

Sisemore, John T. *Church Growth Through the Sunday School.* Broadman Press, 1983. 156 p. Southern Baptists have used the Sunday school as a primary structure for growth better than any other denomination. Here is how they do it. This excellent book takes a balanced view of church growth and then stresses adult evangelism and the adult Sunday school as practical keys. You will not want to miss this one.

Tippett, Alan R. *Church Growth and the Word of God.* Eerdmans, 1970. 80 p. (Out of print.) A brief, but important, foundational church growth work. Tippett, now retired, was an early colleague of McGavran at Fuller.

Towns, Elmer L. *The Ten Largest Sunday Schools and What Made Them Grow.* Baker, 1969. One of the earliest books on what is now known as American Church Growth. It sounded an optimistic note when the national mood was gloomy.

———. *America's Fastest Growing Churches.* Impact Books, 1972. This studies the top churches in the annual listing of the 100 largest Sunday schools. It has good insights into the sociological cycle of church growth.

———. *Great Soul-Winning Churches.* Sword of the Lord, 1973. This looks at the spiritual dimensions of church growth, stressing the divine call of the pastor and the spirituality of the soul-winners in the church.

Towns, Elmer L., John N. Vaughan, and David J. Seifert. *The Complete Book of Church Growth.* Tyndale, 1981. 400 p. An amazingly thorough textbook on various case studies of growth analyzing a number of approaches to ministry in American churches including a substantial chapter on "The Fuller Factor."

Vaughan, John N. *The World's Twenty Largest Churches.* Baker, 1984. An amazing piece of research which identifies, describes, and analyzes the top superchurches. An indispensable resource for the church growth student.

Wagner, C. Peter. *Your Church Can Grow: Seven Vital Signs of a Healthy Church.* Regal, 1976. Rev. ed. 1980. 170 p. Wagner's first book on American church growth has now become a basic document in the field. It is in its 13th printing with over 100,000 copies in print.

———. *Your Church Can Be Healthy.* Abingdon, 1979. 120 p. A description and analysis of the causes and symptoms of eight major growth-inhibiting diseases of American churches.

———. *Your Spiritual Gifts Can Help Your Church Grow.* Regal, 1979. 260 p. Written from both a biblical and a practical point of view, this book shows how activating twenty-seven spiritual gifts can have a beneficial effect on church growth.

———. *Our Kind of People: The Ethical Dimensions of Church Growth in America.* John Knox, 1979. 170 p. (Out of print.) The only book-length treatment of the homogeneous unit principle of church growth and its application to American churches.

———. *Church Growth and the Whole Gospel: A Biblical Mandate.* Harper and Row, 1981. 200 p. Taking the critics of church growth seriously, this book probes the relationship of church growth to social ethics in depth. It is a scholarly theological statement that brings new light to the issues.

————. *Helping Your Church Grow.* David C. Cook, 1982. Four C-60 audio cassettes, six 32-page workbooks. Recorded specially for this study pack, these cassettes include motivation for growth, pathology, how church groups influence growth, pastoral leadership, and spiritual gifts.

————. *Leading Your Church to Growth.* Regal Books, 1984. 224 p. This is the first book dealing exclusively with how both clergy and lay leadership can influence church growth for good or for bad, depending on how they perform. A substantial chapter on lay leadership is also a first. The book advocates strong pastoral leadership to equip the laity for ministry and shows how this can be developed into a positive growth factor.

Waymire, Bob and C. Peter Wagner. *The Church Growth Survey Handbook.* Santa Clara, Calif.: Global Church Growth Bulletin, 1980. 40 p. This 8½ x 11 inch workbook is a step-by-step methodology for doing church growth research. It is the authors' hope that it will serve to standardize the recording and reporting of church growth worldwide.

Williamson, Wayne B. *Growth and Decline in the Episcopal Church.* William Carey Library, 1979, 160 p. (Out of print.) The author is an Episcopal priest who applies church growth principles learned at Fuller to his own denomination.

Yeakley, Flavil R., Jr. *Why Churches Grow.* Anderson, 1977. 85 p. A social scientist summarizes his Ph.D. dissertation on the reasons for growth among the Churches of Christ.

Zunkel, C. Wayne. *Growing the Small Church: A Guide for Church Leaders.* David C. Cook, 1982. 110 p. This is an extremely practical manual (8½ x 11 inches) with extensive professional artwork for teaching the contents to others. It is much more than theory. If its principles are followed, the progress for growth in almost any small church will be good.

INDEX

311